Fishing Lessons

Also by Paul Quinnett

Pavlov's Trout
Darwin's Bass
Suicide: The Forever Decision

Fishing Lessons

Insights, Fun, and Philosophy from a Passionate Angler

Paul Quinnett

Foreword by
Patrick F. McManus

Andrews McMeel Publishing
Kansas City

www.andrewsmcmeel.com

98 99 00 01 02 RDH 10 9 8 7 6 5 4 3 2 1

Library of Congress Cataloging-in-Publication Data

Quinnett, Paul G., 1939–

Fishing lessons : insights, fun, and philosophy from a passionate angler / Paul Quinnett.

p. cm.

ISBN 0-8362-6839-3 hd

1. Fishing—Anecdotes. 2. Fishing—Psychological aspects. 3. Fishing—Philosophy. 4. Fishing stories. I. Title.

SH441.Q57 1998

799.1—dc21 98-3986

CIP

For Pam (a.k.a. Ann)

Contents

Foreword

Paul Quinnett and I had just sat down at a table in a Japanese restaurant when a lady, the owner it turned out, rushed up and began sternly berating us in Japanese. I was shocked and embarrassed, unable to think what odious offense we must have committed, although in such circumstances Quinnett is always suspect. Paul instantly fired back at the lady, his retort delivered just as sternly. This startled me even more, but to my relief the owner laughed and clapped her hands. Clearly, this was some sort of long-standing joke between them. But I was still no less astonished. Not only had Paul responded to the lady in kind, he had done so in *fluent Japanese!* It's not every day you lunch with a fifty-five-year-old, six-foot-four American friend who happens to be a clinical psychologist, book author, essayist, magazine-article writer, columnist, humorist, teacher, lecturer, public speaker, entrepreneur, raconteur, and—this above all—dedicated fisherman, who suddenly starts spouting Japanese. I couldn't have been more surprised if he had started speaking in tongues. I suppose that's next! Lord only knows for what reason he learned Japanese, except possibly to order food in Japanese restaurants. That may seem excessive, but then again Paul Quinnett is nothing if not excessive.

One thing you will learn about *Fishing Lessons* when you read it is that it doesn't contain a single fishing lesson. Well, maybe one. That is: Fish more! No matter how much you think you fish, I can tell you right now that Paul Quinnett would scoff at your pitiful effort. You say you fish every Saturday all year long? Stop! Say no more. You'd make Quinnett laugh out loud. Paul himself, busy as he is with all his activities, only manages to get in what he regards as the minimum amount of time one should devote to fishing, if one wishes to preserve, or recover, one's mental health and proper perspective on life in general. He makes certain he fishes at least *eighty days* a year! And not just in the fifty lakes scattered around his rural home but all over the country and in foreign lands and distant seas as well.

Allow me to clarify a bit. *Fishing Lessons* is about lessons. The lessons, though, aren't about fishing, although they tend to arise out of fishing. The lessons are about moderation and excess, success and failure, proportion, life and death, hope, humor, ethics, love and war, and so on, but they also are about Paul Quinnett fishing, endlessly fishing.

I have been studying Paul for a long time, because he is a person well worth studying. He is the busiest human being I know, have ever known. He goes through life as a kind of blur to most of us observers, but suddenly the blur stops, and there he is, up to his hips in water, casting a bit of fluff out toward some dimpling blue water, and we are rushing past headed for our next rendezvous with the future. How does he do it? That is the question I constantly ask myself. As one of the leading experts in the world on suicide, he spends a good part of his life in the company of people bound up in terminal despair and desperation. Does he ever recommend fishing to these patients as a therapy? "Only a fool wouldn't," he says. And I have to believe him. Quinnett is the sanest person I know. What is it that makes him so? If not the fishing, what?

Fishing Lessons provides a lot of the answers about Paul Quinnett.

One of my favorite essays in this collection is the one in which Paul as a boy triumphs over chicken manure, or the shoveling there of. Most people, in my opinion, could not learn a whole lot from chicken manure, but Paul extracts a life lesson from it, as he does from almost everything. Forget all those other books about the secrets of highly successful people. You want to know about what really leads to success, you read Paul Quinnett on chicken manure.

Even as he jets hither and yon about the world delivering speeches and accepting awards, there's almost always a rod case in the overhead compartment. That's Paul's way of keeping one foot on the ground and, as you will learn from his essays, back in the nineteenth century. Adept as he is in navigating through the Age of Information, he is not fond of it.

"Frugal" is how Quinnett describes himself, and there are lessons in this book about frugality, that's for sure. Paul throws nothing away, not even fish carcasses. His story about his attempt to create fish fertilizer in a barrel in his backyard from filleted-out fish carcasses is one of my all-time Quinnett favorites, and I know it to be true. There in the backyard of this distinguished psychologist is a odorous timebomb brewing and bubbling and sending out fumes so potent that distant neighbors are out on their decks scanning the neighborhood with binoculars in search of the culprit. Paul, of course, is the number-one suspect. Then comes the day of his wife Ann's garden party in the Quinnetts' backyard and . . . Well, it's simply too horrible for me to go into here. You'll just have to read the essay.

The thing I hate about reading Paul's essays is that I always end up with a powerful urge to improve myself. So I lie down with a wet cloth on my forehead, and after a while the urge goes away. But never entirely. His essays always leave me viewing life a little bit differently.

On such occasions, there's only one thing to do: grab a rod and a book of flies and head out to the nearest lake.

Years ago I predicted in print that Paul's book *Pavlov's Trout* would become a fishing classic, even though it wasn't really about fishing either. I believe that prediction of mine has proved out. So I'm certainly not going to make the same prediction about *Fishing Lessons*. It's bad enough when you have to put up with a friend who has written one classic. Two would be just too much to bear.

—Patrick F. McManus

Introduction

In this first sentence my job as an author is to grab you by the lapels, snatch you up on your toes, and get a hammerlock on your attention. I can do this for three reasons: I am six feet three inches tall, a clinical psychologist with judo training, and, book reviewers say, a crackerjack writer.

I believe I now have that hammerlock on your attention, so I will ease you back down onto the balls of your feet while I explain a few things.

When two people meet—say, on an airplane or in a bookstore—they predictably exchange two bits of information. On the basis of these disclosures and the needs and personalities of the two people involved, the conversation either goes forward or ends. The pieces of information are not names; they are the answers to two critical questions, "Where are you from?" and "What do you do?"

People exchange names only after they have found something in common to build upon, or have somehow warmed to each other. Of these two questions, the occupation question is by far the more powerful predictor of the future of the relationship.

Because of the built-in relationship between reader and writer, unfortunately you can't tell me about you, but *I* can tell you about *me*. Thus, half our problem is solved. So here goes.

I was born in Los Angeles, grew up near San Bernardino, and currently live on five wooded acres in the countryside of eastern Washington not far from Spokane, where, to correct a common misperception about Washington State, it doesn't rain much. I live here and not in the city of my birth because here there is beautiful country and fifty lakes and streams within a fifty-mile radius of my home, all filled with fish. I grew up partly in California, Iowa, and Oregon and have spent time in Asia, Europe, Mexico, South America, and Canada, and have wasted a good many fishing days loitering in big cities from Tokyo to New York to Paris. Owing to my work and fishing habits, I travel a great deal. At base a homebody, I am always glad to be back in eastern Washington, mellowed by the familiar, soothed by breezes in the pines, and once again fishing my home waters. Like Mole in *The Wind in the Willows*, I can smell my home when near it, and am glad of heart when I am once again returned.

The answer to the second question: I make my living as a clinical psychologist, a suicidologist, an author, and a fishing/travel writer. I have always lived two lives, and usually three. I can do this because I don't seem to need as much sleep as other people, and enjoy long runs of high, productive moods with only a few down days in between, and yet my behavior does not quite meet the diagnostic criterion for a serious mood disorder. I am blessed with a steady source of positive energy and have trained myself to use it well—habits I describe in an essay included here, "AOG."

At present, my staff and I at Greentree Behavioral Health are launched on a national crusade to help reduce the terrible toll suicide is taking on Americans, their families, friends, and businesses, and on our national economy. Having developed a public health training program to teach every American what he or she can do to help prevent suicide by a coworker, colleague, loved one, or family member,

I was fortunate enough to be supported in my research by Eli Lilly & Company and to convince Carrie Fisher to host a short video that introduces the one-hour training program. When someone asked me how I was able to get Carrie Fisher to host the video, I replied, "If you have to ask that question, you don't understand The Force."

Whatever The Force is, I have been blessed with more than my share. Good fortune has always been mine, in love, in work, and in angling. I cannot guess why.

I have done many things in my life: picked berries, delivered papers, worked on a chicken ranch, surveyed land, spent a year in the U.S. Forest Service, labored in a steel mill, washed dishes, pumped gas, served my country as a soldier, and have been a student of many things, a public speaker, and a college professor. Despite many delays, detours, and disaffections, with the help of a loving wife and supportive parents, I finally managed to earn a master's degree and Ph.D. in clinical psychology, complete an internship, and, after licensing, land a real job. Since that first job in a state mental hospital, I've written a few books and hundreds of articles and stories for all the major outdoor and fly-fishing magazines as well as *Newsweek*, the *New York Times*, *Psychology Today*, and a long list of professional and trade journals. Along the way I somehow conquered my childhood stuttering problem and overcame a terrible fear of public speaking, so successfully that I am now able to underwrite several fishing trips each year on my speaker's fees alone.

I don't know exactly how I did all this, but I did it. Someday I may lay down the rod and try to figure it all out. In the meantime, I plan to enjoy the mysteries of life, stay in love with life and my wife, Ann, and go fishing as often as possible.

Clinical psychologist, suicidologist, author, and crazed fisherman—in this book, I attempt to bring all these people together into one, integrated voice. *Fishing Lessons* rounds out the trilogy that began with *Pavlov's Trout* and *Darwin's Bass*, the first books ever written on the psychology of fishing. Made up of notes, sketches, stories, essays, vignettes, and bits of fluff fiction, *Fishing Lessons* is the book I've been promising my friends for years. "Write something more philosophical," they say. Here it is.

In the pages that follow, I share what I've learned about people, about fishing, about life, and about me. Some of the pieces may be lunkers, and some fingerlings, but since this is a catch-and-keep book, you may take what you like and leave the rest. To keep things zesty, I've included some one-liners that occurred to me while fishing the bright waters. Consider them salt and pepper.

I have fished, now, for fifty years. Perhaps fishing has become my religion. If fishing has become my religion, it is a religion more catholic than most. Nonexclusionary by its nature, fishing embraces all creeds and colors, all manner and kind of man and woman, gay or straight, whole or broken in body or spirit; every seeker, every pilgrim, every hopeful traveler who believes that in the art and sport of angling something purposeful, meaningful, traditional, wonderful, fun and spiritual can be found.

There, now, I've let go of your lapels. Thank you for your time.

Paul Quinnett
Cheney, Washington
1998

Fishing Lessons

The First Lesson

I live on a gravel road in the country. Quite deliberately. Ann-of-the-Three-Decades-and-Counting and I quarreled about how far out in the country we would live when last we moved, and while I did not win the war for a home on the banks of a wild trout stream, I did win the skirmish for a few wooded acres on a county road and a cedar home well beyond any city limits sign.

Compromise makes marriage possible; frequent compromise makes it delightful, provided you don't hold grudges when you lose. And you will lose. If you never lose a fight with someone you care about, you are either single or divorced, or will be. Want a long love life? Give in once in a while, and give up getting even.

Of all the places on the planet's surface where Ann and I might live, we live where we do because within a fifty-mile radius you will find all our children and grandchildren and, to appease the grouch of the company, more than fifty lakes, rivers, and streams filled with fish.

This living close to family and fishing water doesn't seem a lot to ask of life, and I figured to ask it right off while I was still too young to know that you're supposed to put off all good things until you deserve them.

Or until you earn them.

Or until you've paid your dues and it's time to collect.

But I was lucky. I didn't know this rule. I was so stupid I thought that if you wanted to live with your family in the middle of some of the world's finest fishing you ought to just go ahead and move there and have done with it. I mean, how dumb can you be?

More, I live where I live in spite of admonitions not to. Many of my more ambitious professional acquaintances were shocked when I moved from the Seattle metro area to remote eastern Washington to begin my career. "My god!" they winced. "It's a desert over there, an intellectual wasteland. Have you lost your mind? They haven't even paved the streets yet!"

I did not explain to them that any intellectual wasteland is your own damn fault, or that what I wanted was a virtual wasteland, one crisscrossed by gravel roads that ran to nowhere and from nowhere to fishing water. Like native New Yorkers, they would never have understood. I did not bother to point out to my friends that waste, like beauty, lies in the eye of the beholder. Besides, I detest pavement, and there is a shortage of pavement in rural eastern Washington.

Let me be clear about this: I don't detest pavement, I loathe it. Pavement has been fast on my heels all my life. I have spent my life outrunning the hot breath of the paving machine. Where pavement moves in, nature moves out. Pavement wasted the Los Angeles of my birth. Pavement ruined the Southern California hills of my childhood. Pavement stalked me from the West Coast to the East Coast and back again. Pavement ran me out of Seattle. Thus, I hide in the woods in my cedar home along a gravel road and pray that the brainless paving machine never finds me.

I do not regret my decision to remain a little fish in a little pond in the wasteland. In the spring or summer or fall, in the late afternoon, I can drive from where I live to one of a dozen lakes and cast flies for trout, or bugs for bass. Or I can stay home, build a campfire in the brick-lined fire pit under the pines in my backyard, fix a toddy, and be content with the thought that I could go fishing if I wanted to. It is not so important that a fisherman go fishing every day, but that he knows he can. Being close to the things your true heart loves is the surest source of joy, whether family, friends, or fishing.

A much-loved friend died a few years ago. She loved life and life loved her. I gave her eulogy and wept like a baby afterward. She was the older sister I never had. After she'd had a couple margaritas, she often said, on the meaning of it all, "Go home early once in a while. Have a drink, cook a big steak, make love. The first lesson in life is to enjoy." Then she would grin over the rim of her margarita and add, "And so is the second and third lesson."

How to Make Friends Without Half Trying

In my work as a suicide prevention specialist I travel a lot, fly a lot, speak a lot, sleep in motels a lot, and get to meet a lot of wonderful people. When I can, I wear a favorite fish necktie. A fish tie often triggers the query "Are you a fisherman?" which naturally leads to fishing talk and, sometimes, even an invitation to go fishing.

If you want to make new friends and help bring peace and understanding to the world, wear a fish necktie, a fishy T-shirt, a clearly marked fisherman's cap, a silver fish pendant, or trout fly earrings. However you say it, say "fish" and the world will come to you.

My personal favorite fish tie is a Huntington design with small rainbow trout stacked one on top of the other in a repetitive pattern of red-striped fish on a black background. Very spiffy. So spiffy, in fact, that when I saw it around the neck of a friend I said, "Brett, I've got to have that tie!" Brett Haney, a pharmaceuticals representative for Eli Lilly, and well trained in customer service, unknotted the tie, whisked it off his neck in a single sweeping motion, and handed it to me with, "It's yours."

"Oh, no, Brett, I couldn't take your tie," I demurred.

But I did.

Wearing a fish invites people in, even welcomes them. Maybe

when you say symbolically "I fish," you also say "I am friendly, thoughtful, easygoing, apolitical, ethical, amiable, gentle, a bit philosophical, a lover of nature and someone interesting to know."

It works for me.

It is always easier to grasp the meaning of life in a hot bite.

Sex and the Single Fisherman

Not long ago, a young fly-fisherman asked me if I thought it a good and novel idea to invite a girl to go fishing with him. I told him it was a fine idea, if hardly novel. Then I queried him as to whether his plans for the young girl were honorable.

"Oh, yes, sir," he replied. "They are! They are! I'm taking her to Kelly Creek."

Thus reassured (Kelly Creek being the best cutthroat stream in northern Idaho), I gave him my blessing.

Many outdoorsmen are of the opinion that our young friend here is wrongheaded, that sex and fishing do not go together. This notion is primitive in the extreme, even sexist. In fact, there are no two things I can think of that go together better than sex and fishing, unless they are fishing and sex.

I got my start with sex and fishing in 1956, back in the days before much was known about sex. All my fishing pals seemed to know a great deal about the new fiberglass fly rods, but no one seemed the least bit knowledgeable about sex. I would have to learn the hard way—directly from a girl. As I gradually gathered courage to act, I realized that asking a girl for a date (even to go fishing) was considerably more difficult than tying a full Royal Coachman on a no. 20 hook.

Veda Wingate was one year my senior and possessed several fine qualities, among which was the important fact that she hardly ever turned down a date. And then there were those promising rumors that she knew about kissing. Best of all, she went out with boys who, because of insufficient means, were forced to borrow their fathers' cars in order to take a girl out. I called her. She said yes, and I quickly tied up a dozen caddis flies.

As the day of the date with Veda neared a pimple about the size of a grapefruit appeared on my left cheek—a probable result of the anguish and mental torture any young man suffers prior to such a first adventure. No amount of doctoring brought any relief. Mother assured me it was only a tiny blemish and daubed it with some makeup. The result: a powdered golf ball. If the fishing was slow, I'd have to kiss left to right.

My father wasn't much of a rake in those days, and his taste in cars ran to gray-green four-door Buicks. Hardly suitable wheels—I'd wear sunglasses to avoid recognition by my peers. And since we were headed for Lytle Creek, where one could encounter the odd rattlesnake, I strapped on my .22 pistol.

An hour before daylight, I wheeled up, parked, and approached Veda's house.

"Your date," gasped Mrs. Wingate in a half scream, "is here!"

As a member of the ducktail and pomade fraternity of the fifties, I had come to expect some register of alarm from adults. I guess it was probably the powdered golf ball and the dark glasses (I'd forgotten to remove these) that caused her to sag against the doorjamb.

I was wrong. It was the pistol. "My god, Harry," I overheard her whisper to her husband, "he's taking her on a holdup."

Mr. Wingate, a steel worker of towering proportions, did an admirable job of grilling me as to my intentions while I waited for Veda to come downstairs. I gathered he was not a fisherman and remember mumbling something inane and highly improbable about attending Harvard after graduation, at which Mr. Wingate, apparently unconvinced, cracked his knuckles.

"Daddy liked you," Veda said, as she slid into the seat next to me.

"He never said a word," I said. "How could you tell?"

"He didn't threaten to break both your arms if you kissed me. Daddy always says that."

Greatly relieved, I studied Veda's face in the soft light. She had dark eyes, terrific teeth, and a pair of lips that caused me to slam the Buick into reverse and bounce it off her father's Ford.

Pressing the speed limit and mindful of any Fords slipping up behind me, I soon learned that Veda was a painfully thoughtful girl. She said nothing about the golf ball or the sunglasses, or that I seemed preoccupied with my rearview mirror. She even kept silent as I sideswiped a parked Nash Rambler, the immediate result of her placing her hand on the inside of my thigh.

Once out on the open road, I began to relax. For a teenager I was quite eloquent, and during the next hour I regaled Veda with all the fishing yarns and stories I could cram into four complete sentences.

"Why, it's lovely," Veda remarked when at last we arrived at Simpson's Glide on Lytle Creek, the spot where I had planned to show Veda the ropes and maybe even teach her the rollcast. "But, gee, it looks cold outside," she went on. "Can't we sit here for a little while and keep each other warm?"

Unprepared as I was for this open invitation to romance, I made my first move—quickly and without hesitation.

It wasn't the loud slap I delivered to her forehead with the back of my hand as I blithely slipped my arm around her shoulders so much as the can of worms I dumped into her hair that unsettled me. But Veda was a class date—she kept her screaming to a minimum and said not one single word about why a fly-fisherman had worms in his possession in the first place.

Once the worms were recaptured and my arm was securely around Veda, I spent the next forty minutes ignoring the obvious signs of interrupted blood flow in my right arm. I might well have lost the limb altogether had Veda not remarked that my brow was covered with perspiration.

"Does your arm hurt?" she asked.

"Of course not. Probably my malaria acting up," I replied. And it was true. My arm didn't hurt. The searing pain had passed twenty minutes earlier. I was, in point of fact, somewhere near the gates of heaven; my arm around a beautiful girl and a rise just beginning on Simpson's Glide. What did it matter if my casting arm might have to be amputated?

At about this juncture, Veda reached up with her hand and locked my now-defunct fingers in hers.

"Why, your hand is icy!" she said. And with that cogent medical observation, she whipped my now-wooden arm up over her head in one swift movement and brought the remains to rest in her lap, where she began to rub it with great vigor. This caused me some minor discomfort. I passed out.

When I came to, Veda was snuggled down against my fishing vest playing with my nymphs. I had learned my first lesson about sex and fishing: Never cast your arm where you can't make an easy retrieve.

Meanwhile, a nice hatch was under way on the stream. And while I studied the rising trout, Veda lifted her sweet face to mine, looked deep into my still shaded eyes, closed hers, and opened her lips slightly. At the time, I thought she meant to comment on the rise but didn't know what to say. After all, the girl was a beginner and knew nothing about caddis hatches and such.

When at last the trout were slapping insects with a fury up and down Simpson's Glide, I was overpowered by two great urges—one of which was to lay a fly on that busy water. I made my second move.

Moistening my lips (this was the extent of my knowledge about sex), I launched a kiss. Veda responded beautifully, making a midflight correction on her own, which permitted me to land within an inch of the target, albeit an inch high. I had learned my second lesson about sex and fishing: You close your eyes *after* you lock lips.

Then we got to fishing. I explained all the details: floating lines, tippets, dry flies, wet flies, and how, when, and where these don't work. It was at least the finest day I had ever spent on a trout stream, although I regretted how little close-in coaching Veda required to master a decent backcast. She was so good that all the worms survived the day.

Then, suddenly, the hatch and the day ended. Still a neophyte about fishing and sex, I took this as a signal to return the girl to her home, where, without warning, Veda swept me into her more experienced arms and kissed me full on the lips, right there on the front porch in broad daylight.

I don't know how long that kiss lasted, but it buckled my knees and, somewhat unfortunately, caused a no. 6 streamer hanging from my vest to snag her angora sweater precisely at the bustline, bringing about a most pleasant intimacy.

While Veda chuckled and whispered sweet nothings, I immediately set to work to remove the fly. I was busy with both hands when the door behind us suddenly swung open.

I don't recall Mr. Wingate's opening remarks, but I do remember deciding that trying to extricate the streamer (even though it was a favorite pattern) from Veda's sweater seemed an awful waste of time, so bidding a hasty farewell, I started down the steps, trailing a length of leader from my heart to hers.

Like a big fish on the hard run, the leader snapped as I cleared the porch. It is surprising how little strength there is in a 6-pound tippet when a young lady's father has spied you with both hands in the vicinity of his daughter's bosom, or how fast a pair of recently buckled knees can carry a properly motivated young man.

Gaining speed, I stumbled through a privet hedge, piled into the Buick, and, hitting the wrong gear, slammed Dad's car into Mr. Wingate's Ford (which balanced off a fresh dent in the opposite fender) and started for home, leaving what we used to call a "patch" of black rubber down the entire length of Elm Street between Sixth and Seventh Avenues.

Years later in college I met a girl who knew all about fly-fishing. Her name was Ann. She had a terrific backcast. She dressed her own lines. And then, one slow day on the Logan River as we worked out our relationship, a Muddler Minnow from her vest snagged in my shirt. Unable to get free, I married her.

I Led Two Lives

When I was a boy back in the 1950s we enjoyed a popular TV series called *I Led Two Lives*. As I recall, the hero was an undercover FBI operative with the unlikely name of Herb Filbrick. Herb's job was to penetrate Communist cells, get the goods on subversives, and defend the republic against dangerous pinkos. I don't remember much else from the series, except that as Herb wormed his way into the confidences of the enemy, he wore a worried look and mopped his brow frequently. Only a lad, I vowed if the Russians didn't nuke us into oblivion and I ever grew up, I would never work undercover or lead two lives. Now, of course, I do.

In one life I am a fly-fisherman and fishing writer, pleasant and easygoing on the outside, pleasant and easygoing on the inside. What you see is what you get. In my other life I am a clinical psychologist, professional on the outside, professional on the inside. If you meet me in a casual setting I will be a fly-fisherman, not a psychologist. Except to dear friends, family, colleagues, and clients, Paul Quinnett the psychologist has been undercover for twenty-five years.

I first went undercover in the early seventies, or about the time I learned that being a clinical psychologist was a real conversation ender. Back then, if you told a fellow airline traveler you were a shrink, you could hear the *Wall Street Journal* pop open to cut off any budding relationship.

If I wanted conversation I was a fishing writer. People talk to writers and fishermen. If I didn't want conversation I was a clinical psychologist. Thus did I begin to lead two lives.

Years ago social psychologists learned that the second piece of information two strangers exchange, well before names, is occupation.

FIRST STRANGER: Yes, this flight to Chicago takes about two hours. And what do you do?

SECOND STRANGER: Two hours isn't bad. I'm in sales. And you?

FIRST STRANGER: I'm a stockbroker. Small caps, mostly.

The answer to the occupation question determines whether the conversation is going forward or has just ended. If you want conversation on your next flight to Chicago, be a film director, an exotic dancer, or a fishing guide. If you'd rather catch a nap, be a funeral director, insurance agent, or IRS auditor.

Once upon a time we therapists could simply announce our profession and quash those pesky conversationalists. But thanks to Phil and Oprah and Sally and the rest, what was once intimate, private, and pathological has become public, popular, and entertaining. Twisted love, fratricide, kinky sex, infidelity, cross-dressing, alien abductions, suicide, and terminal acne have been so sensationalized and accepted into the great American, within-normal-limits cultural consciousness that it is no longer safe to say you're a therapist.

Just once, a few years back, I came out from undercover on a flight from Los Angles to Miami. Shortly after takeoff the fellow next to me introduced himself. A building contractor, he was headed to Guatemala or someplace to do some charity work for his church. He asked me what I did.

"I'm a clinical psychologist," I said, taking off my fishing-writer mask.

"Wow!" the man blurted, clapping his hands together. "That's great! I'm impotent and have stress diarrhea!"

I recovered with, "But I'm not a very *good* psychologist."

Too late. Except for returning spacecraft, that was the longest known flight from anywhere to Florida.

Only one other time was the psychologist in me tempted to come out to a stranger. On a flight from Spokane to Minneapolis a couple of years ago I was seated next to a vampire. I know it was a vampire and not some kid playing with the minds of the middle class because he had pasty white skin, long nails, funky jewelry, a black cape, and a perfect pair of those long, needle-sharp fangs tucked behind his smile.

I checked the fangs out three times. Without being obvious, of course. You don't want to be too obvious with a vampire. When the vampire smiled at me, I quickly looked away. I'm not sure what you're supposed to say to a vampire, other than to avoid the obvious "Are those teeth *real?!*" I've seen lots of ticked-off vampires in the movies and they're not the kind of people you want to tick off. Unsure of how receptive vampires are to psychological inquiry, I just kept my occupation to myself, my nose in a novel, and tried to act casual.

If talk shows have made being a psychologist impossible, now Robert Redford's *A River Runs Through It* has made being a fly-fisherman impossible. Perfect strangers who know nothing of fly-fishing can, with the slightest opening, bore your ears off with fishing prattle—which means I now need a third life.

So I've been thinking . . .

My dentist assures me he can fix me up with a set of portable but very convincing vampire canines. Sure, I'll be the same tired, middle-aged, undercover fishing psychologist traveling tourist class, but when I need a nap instead of a conversation or a consultation, at least I'll be able to control the outcome.

When I choose to nap over giving free curb service to my psychologically needy fellow travelers or giving fly-fishing advice to beginning anglers, as the plane starts down the runway I'll just turn toward the window momentarily and slip in the vampire choppers. When the stew comes by for the drink order I'll turn, smile broadly to my traveling companions, and say, "Cranberry juice, please . . . warm if you've got it."

I think I'll get my nap, and any worried looks and brow mopping won't be by me. I mean, once people find out what line of work you're in they can lose interest pretty fast.

I have made it a matter of policy to disbelieve all fishing stories on their first telling; they begin to have the ring of truth, however, after I've repeated them several times.

A Favorite Fishing Place?

H-m-m.

People ask me that a lot. When they do I'm stuck for a ready answer.

Favorite fishing places are not like husbands or wives or girlfriends or boyfriends; you can have several and still not get into any real trouble. But if threatened with the perfect torture of never fishing again, I suppose I could name one very special place: Cutthroat Creek.

Cutthroat Creek does not actually exist, at least not by that name. In the West where I live there are hundreds of Cutthroat Creeks, nearly all of them threatened by commercial logging and mining interests. You may have your Cutthroat Creek; I certainly have mine. To protect his own, our local outdoor newspaper writer, Rich Landers, calls his favorite Cutthroat Creek Cutthroat River. I call mine a creek.

Wild cutthroat creeks share certain defining characteristics: They're found only in unroaded, uncut watersheds; they have cold, clear, year-round flows, deep runs, deeper pools, and shallow rocky flats that make up mile upon mile of heartbreakingly perfect habitat for wild trout. Because the water rushes from God's own high-mountain tap, Cutthroat Creek is too cold for invading rainbows or foreign brown trout, and so you only catch wild, native fishes—fishes older in time than man's first imagination of himself, or God.

Of the fishes in these waters, Westslope cutthroat trout are the most numerous in the catch, followed by mountain whitefish, bull trout, and the odd sculpin. Early in this century bull trout got a bad reputation and a bounty on its head for eating other fish's fry, which is what all trout do if given half a chance. Currently the bull trout is in a dead-heat race to see whether it can outlast its negative publicity and the silt from the next logging-road washout.

Let me note here that there is nothing more thrilling than to be fishing some little Cutthroat Creek and have a five- or six- or seven-pound bull trout rush up from the dark bottom of a deep pool and grab the ten-inch cutt that took your dry fly. A huge bull trout that comes screaming out of the depths to attack a shaker leaves your line slack, your mouth agape, and your heart pounding. Seeing and temporarily feeling the power of such a great predator is as rare and wonderful a gift as hearing a wild wolf howl.

The best Cutthroat Creeks are still wild enough to hold bull trout. You can even fish intentionally for them. But most folks lack the patience. I have fished for them, and I know a few anglers who do, but most fishers rely on the steady eating habits of the Westslope cutthroat trout.

The best cutthroat fishing is always catch-and-release after a long walk. The farther you walk the more pristine the water, the wilder the fish, and the wilder the fishing. Hike two or three or four miles from the nearest road—where even the trails peter out to ferns and blowdowns—and you will find wild cutthroat trout fishing the spiritual equivalent of a rousing salvation hymn by the Mormon Tabernacle Choir.

On one hike into a remote Cutthroat Creek some years ago I caught and released more than 100 native cutts up to thirteen inches in three hours of fly-fishing. The angels sang. This is not bragging; anyone could have done it.

Cutthroat Creek is so fine and forgiving, and the trout so beautiful and willing, that even beginners can watch these jeweled treasures rise through crystalline waters to eat their offerings. Since every insect is a meal in such competitive climes, the type of offering doesn't matter much, so as long as it's buggy. And for a beautiful place in which to fish, well, I have it on good authority that God fishes in the same zip code.

I've caught and released my share of trout from Cutthroat Creek, and probably more than my share. With plenty of pleasures banked, now I like to hike up Cutthroat Creek, catch a few trout, and then find a grassy bank and an ancient cedar tree spared from the sawyer's saw, and just lie back and listen to the way the world was a million years ago. If I know ahead of time that I have only one more fishing trip before I begin my personal Great Adventure, it will be to Cutthroat Creek.

Cutthroat Creek is the fly-fisherman's equivalent of that home Robert Frost once wrote about. For trout fishermen, "Cutthroat Creek is the creek where, when you really have to catch a wild trout, they have to let you catch one."

Fishermen Never Run

Some of my best friends are runners. My older brother once ran the New York City Marathon in three hours and forty-five minutes. I like runners. I just wish they wouldn't talk about running at the dinner table.

Fishermen never run, or if they do run it is to chase a big fish down a river before it breaks them off. Fishermen do not abhor running, they just don't see the point in it.

Mind you, I live in running country. Spokane's Bloomsday Race is supposed to be the biggest road race in the world. Though I've been called names for not running in Bloomsday, I am not even tempted. After all, the Bloomsday run takes place in the middle of spring fishing.

Several years after Bloomsday took over the minds and bodies of otherwise normal people all over the planet, I heard about a new organization, the Thoreau Sauntering Club, a group devoted to a more reasonable approach to getting from one place to another on foot. I liked what I heard. They didn't sound righteous about sauntering. Better still, they didn't sound as though they were in a big hurry about much of anything. I sent them fifteen bucks for a T-shirt.

Six months later the shirt arrived, together with a brief printed message about the club and a note from the founder. The Thoreau

Sauntering Club does not meet, has no fees or schedules, accepts anyone as a member, and is striving for nothing in particular. On the club's T-shirt the club president, Patrick Kelly, had printed Calvin Coolidge's now famous 1928 response to the question of whether he wanted a second term: "I do not choose to run."

Kelly (whom I once met in the Napoleon Bar in New Orleans before his untimely death in 1990) suggested that interested persons, and especially fishermen, read Thoreau's 1862 essay entitled "Walking" for a definition of what sauntering can and should be. In his accompanying correspondence he said that he had started reading the essay in 1966, but had yet to finish it.

Where, Kelly asked, would we all be if Robert Frost had been in a hurry when he came to those two roads that diverged in a wood? What would have come of his passing through our lives if the poet had taken the road more traveled—you know, to shave a few seconds off his time?

Although the club is now defunct because of Kelly's death, the spirit of the Thoreau Sauntering Club still suits me fine. I like to walk and do not choose to run. True, I can get fishing in a hurry, but taking my time is a greater comfort. Fishing carries you into nature, and to understand nature you must see, smell, hear, taste, feel, and absorb her. You can't get your mind or heart around nature while at a dead run.

I have tried running. I didn't like the way it hurt and wore on my hinges. I once chased a bull moose through a Canadian muskeg swamp (trying to get a photograph), and the sucking action of the muck on the things that hold my knees together caused a great and painful stretching—a medical condition later diagnosed by my orthopedic surgeon as "temporary stupidity in a forty-year-old." Afterward, I could go uphill fine; downhill I had to walk stiff-legged, like Frankenstein.

So now when I walk in the woods in search of fish or wildlife I save my running for those occasions when a camera-wielding moose is chasing me.

Sauntering fishermen seldom need arthroscopic surgery; serious runners know their surgeons by their first names. But this isn't the worst part of running. The worst part of running is how it seems to aid and abet America's hurry-up sickness. We want our kids to learn speed-reading. We want them to get Shakespeare in an afternoon. If we're going to speed-read the Bard, why not jog through the Smithsonian or Rollerblade through the Louvre? I mean, why fool around?

One last thing. I can't think when I run. Sauntering, on the other hand, stirs the philosopher in me. I am much more likely to have a useful thought, even a modest insight, if my breathing is not labored. Personally, I have found it almost impossible to wrestle with life's great ironies while gasping for air.

Like Patrick Kelly, I have not yet reread Thoreau's "Walking." We moved to the country in 1979 and my plan was to get to Thoreau right away.

And I will.

Any day now.

Thanks, Dad

The other day one of my favorite fly-fishing catalogues arrived by the afternoon mail. I quickly dashed two fingers of Canadian bourbon over an ice cube, relaxed into the big blue chair under the good reading light, and began thumbing through the catalogue in hopes of finding something I don't already own two of. It didn't take long.

Portable Fly-Tying Vice.
Don't get caught without the right pattern during a hot bite.
Screws into any available wood surface.
Only $123.95.

As I now do all my serious shopping from the big blue chair, I reached for the phone. "Wait a minute," I said to myself. "I already have a portable fly-tying vice, the antique one my father gave me a long, long time ago." And with that, I cradled the phone and paused to recall the episode.

I was leaving home for college. Dad, a flytier himself and the man who taught me to fish, handed me what is now a genuine antique vice built on a large wood screw. "Just in case," he said, passing me a little packet of feathers, floss, thread, and hooks.

"In case of what?" I asked. "I already have a fly-tying vice."

"Son," he said, "keep this little kit in your vest pocket. It's one of life's necessities. Someday you'll find that little vice will come in handy. It's a very important part of a fisherman's equipment."

"How so?" I asked.

Dad smiled. "Someday when you are far away in the backcountry, fishing alone for days on end, you may grow lonely. One day you will find yourself yearning for the sound of another human voice. Then you'll remember this little fly-tying kit."

"So?"

"Trust me," he said. "When that day comes, just take the vice out of your vest pocket, screw it into a log, lay out your kit, insert a hook, and start to tie an elk-hair caddis. And in ten seconds flat there will be another angler at your shoulder saying, 'That's not how you tie an elk-hair caddis!' "

A little-known law of gravity holds that a canoe is always heavier on the portage out than on the portage in.

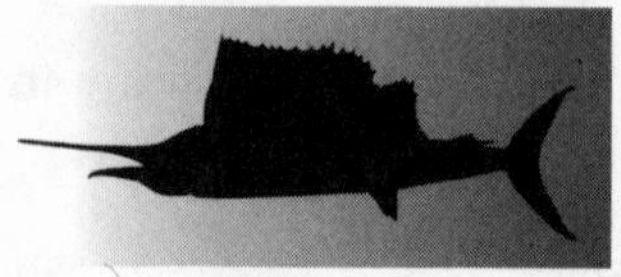

Journal Entry:

Missouri River, Early Spring

Fishing is a great leveler. Rock stars, schoolgirls, expert fishing guides, ordinary folk, or extraordinary folk—the fish don't much give a damn who catches them. Or who doesn't catch them.

Why else would we worship them so?

Fish are sufficiently indifferent to human desire to be deities, which no doubt accounts for so many fishing prayers. When a fish takes our lure or bait, it is as if we are, for a moment, acknowledged by a life force we can neither predict nor control. The slightest recognition by this life force fills us with joy.

We may not be remembered or respected by our own kind, but if noticed by a fish—even for a moment—we are able to salvage a bit of meaning from the Great Confusion. Distant, fickle, capable of existing entirely without or in spite of us—no wonder we angle for the blessings of these little finned gods. Safe in their deep, they don't give a rip if we live or die. What greater remedy for the sin of pride than to be dismissed by a mere fish?

On the Missouri River this early May afternoon I watched the rainbow-trout gods toy perfectly with three human beings: my professional guide (a friendly, persistent man filled with hubris who bragged mightily about how many fish we'd catch this day), an innocent, first-time, never-touched-a-fly-rod-before lad, and me.

You know what happened.

After four hours of casting the same black leeches to the same spawning rainbows on the same gravel bar before us, the boy had caught seven fish, I four, and the guide none. Zero. Zip. Nada. Nothing. Not even a touch. As the Good Book says, "Pride goeth before . . ." and all that.

"They were especially cruel today," remarked the utterly humbled fishing guide as we started up the hill to the truck.

"Who?" I asked.

"The rainbow gods."

"Yes," I said. "Yes, they were."

At the truck, stripping off my waders, I glanced back to the river to see the boy's rod doubled over once again under the weight of yet another big trout. I thought to myself that it is good to worship a god you can count on in the clinches.

"No Fishing!"

I don't deny it, I've fished behind "No Fishing" signs. As a boy I cut my fishing teeth trespassing. The only fishing within biking or hiking distance was Miller's Pond, and it was posted all around with big, black-and-white "No Fishing!" signs. I would read Mr. Miller's "No Fishing!" signs, and the little criminal in me would twist "*No* Fishing!" into "*Hot* Fishing!"

Unless you've been a boy or raised one, it may be hard to believe that boys are *supposed* to cave in to temptation once in a while. It's how we learn. We come upon some opportunity or other and ask, "Is there anything around here a fellow really shouldn't do?"

No matter the answer, we'll try it. A child psychologist assures me that if you want a navy bean up a boy's nose, say to him, "Now whatever you do, don't put that navy bean up your nose."

Forbidden fishing was about the easiest, least complicated sin I ever committed. Besides, I could hear old Mr. Miller's pickup coming for better than a mile, by which time I was safely through the trees and back over the posted fence.

Despite my parents' valiant efforts, most of the Christian guilt load I was supposed to carry for my trespassing crimes slipped. The knots came untied or something. Most of the guilt ended up in a heap at my feet. I guess I never thought to pick it up again.

From my Bible classes as a small boy I learned that if you sin in your heart you might as well go ahead and sin for real, since you have to do the time anyway. I figured that if they were going to charge my account for sins I'd already *thought* about doing, it didn't make much sense not to go ahead and have some fun.

To me, trespassing to fish was never a high crime; it was a borderline sin at best. It wasn't on the same level as fishing out of season, killing more fish than you needed, or damaging someone's property to get to the fish. If anything, trespassing to catch fish was a kind of sport.

A peasant's sport, it turns out. Not until years later would I learn from history that in Europe the royals owned all the land and water and put up signs and fences to keep the riffraff out and the game to themselves. Except for a possible French king's bastard on my father's side several centuries back, and some royal Scottish Guthrie blood on my mother's side, the odds are that most of my kin were white trash, meaning mostly poor Scots, shanty Irish, potato eaters, poachers, and trespassers. My guess is that the only time most of my ancestors spent in royal courts was when they were on trial. If we'd had one, our family crest might have read "Swipin' fish, fur, and feathers from them what owns 'em but aren't lookin' is no sin in God's eyes."

There's an old Native American belief that when thieves die they have to carry everything they ever stole on their backs throughout eternity. Luckily, I'm not a Native American, because if "stole" means stealing fishes from Miller's Pond, then I'd be needing an eighteen-wheeler tractor-trailer just to pack the bluegills. Miller's Pond was loaded with bluegills.

Trespassing as a boy taught me a great deal. I learned how to keep my eyes peeled, how to listen carefully for the sound of a distant truck engine—Mr. Miller's—how to trust fear, what a friend paranoia can be, and how to duck and run low through the bushes when an enemy bigger than you approaches—all important lessons I didn't have to relearn in the U.S. Army.

There was a delicious taste of fear to be found fishing forbidden waters. The feeling tingled with the risk of being caught, convicted, and hanged by the neck until dead for stealing a two-pound bass. And there was that special lightness of being when, once again safe on the other side of the "No Fishing!" signs, you knew you'd gotten away with it one more time.

It was a considerable disappointment to me when, after a couple of years of heisting spiny rays from Miller's Pond, one day Mr. Miller decided to walk down from the farmhouse instead of drive.

He slipped silently up behind me and whispered, "Catching any?"

Wound as tight as a tick with two years of pent-up paranoia for power, I shot out over the pond like an electric bullfrog and nearly landed on my bobber.

Sputtering as I came up out of the water, I stammered, "S-s-some."

Old Mr. Miller smiled, looked at my stringer in the water, and said, "Next time stop by the house and ask. I like to know who's here. Good luck, kid."

Freud's Flounder, or How I Taught the Good Doctor to Fly-fish

When I first began the study of modern psychology some forty years ago, Sigmund Freud was considered a god, or simply God, depending on how close you felt you stood to the father of psychoanalysis. Now the master has fallen on hard times. Freud still has followers, but nobody pays much attention to them anymore. For a time I even considered myself a Freudian, owing in part to the alignment of the stars following his death and my birth a few months apart in 1939—a celestial event portending small things indeed—and the fact that I taught Sigmund Freud to fly-fish.

This essay is called "Freud's Flounder" for good reason. When you've already written books entitled *Pavlov's Trout* and *Darwin's Bass*, your duty is clear. I did promise my wife, however, that I would never write *Solomon's Salmon* or *Plato's Pumpkinseed.*

Freud's impact on humanity is staggering: He pretty much invented the study of modern psychology all by himself. You cannot open a car door in a parking lot at a convention of the American Psychiatric Association, the American Psychological Association, or the National Association of Social Workers and not knock over a regiment of venerable professionals who cut their teeth on Freudian theory, Freudian principles, and Freudian thought. Fully integrated into the mother tongue, the terms *id*, *ego*, *superego*, *repression*, *rationalization*, *projection*, *sublimation*, *reaction formation*, and dozens of others festoon our language with meanings we never had before Sigmund invented them. Even people who move their lips when they read speak fluent Freudianese.

Freud's writing was the lure I fell for as a young man fishing for ideas to help explain human behavior, including my own. Reading Freud carried me into the most fascinating career possible, and I owe him a great debt—which is why I taught him to fish the dry fly.

So far as I know Sigmund Freud never fished while he lived. Fishing might have changed his views on the nature of things. Had he taken up the study of angling with the same passion with which he took up the study of the human psyche, he might not have developed such a bottom-up, parallax, screwball, flounder-eyed view of mankind. Mind you, I say this with all due respect.

Had Freud fished, I believe he would have been a deepwater bait fisherman. He'd have wanted to probe the depths. He'd have gone for fluke and halibut and all the flounders. Yes, the flounder would have been his fish.

Freud's flounder is just the sort of furtive, deep-dwelling, dark-on-one-side-light-on-the-other-side mystery fish that would have piqued the Master's lust to analyze. I can see him studying the bright eyes of a fresh-caught flounder flopping on the deck of a fishing boat.

"H-m-m. Curious. Yes, very curious indeed. It has both a light and dark side, a sort of id and superego, and yet its eyes are on *one side*. And it changes its coloration at will. A repressed, conflicted creature if ever I saw one!"

You have to face it, Freud was an odd duck with odd ideas. Most of what he read into ordinary reality sprang forth from the creativity of a too-fevered brain. The idea of penis envy comes to mind. I don't know how, but Freud lectured on phallic symbols and penis envy with a straight face. Still, he enjoyed fine cigars and a good joke, too, and once remarked to a class of students—smiling as he stuck a thick stogie into his mouth—"Sometimes a cigar is just a cigar." God knows what he'd have made of whipping a nine-foot fly rod back and forth, especially by one of our lady anglers.

Psychoanalysis is dying. Some say it's already dead and beginning to stink up the joint. What scientific research hasn't finished off, managed health care will bury alive. One hundred years from now Sigmund's work will be but a footnote to the history of human thought. "Whatever happened to Sigmund Freud?" they will ask.

Well, here's one answer, albeit a fanciful one.

Sigmund Freud died just before I was born. Where, you may ask, did Freud's soul go? What did the stars say at his death and my birth? More than one religion believes in astrology, the transmigration of souls, reincarnation, and other such difficult-to-prove articles of faith, so why shouldn't I?

As proof of my theory about what might have happened to Freud's essence, I here offer a brief summary of an evening many years ago when, after a long afternoon of fly-fishing in one of Utah's finest trout streams, a college friend and I lay on our backs under a darkening Rocky Mountain sky and grasped upward and inward in an attempt to understand the nature of things.

I explained to my pal, Steve, that in light of the Eastern mysticism I was reading at the time it seemed a quite reasonable hypothesis that Freud's soul might well have transmigrated into my body at the moment of my birth on November 17, 1939. After all, reincarnation being what it is and all, what else could account for an otherwise mediocre's student's straight-A average in my psychology courses?

"What else, indeed!" cried Steve, slurring his words. "Makes sense to me! Now pass the wine."

I took a swig, recrossed my legs, and gazed up at the Big Dipper. "Makes sense to me, too," I echoed. "Which means I taught Old Siggy to fly-fish . . . if you can fish in the afterlife. And if he can, I bet he enjoys it as much as I do."

"I'm sure he does," Steve said. "Now, will you please ask *Dr. Freud* to pass the wine bottle?"

It has always amazed me how perfectly reasonable theories as implausible as psychoanalysis, astrology, reincarnation, and the transmigration of souls sound after a wonderful day of fly-fishing—especially when you are lying on your back on summer grass next to your fly rod under a canopy of stars with a good friend, and the two of you have just polished off a half gallon of cheap red wine.

Fish are held together with bones. Without bones they would be invertebrates and therefore no more difficult to catch than clams. When I meet someone who does not eat fish because they are "bony," I must assume they do not understand what holds the world together.

One Fly Rod for Socrates, and Ten for Me

I read somewhere that experienced fly-fishing enthusiasts in America own, on average, ten fly rods. As an average fly-fishing enthusiast, I meet the standard and then some. I am not sure if this is a good thing, a bad thing, or something I should worry about. I do know that materialism, like a pair of shorts, creeps up on you.

On observing a multitude of wares for sale on the streets of ancient Athens, Socrates cried, "How many things I can do without!"

Socrates was a man. I am a man. But I am not Socrates.

For years and years when I scanned new fishing catalogues each spring, I did not shout, "How many things I can do without!" but rather, "How many things I *cannot* do without!" Thanks to years of gadget buying, I'm better now, but hardly cured.

I readily confess my materialistic leanings, and make no bones about the fact that there are few things of which I am more fond than a really fine fly rod.

Or a precision fly reel.

Or a boat with a keel to tame the rough sea.

Or a Gore-Tex jacket that protects me from wind, rain, sleet, and snow.

Or a pair of polarized sunglasses that give me the eyes of a heron.

Or . . .

If for every marketing person there is a mark, then for the Orvis company I am he. Maybe I am living proof of the philosopher William James's observation, "There is a very thin line between what's me and mine." Or maybe I am just an average fisherman who enjoys nice things.

In these modern times it is increasingly difficult to sort out that which is me from that which I have purchased to make me who I'd like to be. People are always more than the sum of their costumes, but it is becoming increasingly difficult to tell the people and the costumes apart. You have to hand it to the marketing people; they sell us things we never knew we needed until they told us so.

I'd like to think I am the sort of person who needs little, eats brown rice, and can get by without expensive toys. But then I see a nifty, collapsible wading staff and say to myself, "Naaaa" while I reach for my billfold. Over the years I've come to accept this small character flaw, if indeed it is a flaw in an America made robust by commerce and trade and the personal Gold Card.

Socrates eschewed things material and lived a life of the mind. I do not eschew things material and only *try* to live a life of the mind, some days spending up to twenty minutes at a time there.

To help rationalize my materialism, I have read a little about Socrates and ancient Greece. I believe I have found at least one reason why the philosopher could look at a great display of goods and say of them, "How many things I can do without!" Except for a few clay pots, a string of pearls, some silk from the Orient, a bit of silverware, imported wine, a fatted pig, and maybe a dagger or two, ancient Greece wasn't all that much of a shopping mall. What are these items compared to a G. Loomis fly rod, a Tibor reel, a float tube and fins?

Perhaps Socrates could afford to live a life of the mind because, in his time, there weren't all that many other places to live.

I have worried lately that the reason the world seems to be producing more consumers than philosophers is that it is near to impossible to live a life of the mind anymore. Our heads are so cluttered with toys and tools and must-see TV that our brains no longer have time to produce a mind. A mind is, after all, that fragile, impossibly complex, naturally selected, ephemeral, wispy, neurophysiological epiphenomenon the brain produces to enable us not only to survive but to live life with gusto. While I like Bill Gates, I believe the human brain ought to aspire to being something more than a receptor site for the World Wide Web.

With the senses packing in so much nonsense, our brains haven't enough energy left over to power up our minds. People everywhere seem unaware they even have a mind, and some wouldn't recognize their own mind if they bumped into it on the street. Not long ago one of my patients remarked, "I must be out of my mind, that is, if I have one."

Whatever your passion, it is during your quiet time within that passion that you will find your mind. For me, that quiet time is fishing.

Angling is how I get reacquainted with my mind. After a couple of hours of silent casting, and as I'm reeling in to go home, my mind will say, "So, don't be a stranger!"

Sometimes when you are fishing your mind will wander away and bring back the damnedest things. Solutions to problems. Insights about people. Ideas so fresh they demand writing down.

It may sound easy, but not thinking about anything in particular, and just *being*, is a very hard thing to do. In this state of unfocused focusing, you don't chase your mind away by chanting a mantra. You don't numb it up or down with booze or drugs. You don't hand your brain a pick and shovel and say, "Dig here! Find my mind!"

Rather, you just fish and be, and be and fish. If you're lucky, your mind will slip out of its tight shoes, wriggle its toes, and find you.

When you are quiet and engaged in unfocused focusing, things deep in the great unconscious unfetter themselves and start to drift around, like cotton from a cottonwood tree on a breezy day. Somehow these loosed seeds float through your mind and find each other. Where they fit together, they come together, and a new idea is born.

There are no new original ideas in the world, only new juxtapositions of old ones—all of them handed down to us by generations past. If for no other reason than this, we should honor our elders.

Were Socrates alive today and living his life of the mind, he might be a fisherman. He might even be a fly-fisherman. Whatever sort of fishing he enjoyed, something tells me he would keep his angling simple, his life uncluttered. He wouldn't watch much TV and he wouldn't hang around the mall. Rather, you'd find him out on a stream somewhere, or sitting by a campfire under the stars, thinking. He'd be the most interesting man imaginable to talk with, and he'd own but a single fly rod.

Fly-fishing Nazis

"Paul, I know you're into fishing," said the caller with a Dakota drawl, "so I was wondering if you could help me. My father's birthday is coming up and some of us in the family want to get him a warm box. He's talked about getting one, but we don't know exactly what a warm box is."

A small fishing reputation will occasionally get you phone calls like this. I asked the lady, "Could you tell me more?"

"Well, what he wants has warms on the bottom. Then, when you want warms on the top, you just turn it upside down. I think you can sit on it, too. I don't know how big it is or what it costs, but could you tell me where to find one?"

"H-m-m," I said, temporarily stumped. Warms? What warms when you turn it upside down? Some kind of high-tech outdoor stool for ice fishermen?

As a fishing writer, I get all sorts of new gadget announcements in the mail, but I'd apparently missed a fishing stool that warms when you turn it upside down. Puzzled, I asked the caller, "Does your father ice-fish? Bait-fish? Fly-fish?"

"I don't know," she said. "I think he uses a bobber."

"Warms?" I asked. "Are you sure you don't mean worms?"

"Warms, wooorms, whatever you call them is okay with me, I just want to know where you find one of these fancy boxes."

With the mystery solved, I gave the young lady directions to the nearest sporting goods store. Having found a worm box with lids on both ends, she called later to thank me, thus saving my small reputation.

Perplexed at taking so long to hear "worms" in "warms," I began to roll the mystery around a bit. It occurred to me that the reason I had so much trouble with the lady's request was that perhaps I am becoming a fly-fishing Nazi. I've always hated fly-fishing Nazis, so I wouldn't like it much if I became one myself.

A fly-fishing Nazi is someone who believes there is only one way to fish properly, and that is with artificial flies. The worst kind of elitists, they consider any other approach to fishing unacceptable, and strongly suggestive of questionable paternity and a room-temperature IQ. Such people tend to be full of themselves, high-toned pompous asses who, when you really get to know them, you wish you hadn't bothered.

It is true that over the years I've given up fishing with worms and frogs and minnows and salmon eggs and cheese and marshmallows and such, and switched almost entirely to artificials to catch fish. I suppose you could call it a fishing journey from "I fooled you" to "I *fooled* you." There is nothing unusual about this evolutionary journey through sportfishing, just so long as you don't end up thinking the trail leads to some high moral ground that permits you to look down on others. It doesn't.

At this phase in my own development as an angler, I'm admittedly enchanted by fly-fishing, and especially flies. Trout flies, bass flies, salmon flies, steelhead flies, crappie flies, pike flies, barracuda flies, bonefish flies . . . You name the fish and the fly that will catch it, and the same fly will catch me.

I tie most of my own flies and even have a bogus fly named after me. This may sound like some great accomplishment, but compared to the achievements of the real contributors to fly-fishing, it is indeed a low honor. Most flytiers can contribute a new fly to the world of fly-fishing with a little thread, a hank of yarn, a couple of feathers, and a stiff drink. Whether the creation ever gets used by others and develops a fish-catching reputation is something else again.

Two things have kept me from becoming a fly-fishing Nazi.

First, my roots reach deep to Midwest rivers, farm ponds, bluegills, catfish, and angle worms. A fisherman should never forget his beginnings, nor be ashamed of them.

The second thing is a plain fact few fly-fishers are willing to acknowledge. Trout, bass, salmon, steelhead, bonefish—you name the game—most could care less about what pattern is presented to them, so long as it is presented properly.

Sure, all fly eaters can be fussy from time to time, zeroing in on one mayfly and not another, but the cold truth is that catching fish with flies is as easy as pie when the fish are hungry. When the fish are famished—and so long as the fly doesn't do something weird once it's on or in the water—the only fly that matters is the one that fits in their mouths.

Starved for nourishment, fish and fisherfolk are not much different; we eat what is set before us. When we are ravenous caviar is fine, but so is peanut butter and jelly. The fisher who catches a starving fish on a fly and then brags because he did not use bait is not only ignorant, but uncommonly full of crap.

Over the years, in this fishing camp or that, I've met several fly-fishing Nazis. They prove interesting as specimens of snobbery, and demonstrate what can happen to a small person when he finally finds something at which he is successful, but they tend to fall into a class of people about which an old fishing buddy once remarked, "With all that deep water around, I can understand why you'd take a pinhead like that fishing, but what I can't understand is why you'd bring him back."

There are two things you can count on in life: Sooner or later the trout will rise, and whatever it is they're rising for will not be in your fly box.

The Kiss of the Piranha

Some things you should do when you're young, and well before something called sound judgment sets in. Sound judgment can take an awful lot of fun out of being alive. Too much sound judgment and you may never catch a piranha on a fly.

I was forced to think about all this one afternoon while flying over the Amazon rain forest in a light plane, when both engines coughed and stopped. With the props stilled, the aircraft didn't nose over into a steep dive, but coasted along in its glide path, silently slipping through a blue sky high above a horizon of jagged jungle peaks. The pilot offered no explanation for what had happened, and I was too upset to ask.

When I was young and dumb and unencumbered by even an ounce of sound judgment, I vowed to live life any way but dull. I hoped that even if I grew up someday, somehow I would still be a boy. At least inside. I've always believed that women fall in love not so much with the man they meet, but with the boy they find inside. I'd never regretted this aspiration to always remain a boy . . . until those engines quit.

My first thought was not panic, but a quiet reflection that the show, as much as I might not like it, was over. Right now. Right here. No more family. No more fishing. No nothing. Time was up. That time comes for all of us, and that time had now come for me. For some reason I recalled W. C. Fields's line, "It's a funny old world—a man's lucky if he gets out alive."

But just as I began to count my blessings and add up my regrets, the twin engines roared to life again. The fisherman in the seat next to the pilot called back to the rest of us, "He was just switching wing tanks! Let the one run out first and then restarted!"

Whew.

I had my life back. Just between you and me, I do not think it is nice to let the poor gringo tourist free-fall for several seconds into what's left of the Amazon rain forest without first telling him why. I much prefer to schedule my existential crises for Monday mornings, not for when I'm on my way to a new fishing hole. But then, I suppose this is just the sort of thing that happens to people with not enough sound judgment to stay home instead of traipsing off into the wild Amazonas in search of fish.

After I'd started breathing again and loosened a death grip on my rod case, I realized how badly I wanted to catch a piranha on a fly. Boy, man, and grandfather wrapped into one being, I repeated to myself a favorite old saw: "You may only be young once, but you can be immature your whole life."

Three days later, up the Ventuari River from camp.

Though the official sport was peacock bass, I wanted a piranha. And on a fly. A fly-fisher doesn't travel to the heart of the Amazon rain forest to take a piranha on a plug. Oh, you can, and they won't arrest you for it, but fly-fishers are allowed to be peculiar. I'm pretty sure the other anglers—all spin and bait casters—thought I was peculiar, but we got along famously.

So there I was standing on a rock near some fast water making ready to lay a yellow-and-white Lefty's Deceiver in a piranha hole. With a light rod, I began a series of false casts.

Just once I wanted to catch a fish that can eat a man. There is something wonderfully leveling about this arrangement between man and piranha: If we catch them, we eat them; if they catch us, they eat us.

As a boy I spent many a Saturday morning at the movies watching weekly adventure episodes featuring Johnny Weissmuller as Jungle Jim. Jungle Jim was law and justice in the jungle, but quicksand and wild creatures were the executioners. One of the paybacks you got for kidnapping some scientist's daughter, or killing a few natives while stealing the emerald from the jungle god's forehead, was the kiss of the piranha.

And it was some kiss. Run to ground by Jungle Jim, and while trying to escape by wading a river, the bad guys were suddenly surrounded by thousands of unseen fish with razorlike teeth and big appetites. Cleaned to the bone one bite at a time, the evildoers screamed and sank slowly out of sight. The water boiled and turned red around them. Complete and perfect justice. No high-priced lawyers, no bail, no change of venue, no media circus, no jury selection, no mistrials, no stays or delays or screwing around; just sure, swift, unabridged, unmitigated justice, dispensed coolly and without malice by old Mother Nature herself.

I tied a Lefty's Deceiver to a 16-pound tippet. The piranha in this part of the Orinoco River basin don't get much bigger than five pounds, so I figured 16-pound monofilament would dent their razors and land them just fine. Since piranha don't rise, I made a cast, sank the fly and mended it once. The fly slipped down and into the head of some greenish slot water that, according to my guide, Luis, held plenty of "bluegills from hell."

There was a stiff tug. I set the hook. The fish turned, then, *pop*, the line went slack. I reeled in and studied the end of the leader, which appeared to have been cut through with a pair of nail clippers. Luis smiled. "Wire," he said in his limited English.

But I reached for some special leaders I'd tied back home (20-pound-test with 40-pound shock tippets) and began to tie on another fly.

These little fish I'd come to catch in this remote corner of the globe aren't the earth's only piranhas; the world is full of piranhas: people who relate to the world with vicious, flesh-rending mouths. I once knew a criminal defense lawyer who, rumor held, kept an aquarium full of piranhas at home so that, hand-feeding them raw meat each morning before trial, he could stay in shape. I always thought this was just the sort of intimidating rumor a flashy criminal lawyer might intentionally circulate about himself until, one day, I was served up as an expert witness for one of his famous cross examinations. Didn't like it much. He could rend flesh with the best of them. Turns out the story of his piranha tank was true.

But a 40-pound shock tippet should whip any piranha. A 40-pound tippet is a rope. Laying out a new fly, I made a mend and watched the fake sink into the feeding lane. A silvery flash in green water and a strong tug followed. This time the fish bolted. I broke its neck. The line went slack.

Reeling in, I glanced over to see Luis squatting on a boulder with his straw hat tipped down over his face. If he was smiling, I couldn't confirm it. But I heard him repeat, "Wire."

When it comes to adapting to local conditions, I like to keep doing what works back home, even if it isn't working wherever I happen to be. Ann says it's a gift. Studying the clean cut of the piranha's kiss, I counted my flies and, always the slow learner, tied another pattern to the 40-pound-test.

This time the take required a few casts, but come it did: a sharp tap, then nothing. I stripped in line to find that the green-and-yellow faux-polar-bear-hair fly was still mine, but looked as if it had been trimmed with a barber's scissors: All the hair above the hook's shank had been nipped away. Clean. Some kiss. Luis seemed to be napping.

Finally, I reached for the wire, nine inches of coated 20-pound-test. When the next strike came, the steel held, I tipped the rod up, and the fight was on. A muscled panfish version of Arnold Schwarzenegger, we had a good quarrel, but I won. Luis was standing beside me as I slid the three-pounder up onto the rock I'd been standing on. (I should note that, owing to my childhood exposure to Jungle Jim action episodes, I elected not to wade for piranha.) "Pincers," he said with a smile.

I handed him my pliers. Luis showed me the pointy choppers, carefully cradling the fish so I could see its bright nickel-silvered sides, gold throat, burnished red-gold gill plates, black bar behind the gills, and shape—like a crappie with shoulders. He repeated his "wire leader" lesson and then, according to camp code, released the beauty.

It was late. We quit with the first piranha and headed back to camp for supper.

Stripping off hat and bandanna and letting the jungle air cool my body as we flew downstream in the launch, I felt good and calm inside. I'd realized a dream and come full circle of a boy's life, piranha to piranha in fifty years. I'd beached a man-eater, and, if and when the time came, I'd finally be able to top some pal's fly-fishing story with one of those down-in-the-Amazon whoppers.

As we raced downriver, the sun reddened as it touched the rain forest, lighting up flocks of perched ibis like white candles against a great green drape. A time to talk; I wished my Spanish were stronger.

Then, passing a riverbank Indian camp as evening fell, I could see small boys fishing pools and runs near shore. Squatting on smooth brown rocks where the swift current passed, they had no rods or reels but cast hand lines with hook and bait tied to a small stone. Concentrating on their angling, the fisher-boys jerked their baits back to them in short pulls, hand over hand, and only glanced up briefly to wave to us.

I turned to Luis and asked in my stumbling Spanish, "*¿Qual tipo de pez?*" What kind of fish?

Luis smiled and said: "*Los ninos el pez.*"

"Children's fish?" I asked.

"*Si,*" replied Luis, "*piranha.*"

Humor

Early one spring many years ago I took a full professor of sociology fly-fishing with me. One of his graduate students, I had a plan to suck up to him and get good marks on my term paper. He knew it and I knew it, so the deal didn't smell too bad.

Sociologists are an odd lot, kind of a cross between a proper English gentleman and a pocket calculator. A prissy Irish-tweed man, Dr. Smith wore a shirt and tie to give lectures and a shirt and tie to the pizza parlor; if I hadn't threatened him, he'd have worn a shirt and tie trout-fishing.

The stream we planned to fish was raging with spring runoff. I grabbed an aspen limb and broke it over my knee to make myself a staff; I advised the good doctor to do the same. "Nonsense," he snapped, "I'm an expert wader."

"Suit yourself," I said, bowing to let him take the lead.

Dr. Smith plunged in ahead of me and, three steps into the torrent, slipped under the surface, leaving only a highlander's wool cap floating downstream to mark his disappearance. He went under with a certain grace, sort of the way you might imagine a British aristocrat would sink properly from sight under a roily trout stream: quietly, calmly, with no screaming or flailing of the limbs, and making no more of a splash than a small muskrat.

When Dr. Smith eventually surfaced at the tail of a promising pool some way downstream and grabbed his hat, I wiped the tears of laughter from my eyes, waved, and asked after the pool's contents. Had he seen any respectable trout? Was the pool worth a few casts? Based on the observed aquatic life-forms, what fly pattern did he recommend?

Pouring out of the stream—and with the stream pouring out of him—Dr. Smith failed to respond to my queries. Rather, he cut me a stare that would freeze steel. Gee, I wondered to myself, hadn't he ever seen a Charlie Chaplin movie?

We didn't catch many trout that day, and Dr. Smith never lightened up. Even after I built a fire to keep him warm while we dried his clothes, he was never able to find his smile in the situation. I'm not sure you want to go fishing with anyone who can't see himself starring in a Charlie Chaplin movie.

On a longed-for fishing day, a sudden storm can blow you off the lake. After a six-hour drive, you can arrive at a river ten minutes after the bite stops for the month. You can break your favorite fly rod in a fall, slice open your thumb cleaning perch, stumble backward off a pier while lifting an anchor, crack your head on a bulkhead, get so seasick you hope to die, snag a friend with a hook or have him snag you, and on and on and on in the great and universal comedy of errors that is angling, and life. If you cannot find mirth while thus employed, where can you find it?

It is not enough for a fisherman to quietly endure what is unpleasant or painful or even tragic; he must come to relish it. After all, it is comedy that separates us from the mayflies and the fishes, and only wit between us and the gloom.

A fishing trip without laughter is not much of a fishing trip. To get there, something funny needs to happen, preferably something bad needs to happen that turns into funny, especially something bad/funny that happens to someone who had it coming—the whiner does nicely.

But if this person is unavailable for duty, then something bad should happen anyway. For the true fisherman a story is funny when a beginner loses a big fish, but for the story to rise to comedy you have to use a dying fisherman and a world record.

One of the pleasant things about middle age is losing a fine fish but not losing your temper.

Hawg Plug

Back when I was a kid, and before time became money, I made my own bass plugs. Or, to be perfectly honest, I made my own bass plug. I would probably have made more than one, but as things turned out, the day I lost "Quinnett's Killer" I was so heartbroken I thought I'd never be able to make another quite like it.

"Whatcha makin'?" Richard Hatcher asked as he strolled into my room with a banana he'd pinched from the fruit bowl. Richard was my childhood fishing friend and sometime fellow trespasser on Miller's Pond, where for several years running we had tried to catch Old Barrel Belly, a largemouth bass of legendary proportions who supposedly ate mallards and small dogs for breakfast. Father referred to Richard, a boy of low reputation and dark character, as the Artful Dodger (which didn't mean much to me until I was forced to read Charles Dickens in the tenth grade, by which time Richard, bless him, was off to reform school).

"A bass plug," I said.

"Huh? A bass plug? Why don't you just dip one out of your dad's tackle box? He's got plenty." ("Dipping" was one of the euphemisms Richard employed to shade theft into something less criminal. "Borry" was another favorite—even if what you were "borrying" was a peach from Mr. Thompson's tree and you couldn't return anything but the pit.)

"I got this idea for the perfect bass plug," I said. "It'll be a diver, floater, surface popper, and all-around noisemaker with these two propellers in the back and this scoop in the front. I'm going to call it Quinnett's Killer bass plug. If it works, I'll patent it and make millions."

Richard sauntered over and tweaked the propellers. "Looks like a toy boat to me. Old Barrel Belly will never fall for something as silly as this."

"Who's to say?" I said. "We sure haven't got him to hit anything they've made yet."

"He's old, not stupid," Richard shot back. "And he sure ain't goin' to hit a toy boat. Why don't we just go down to the sporting goods store and pick up that muskie plug we been lookin' at?"

"That plug costs two bucks."

"I didn't say we was goin' to *pay* for it; I just said we'd pick it up, you know . . ."

I reminded Richard (for about the thousandth time) that I wasn't allowed to steal and that if he stopped to think about it, he too would see it was wrong to take something that didn't belong to him.

"Shoot," Richard said, "I have thought about that. Anybody knows it's wrong to steal. It says so in the Bible. What I mean is, we'd only borry it. Why, I'd take it back myself!"

"And what if Old Barrel Belly ripped it off the line and we lost it?"

"Well," he said, "I guess that'd be God's way, wouldn't it? Mysterious and all that."

I told Richard I had some homework to do, but that by next Saturday, Quinnett's Killer would be finished and we'd bike out to Miller's Pond and give it a try. He tweaked the propellers once more, shook his head, and left by way of the kitchen. By the time I remembered I was supposed to keep an eye on him while he was in the house, he'd already cleaned out Mom's fruit bowl.

"If that boy had a scruple," Mother later remarked, "it would die of loneliness."

By Friday night, the paint was drying on the Killer. I was fairly happy with my spawning bluegill design, and was standing back to admire the tiny hand-painted scales when Jerkface (my older brother) wandered by to comment that Killer looked more like something the cat threw up than a fishing lure.

"Wait'll I get the hooks on," I said with confidence. "Then you'll see."

"Why bother putting hooks on it?" Jerkface said. I picked up something sharp.

"I'm sorry. It doesn't look like something the cat just threw up."

"That's better," I said, laying down my X-Acto knife.

"It looks like a toy boat."

But I knew, even at that tender age, that genius inventors had to put up with scorn and ridicule until they proved themselves—just like Spencer Tracy when he played young Thomas Edison in the movies. So I screwed the big treble hooks into the pine, daubed on some eyes, painted a little Q right on the belly, and called her good. Even though Mother got after me for short-sheeting Jerkface's bed that night, it seemed the least I could do under the circumstances.

Early next morning, Richard and I headed out to Miller's Pond in the dark, stashed our bikes in the brush, and crawled under the fence. According to Richard, Mr. Miller didn't like boys on his farm pond, so we always fished the pond at first light before he was up and about his chores. It always bothered me, though, to untie his little pram from the willow tree to which he had nailed the following sign: "Wonder if there is life after death? Trespass and find out!"

"He don't mean it," Richard would say. "He'd never kill a couple of little Christian boys. Besides, he's got more fish than he needs, and we're only going to borry a few anyway. And it ain't like God didn't put this here pond right where He did if He didn't want us to fish it."

It wasn't always easy to follow Richard's crooked logic, but when you were out on Miller's Pond at first light and the air was cool and still and you could see the bluegills feeding just under the surface or watch a school of bait fish being chased along in the shallows by a big bass, his powers of reasoning seemed simply amazing.

I tied on Killer as Richard rowed toward the island Old Barrel Belly was known to haunt. The water was flat and gray and filled with promise. Richard stopped rowing about fifty feet from the island so we could coast into casting distance. I heaved back and let the Killer fly out and over the weed beds. *Kerplunk!*

"Now let that toy boat sit a spell," Richard whispered. "Then twitch her."

We waited. The rings spread out to nothing. About a week later, Richard gave me the nod. Reeling up the slack, I sent a twitch down the line.

Now I know how a lot of fishermen would start to embellish their story right about here and go on and on about what happened: how the water bulged; how a bass the size of a rain barrel surged up and out of the water shaking a plug in a mouth so big you could have parked a Ford tractor in it; how the monster dove into the weeds, cut circles around the boat so fast we looked like two kids riding a washing machine set on spin-dry; or how he made a run that pulled us so fast the pram set up a wake two feet high; or how, just when we thought we had him pooped out, he came straight at us at ramming speed and put a dent the size of a soccer ball in the side of the pram. And then how, on his last great run, the Hawg of Hawgs charged straight down and, finding a log to wrap the line around, broke off to freedom with the Killer still in his mouth, leaving me with my grandfather's old steel casting rod bent into the shape of a coat hanger.

But I wouldn't do that. All I'll say is that by the time I got my thumb off the spool of braided line, the skin on the underside of that digit was so shiny I could see my face in it. "That was him!" Richard cried. "Old Barrel Belly! He must be going blind. Now what's the matter with you?" he said, looking at me questioningly.

"Nothing," I said.

"Then whatcha bawlin' your eyes out for?"

To confess a thing here, I had started to shed a tear or two. It wasn't every day you lost a million-dollar prototype bass plug to the Hawg of Hawgs, and had a mirror for a thumb to prove it. But I couldn't let on to Richard how I felt at the moment. "Burned a blister on my thumb" was all I could muster up to say.

"Well stop bawlin'," he said. "I can't stand to see a fisherman cry. It just ain't natural."

I recovered some and asked Richard why he thought Old Barrel Belly had gone blind.

"Now I ask you, why would a bass take a toy boat? I mean, it ain't normal, is it? Why, that so-called Killer of yours was just about as dumb-lookin' an excuse for a bass plug as I've ever seen. Yep, Old Barrel Belly's gone blind as a bat."

Just then, a great and ugly passion welled up from deep in my breast, and I thought to grab Richard by his scrawny neck and toss him overboard, but as I lurched to my feet, I spied Mr. Miller pounding down the gravel road in his pickup. "Yikes!" I cried. "The cops!"

Richard, who was never one to stand up for his convictions, had no desire to test his theory about Mr. Miller's reluctance to send a couple of little Christian boys to the Great Beyond, and so, stroking like a galley slave who was under combat conditions, he rowed us speedily to shore—and safety.

As footraces go, it wasn't much of a contest. Mr. Miller was an old man, and under the circumstances, we were inspired to attempt a personal best in the hundred-yard dash. You wouldn't think a couple of small boys could hurdle a four-foot barbed-wire fence at a dead run—but we did.

Later, when we'd reached safety and were speeding down the country road as fast as we could peddle, Richard remarked, "Boy! Old Mr. Miller sure is a mean old coot! Selfish, too! Why, the things he called us! You'd a thought he wanted all those bass for himself. And here we only borried his pram. Heck, we even gave it back to him. If he's goin' be that way about it, guess we'll just have to start night fishin'."

"Maybe we ought to go back and apologize," I said. "Maybe ask him if it would be okay if we fished his pond."

"Shoot," Richard said. "Fishin' ain't no fun if it's legal."

I didn't want to do it, but right about then I shoved my ruined old steel casting rod into the spokes of Richard's front wheel. Later he said he did three cartwheels. But it's a lie—he only did two.

In a good fishing camp it is not enough to share equally in the work; each must offer to do more.

Keepers and Dumpers

People can generally be categorized into two groups: keepers or dumpers. So can fishermen. Keepers are people who hang on to everything and believe that even the most useless, worn-out, never-used item has value that demands keeping. Dumpers say, "I haven't used this thing in six months, it's taking up space, so off it goes to the dump."

Somehow keepers and dumpers seem to find each other in life. And they tend to fall in love. I would never dream to question how these things happen.

My father was a fisherman and a keeper. My mother was not a fisherman and a dumper. Their marriage lasted their whole lives. When Father died, Mother had an awful lot of dumping to do. She'd been waiting more than fifty years.

Among other things, Mom dumped all Dad's fly-tying and rod-building materials, fresh- and saltwater tackle, and dozens of boxes filled with lure-making materials. These treasures were dumped onto her sons and grandsons. I took my share home. Even today, when I delve into the pile in search of some thread or hooks or lacquer or something, I find one of Dad's handwritten notes explaining the date the item was purchased, the price, and an explanation for its intended use. Good memories flood in.

I am a keeper, my wife is a dumper. Surveying any given storage room, Ann will say, "Why are we keeping all this old junk, let's toss it out!"

I'm grateful that Ann's instinct to dump does not include husbands.

Yet.

All the research on personality traits suggests that despite a desire to be different, people end up pretty much the way they start out. As the twig is bent in the womb, and especially during the first five years of life, so it grows. If we live long enough, we eventually become like Harschfeld caricatures, with all the lines exaggerated in all the right places.

Keepers and dumpers never change, but they do ripen.

So I was not surprised to hear a story about an old keeper fisherman who saved all manner of fishing tackle until the day he died. After the funeral, his wife and children began the sad and happy task of going through the multitude of things he'd kept, the dumpers among them leading the way.

In his sporting room they found a desk with several drawers. In the top drawer they found spool after spool of old, worn-out fly-fishing lines carefully wrapped around cheap romance novels. On each spool were the following words, handwritten on a tag tied to the line: "fishing line to be saved."

In the next drawer down they found spool after spool of old, worn-out fly-fishing line carefully wrapped around cheap romance novels. On each spool were the following words, handwritten on a tag tied to the line: "fishing line not to be saved."

Sunshine Anglers

Everybody wants a sure thing, or at least a pretty sure thing. Fishermen included. Some fishermen get ticked off when a supposedly hot fishing tip turns cold. "We never got a hit all day," they whine, "and you said you killed 'em just last week."

These are the sunshine anglers.

Fishing is chancy.

Fishing is *supposed* to be chancy.

If fishing wasn't chancy, they'd call it catching.

Fishing is a form of gambling, but not as dumb as playing the lottery. My professional gambling pals assure me that buying a lottery ticket is the true sucker bet. Every time. Any house action that can guarantee funding for new schools and roads needs a lot of suckers to feed the play, which is no doubt why governments are into gaming. As H. L. Mencken said, "No one ever went broke underestimating the intelligence of the American people."

Picking a Lotto number is a sucker bet because it requires no knowledge, no talent, no skill, no practice, no timing, no nothing—except, of course, a childlike belief in magic. In fishing lingo, a sucker is a fish so easy to catch it is not considered sporting to do so, which is no doubt why people who throw their money away in lotteries came to be called by the same name.

Conversely, fishing is not a sucker bet; fishing is more like blackjack. The more you know about the house (habitat), the game (fish), and the odds (water, food supplies, and weather conditions), the more you stand to win (catch fish).

If fishing is gambling, at least it is *intelligent* gambling, in which luck only plays a small, undiscovered part, and then only for the other guy. Luck is such a primitive concept I'm surprised any fisherman who didn't drop out of grade school even believes in it, let alone bets on it.

To win at fishing—and blackjack—you have to have two things: brains and skill. And you have to play. You can't win at blackjack thinking about it, and you can't catch fish thinking about them either—you have to *go fishing*.

The only way to find out whether you're going to win at blackjack, or catch fish, or fall in love, or succeed at business, or make it big in whatever you hope to make it big in, is to lay down your bet and play. No bet, no play, no chance of winning. That's the way life works.

Sunshine anglers want a sure thing.

"Are you sure we'll catch fish?" they ask.

"I don't want to go fishing if we don't catch some," they say.

"How do you know we won't be wasting our time?" they query.

Once the diagnosis is in, I never waste a minute trying to convince sunshine anglers to go fishing.

And I never ask a sunshine angler to go fishing twice. If they want a sure thing they should stay home, watch TV, and play the lottery. At least then they can count on the outcome.

And Cain Outfished Abel

Competitive fly-fishing is not new: my older brother John and I invented it in 1953. Not a year apart in age, we also invented sibling rivalry. For the record, and for this little story, John is Cain and I am Abel. Except for my father's intervention on Green Lake one summer day, my brother and I might have repeated that dark episode of biblical history.

It is not entirely clear whether the original Cain and Abel were fly-fishers—the information was lost somehow in translation from the ancient Greek. We know that artificial flies were used in antiquity, and that cane rods go all the way back to the beginning, so it seems a reasonable hypothesis that Cain and Abel were flycasters, taught to fish, no doubt by their father, Adam. Without cane rods and hand-tied flies, it is hard to sustain the notion that the Garden of Eden was truly paradise. I cannot get my mind around a "No Fishing" sign in paradise, whether on this side of heaven or the other. Hell, I'm sure, is lousy with "No Fishing" signs.

The birthplace of modern competitive fly-fishing in 1953 was the inlet stream to a high mountain lake, Green Lake. The game was rainbow trout, the prize, cash. Two dollars, as I recall. The weapons of choice were cane rods and no. 12 dry flies. The trout were unwilling participants, and Cain, having sprinted ahead to claim the best casting rock, was outfishing Abel three to one.

"That's four!" he cried. "That's five!"

Try as I might, I could not cast a fly as well as Cain. Thirty minutes into the competition, I had yet to hook a trout.

"Ha! That's six!" Cain was eating Abel's lunch.

Hating a brother is not the same thing as hating a stranger, it's better. Much better. Only when you hate kin can you appreciate the really vicious, truly special, fratricidal fury that can build up between you and a blood brother. This is the same person you've been forced to apologize to, to shake hands with to avoid slaying, and the very same person on whom you are obliged to throw away perfectly good money on a birthday gift for an event that should never have happened in the first place. Having two brothers whom I once hated but now love, it comes as no surprise to me that Brother's Day is not celebrated, or that you can't find a card and envelope big enough to hold a letter bomb, or that, even if you can find a card with a written thought, it never bears the proper dose of malice. If not monitored and repaired by loving parents, what comes of this delicious brother-to-brother love-hate relationship is the same iced-down, razor-sharp, black-hearted malevolence Sicilians feel for an errant family member just before they go on the slaughter. Whatever this ancient Cain-and-Abel thing is, I can tell you this: Until you outgrow it, it's pretty wonderful.

Cain caught his seventh trout, turned, and smirked. I reached for my sheath knife. But being a good Christian lad, I would never harm a hair on my brother's head, especially with no place to dispose of the body.

On the pretext of seeking a more profitable rock from which to cast, I hiked upstream to a ford, crossed, and slipped up on Cain's backside. Unlike in modern competitive fishing, there were as yet no rules to encumber the contestants. Finding a long ugly pole lying nearby, I picked it up and touched Cain in the back as he leaned forward to deliver a cast. Amazingly, this tiny bit of pressure caused him to lurch forward, lose his footing, and tumble into Green Lake. From a quarter mile downlake Father called, "Was that a rise?!"

There followed a great deal of shouting and screaming. Cain had a few remarks to make as well. Then he came boiling up out of the water with that same red-eyed rage I'd seen the last time he tried to kill me, so I took off running toward Dad.

A lot of people think Abel was innocent and that Cain, the bad boy, killed him for no good reason. This is highly unlikely. My money says Abel had it coming.

Thanks to our father, the first competitive fly-fishing contest was aborted without bloodshed. No money changed hands. Ordered back to camp and forbidden to fish the remainder of the evening hatch, father punished the both of us, apparently on the theory that he would be right half the time, which, if you've ever raised children, is quite an acceptable average.

Father also made it clear that competition and wagering had no place in the world of fly-fishing. For my money—except to raise funds for charitable causes—it still doesn't. The thought of competitive, cash-money fly-fishing causes me to rise up sharply in my bed in the dead of night. After all, I know how Abel died.

You're probably wondering whether Cain ever got even with Abel. Of course he did. On the downside, I found stones in my backpack. On the upside, Cain found pine cones in his sleeping bag. True, Cain outfished Abel, but Cain never got much sleep.

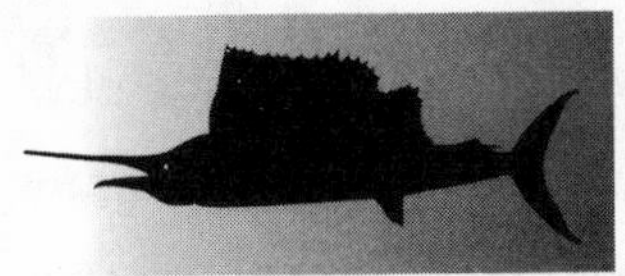

Journal Entry:

Cutthroat River, Summer

Fishing with brother Jim and introducing my niece, Erin, to fly-fishing for wild trout. She's a quick study.

Hiking back up a long, steep trail from a favorite bend in the river got a little harder today. At the halfway mark I leaned against a large Douglas fir and puffed hard. In years lived, I'm past double nickels now. But I'm not complaining. Most Russian men my age are already dead. Most Romans got only thirty-seven years before checking out. My grandfather got sixty-four years, and his father, who fought in and survived the Civil War, got less than sixty. No, I'm not complaining.

Modern medicine has given us longer life, but at a price: the longer we live the longer we get to be sick. Eighty-seven percent of Americans die slowly, and expensively. I'm not sure this is the deal we were all looking for when we spent all those tax dollars on medical research.

Considering the prospect of going slowly, keeling over with a heart attack at the end of a fishing trip—not the beginning, for Pete's sake—can look pretty good, especially if you've just finished a week consulting in a nursing home. Since everyone's got to do it, and if you can do it without having to put a bullet through your brain, then why not take the coronary express?

Except for the dying part, getting older has good things and bad things about it.

Among the good things about growing older is that you don't feel as strongly about things as you did when you were young; this means you are less likely to die quickly doing something foolish, like driving off a cliff while watching fish dimpling smooth water, or wading too deep to reach a trout too far.

Among the bad things about growing older is that you don't feel as strongly about things as you did when you were young; this means you are less likely to die quickly doing something foolish, like driving off a cliff while watching fish dimpling smooth water, or wading too deep to reach a trout too far.

I made it up the trail and back to camp fine. We built a campfire, broiled steaks, and talked the stars out of their hiding places. Wonderful weather, wonderful fish, wonderful life. When it's time for my tippet to snap, I hope it snaps all the way through, and quickly.

Why Fly-fish?

People ask me why I fly-fish. "I can't help myself," I say. "I had an abnormal childhood." Some kids are raised on milk and cookies, Saturday-morning cartoons, and baseball. I was raised on dry flies and trout streams. I blame it all on my father, a bamboo-rod man who tied his own flies. It is good to have had such a father.

I love all fishing, but fishing with the fly is somehow special. The quick list of reasons to fish at all include raw joy, mental therapy, physical exercise, spiritual renewal, camaraderie, and campfire talk of rods, reels, religion, politics, astronomy, geography, sex, death, and fishing. In the right company, even an average fishing trip is a raw gemstone that can be polished into a thing of value, not unlike an Oregon river agate you can carry in the pocket of your mind. These reasons are but a good start.

The whys of fly-fishing are as wide as they are deep, and certainly every fly-fisher has his or her personal reasons. With a lifetime of fly-fishing behind me, here are mine.

It is generally harder to catch fish with flies, and harder, in this age of ease and comfort, is better for us. Adversity develops character, prosperity discourages it.

Fishing with a fly is always a great deal more than it seems; simple on the outside, complex on the inside. Thus, fly-fishing is a challenge to the intellect, at once stimulating and demanding, but offering great promise.

To fly-fish well, you must invest effort to master even a bit of it, and without effort, nothing worthwhile can be accomplished.

There is no perfect mastery of fly-fishing, even among its greatest practitioners. Because this is so, humility and sharing among fly-fishers is commonplace, thus enhancing goodwill while advancing civility.

Fly-fishing is beauty and light and wonder and grace and religion all rolled into one. To fly-fish the bright waters is to dwell for a time in nature's palm.

There is a constancy in fly-fishing, a constancy that calls you back no matter how long you are away. No matter your travels or travails, fly-fishing will always be there for you, waiting with the trout in the riffle, or the black bass under the lily pad, or the bonefish tailing before you across the sunlit flat. In the journey of life, such fidelity is rare.

Last, fly-fishing takes place in the loveliness of God's own neighborhood. If you pay close attention, you may even see Him casting to the pool above you.

If you go fishing often enough, pretty soon the really respectable people will start to avoid you.

Das New Boot

"You're not going to start that again," Ann asked as I adjusted my pillow next to her in bed.

"Of course I am," I said. "A man my age has certain needs."

"But, dear," she said, "do you have to do it every night?"

"Yes," I replied. "At least until I get everything figured out."

Then, adjusting her own pillow, Ann rolled away and turned out her reading light. Then she cracked, "I hope someday we can get back to normal married life, whatever that is."

Hurt and upset by her sharp remark, I picked up all the new boat catalogues I'd spread across our king-sized bed and tossed them on the bedroom floor. So much for love and understanding in my hour of need.

As every married fisherman or fisherwoman knows, the bonds of matrimony are so heavy they require two people to carry them, and sometimes a canoe. Truly happy unions require not only a canoe, but a sixteen-footer with a fifty-horsepower motor and a couple of float tubes.

New boat quarrels are so common in fishing couples that marriage counselors should be required to take special seminars in how to settle them. As the lawyers say, "Behind every nasty divorce is a twenty-footer." To avoid the problem all together, I quote a personal ad from a major newspaper: "Wanted. Woman fisherman who loves kids and owns a boat. Send photo of boat. P.O. Box 999, Salmon, Idaho." I've seen the identical ad placed by a woman angler.

At last count I own only four fishing boats, not including my float tube. Each boat has a perfect use and perfect justification, none of which will I bore you with. As every fishaholic knows, four fishing boats is hardly enough. But it's a start.

To a fisherman, owning a fishing boat comes as close to owning a magic carpet as one can get with monthly payments. A spiritual, feminine vessel, a boat returns us to the waters from which we all arose. A boat is never just a boat, it is a miracle of the human mind and a thing of beauty.

As a small boy I lusted after fishing boats. I wouldn't know what lust was for several years, but what I felt for fishing boats was lust, not love.

Lust is what a man feels for a beautiful woman, and what he hopes she feels for him. Love, if it comes, can come later. It is the same with fishermen and beautiful fishing boats.

Unfortunately, lust is dumber and more impulsive than love. Lust writes the first check for a new boat, and lets love make the payments.

Last, lust doesn't know when to shut up.

"Are you still awake?" I asked Ann after a few minutes.

"Yes," she purred.

"I've got a question," I said.

"Yes?"

"Do you think I can get by with a fifty-horse motor?"

There was a slight pause. "I don't know," she replied. "Do you think you can get by with a concussion?"

Love endureth all things, but lust for a new fishing boat testeth it mightly.

I have never understood Ann's tolerance of me in these and similar matters; it is one of the great mysteries of our relationship, and one I do not intend to examine too closely.

When a fisherman says he'll only be gone half a day, he means the first twelve hours.

Lake Inconvenience

Lake Inconvenience is not its real name, just its reputation. Lake Inconvenience is the place I go when I need a dose of something hard to do, something a little arduous and difficult. The trip contains a molecule of danger in it, and we moderns need a small, nonlethal dose of fear once in a while, if only to keep our blood moving and remind us we're still alive.

For all the risk and effort it takes to get to Lake Inconvenience, the fishing isn't all that great. The payoff isn't in fish, but in feeling your pulse quicken.

No matter where you start from, it's a long drive to the lake, mostly on dirt roads. Once you're on the lake, steep, sheer canyon walls surround the water, forming a grand wind tunnel. Caught in a sudden gale, you can be swamped and sunk in minutes, and with no hope of rescue.

There are no beaches on Lake Inconvenience. No homes. No resort. No phone. No campsites. No potty. No access roads. No boat launch. No bait shop. To get there you have to walk or boat or four-wheel-drive, and to drive you have to have permission, which most can't get. All ways in involve risks: rattlesnakes and falls for hikers, busted lower units and shattered props for boaters, and a slide off a narrow cliff for those few with permission to use the only road in.

For a time I had permission to use the narrow, white-knuckle road that had been dynamited out of the side of a cliff face sometime in the 1890s by the landowner's grandfather. Steeper than a cow's face and barely wide enough for a handcart, it had you with half a tire pooching into space on one side and scraping door handles against rock on the other. When we got to the "narrows" in the middle of the cliff, my father used to motion me to stop the truck. He'd say, "I'm an old man, son. Let me walk down. Life's short enough as it is."

But we always got in and out safely, sometimes catching great stringers of crappie, and once in a while hanging an old bucketmouth deserving of a wall mount but better left a breeder of bass dreams. Then one year some idiot left a fire burning on the lake's edge and sent the landowner's winter cattle range up in smoke. "Sorry," he said the next time I asked permission. "I know it wasn't you, but you know how people are."

That left the creek that runs out of Lake Inconvenience. The creek is but two oar lengths wide and the color of dark tea. Used by fishermen for years, it's a public waterway. It snakes a couple of miles through a big meadow to the south end of the lake. Except for a few outsized boulders that seem to move around on their own over the winter, it isn't too bad a passage for canoes and small car toppers except that if you run a motor, and lack a perfect memory for location, those boulders can eat shear pins. Many years ago I renamed the creek Two Pin Creek, since that seemed about the average number of shear pins it took to travel the thing to the lake and back again without having to resort to rowing.

At the rough landing on Two Pin Creek there's no parking lot. No signs. No litter barrel. No "Guide to Local Fishes" sign tacked under a government-made, weatherproof, proper-English directory. There isn't even a to-the-lake arrow for the pilgrims.

Last summer, on my way out of the lake, the man who owns the land surrounding Two Pin Creek approached me. He was in the middle of his summer haying but got down off his swather and came over to talk. He had a purpose.

"Hi," he said, introducing himself and extending a rough farmer's hand. I remembered the landowner from times past even if he didn't know me. "Where are you from?"

I told him.

"Come here often?"

"A few times each summer," I said. "And thanks for letting me park in your field."

"That's what I want to talk to you about," he said. "The county wants to buy a little access and doll the place up. You know, put in toilets and a parking lot. Maybe allow a little camping. But some people want to keep it wild. They say we shouldn't allow any development."

"It is wild," I said, glancing back toward the lake and the high cliffs.

"Mainly, though," said the farmer, "it's fragile country. One fire in this bottom and it can get into the pines. With no roads in, you've just got to let her burn."

I told him I knew the history.

"Can I ask you a question?" asked the farmer.

I nodded.

"What do you think about developing the place? The county wants to make getting in and out easier for folks. Maybe lift those boulders out of the creek. Put in a little paving. Just let in a few folks at a time, you know, on a sign-up sheet."

"Toilets?" I asked.

"Yep. And fire rings on the island. But that bothers me some. Maybe I'd just let them day-camp. But you know how people are."

"I know how people are," I said.

"What do you think I ought to do?" asked the farmer. "You're local enough that your vote counts."

I thought a moment. This wasn't my land. It wasn't even my problem, except in a selfish, fisherman's sort of way. Two Pin Creek was already a public waterway, so it wasn't as though the farmer could keep people out even if he tried. But . . .

"So?" asked the farmer.

"I say to hell with them," I said.

"No, then?"

"No," I said. "Leave it be."

"No to all of it? Even the toilets?"

I nodded again. "But that's just my opinion. Seems like nature is limiting access pretty well as it is." Selfishly, I wondered where I would find another wild place so near home that could keep my blood moving, that could keep a little danger in my life.

The farmer gazed at the creek, and at his uncut hay waving in the breeze, and at the high cliffs that keep Lake Inconvenience hidden in their clefts of stone. It was midday and heat was steaming off the stone cliffs; he took off his straw hat and mopped his brow. "Just leave her be, then, huh?"

"That's my vote," I said.

"Well, thanks," he said, putting his hat on. "That's what my wife says. She fishes and she says you fishermen will stand by her."

I smiled. "Well, some of us will."

A Small Fracture Between Friends

His name was Jay and he was a physician, and I liked him a lot for his intellect and wicked sense of humor, and except for something he did one May afternoon, he would have made of me a friend for life.

Jay and I worked together on an admission ward at a state mental hospital. Except for him, the work in those pre-antipsychotic-medication days could have been frightening and grim. But Jay made it fun and even exciting. The staff loved him. Nurses would do anything for him. When an enormous, drunk, psychotic logger was admitted to the unit one morning and physically attacked one of the attendants, Jay shouted to the charge nurse, "Plug in the toaster!" Then he grinned. "When I'm finished with the son-of-bitch he won't be able to find his ass with both hands." Jay's order of electroconvulsive shock treatment was not medically indicated, nor morally or ethically correct, but it made him a hero with a grateful staff. Even though I knew what he'd done was wrong, it wasn't this that ended our friendship.

Jay flattered me as the new kid on the unit, and made me feel special, a part of the team. He thought I had promise, and told people so. I began to believe I was someone special to him. Jay didn't know how to fish, but wanted to learn, and because I could mentor him in these things he made me feel the teacher, and him the student.

We became good friends, even close. Men don't make many lifelong male friends, so when a potential one comes along we try hard to make it succeed. Twenty-nine at the time, I was only just learning to judge character.

Because of the way fishing works and where and how it's done, because of the way it tests your sense of fairness and sportsmanship and ethics and integrity and even authenticity, a fishing trip is a kind of laboratory for the study of human character. If you pay attention you can learn lessons, not only about others, but about yourself. People are different in different contexts, and the person you're fishing with may be one person back in the office or in the hospital or at a dinner party, but someone else on the stream. And so it was with Jay.

Though Jay never knew it, he taught me that even good and promising relationships do not so much blow apart at a single quarrel over some incident or other as they develop a small crack somewhere that widens and widens and widens, until one day, the two people who thought themselves close look up to see they have drifted far, far apart. I now call this my continental drift theory of human relationships, and Jay helped me to understand it.

Because it rides on a different tectonic plate than the rest of the West Coast, Southern California southwest of the San Andreas fault is headed northwest. The rest of North America is headed southeast. Mostly there are only small jolts and tremblers and barely measurable geologic fits and starts to signal Southern California's northwestward journey, but the different directions of travel between the two land masses is undeniable. And unstoppable. One day Los Angeles, the city of my birth, will rest opposite San Francisco, and there isn't one single thing anyone can do about it.

Human relationships develop fault lines, too. Sometimes two people look as though they fit together perfectly, but in fact they are standing on different plates, plates going in different directions. One day something happens and a fracture line appears. Later the earth trembles again, and the crack widens. With nothing resolved for the better, the two people begin moving in fundamentally different directions, gradually drifting apart. After a time, the separating effect of the drift becomes clearer and clearer to both parties, and unless something quite heroic is accomplished, or a therapist is called in, the relationship will split asunder, sometimes with a final painful argument and the loud thunder of a divorce, but sometimes with the quiet, unspoken resignation that love has died.

All splits between people happen first in the head and heart, not when someone moves out. And sometimes after the split happens in the head and heart, nobody moves out. Living in the same house, in the same rooms, the two lives move quietly through space and time together in parallel but untouching universes, never growing together again, never loving deeply again. Yet both people know, down deep, that one of them is headed north, and the other one is headed south, and that there isn't one single thing anyone can do about it.

On a perfect May afternoon a critical fracture in my relationship with Jay appeared. We were fishing a small, remote rainbow trout lake. A hike-in lake, we fished apart for a few hours and then met back at the truck at two in the afternoon.

"Look at these!" Jay said, beaming, as he puffed and rested from his hike up the trail to meet me.

I studied a cheap, blue-and-white nylon stringer sagging with too many fish. Way too many. Without speaking, I looked into Jay's eyes. I knew he knew the rules because I had taught them to him.

In Jay's eyes I saw no flicker of remorse or guilt or shame or concern or worry for our collective welfare should we be stopped by a game warden. On his lips was the same smirk I had seen the morning he ordered shock treatment for the logger.

Deep below us in the mantle that supports human relationships, something moved. The trembler was so slight I think perhaps I was the only one who felt it. But suddenly and surely there appeared a small, undeniable fracture between us. Jay had started north, and I had started south, and there wasn't one single thing anyone could do about it.

A year later Jay quit the hospital and moved away. I never saw him again, nor tried to.

Fishermen who miss church on holy days are not necessarily out of communion with God.

The Hermit

There is an old man who lives in a small out-of-the-way cabin on a small out-of-the-way lake not so many miles from my home. The country around the lake is dry and inhospitable. The old man who lives in the cabin on the lake is dry and inhospitable. Rumor has it that the old man is a very good fishermen but that, somewhere in his long life, he was badly hurt by a relationship gone bad and soured on the rest of us, turning away from mankind and into himself. They call him "the hermit."

The small bay in front of the old man's cabin is a good catfish hole. I had been fishing in the bay from my rowboat for a couple of hours but without getting so much as a nibble. Catfish can be like that.

Twice the old man had come out onto the porch of his cabin and glared at me. He did not speak and I did not speak, although I tipped my hat to him—which seemed to have the effect of sending him back inside his cabin. The bay and the lake are not his property, but he makes you feel as if you are trespassing.

When I finally gave up, reeled in my line, and reached for the anchor line, the old man suddenly appeared on his rickety, slanting front porch. With one hand on his hip, he shaded his eyes from the sun with the other and shouted, "Any bites?"

"Nope," I called back. "Didn't catch a thing."

"I'm not blind," the old man growled. "Watcha' usin'?"

"Worms," I explained, hoping he might offer some of his storied wisdom about how to catch catfish in the bay.

"No wonder!" he yelled back, shaking his head as he turned sharply on his heel and disappeared back into his cabin. Like a catfish touched, he'd thrashed and spiked me.

The most grievous wounds in life leave no visible scars.

The god of fishing luck is on the side of the angler with the right fly.

A Good and Different Journey

We'd never done it before. Drift a river for trout. But it was time. With fifty on my odometer, it was past time. Like the bartender said, "You keep doin' what you're doin', you'll keep gettin' what you're gettin'." Feeling a rut developing underfoot, I needed a different journey.

"It's time," I told the boy. "We go tomorrow. We'll drift the big river the first day and then drive up to Kelly Creek for the cutthroats after dark."

"Turning fifty bothering you?"

"No more than it should," I said.

"Isn't this a little risky? We've never drifted that river before."

"We've never drifted *any* river before," I said. Then, remembering a line from somewhere, I added, "Only put off until tomorrow that which you are willing to die left undone."

"H-m-m," said the boy. "Does turning fifty make you philosophical, too?"

"Just help me load the boat."

The boy was my middle son, Brian, a small forward for the New York Knicks. He gets only summers off, so when the ice goes out, he gets a little crazy to fish. Just back from a two-week fishing trip to Alaska, he was still raring to go. We packed the long river oars, rods, vests, waders, and such, and filled the cooler with venison steaks and fresh fruit. Only three hours over the passes to the Clark Fork in western Montana, we'd be into the rainbows by midafternoon.

I've always wanted to drift a strange river. I mean without adult supervision. This same son and I rafted the Salmon one fall for chukars and steelhead, but we had responsible guides to keep an eye on us. This trip would be different; we'd be on our own.

"How far will we drift before dark?" asked Brian, as we headed down the grade into the valley of the Clark Fork.

"Far enough," I said. "Think of it as an adventure." Without a prearranged takeout, not knowing how far we might drift, not knowing how we were going to get back from wherever we ended up, all made for a little rush. Not much of a rush, but a rush all the same. At fifty, this late in the twentieth century, you take any rush you can get. But with the highway running side by side with the river, and thanks to Lewis and Clark mapping the river, it wasn't as though we could get lost. Or never see home again. Shoot, I'd picked up fishermen holding up oars instead of thumbs myself.

A kid at a gas station directed us to a put-in near the town of St. Regis, a little stop on the way to the silver country of the North Idaho Panhandle. This far downstream, the Clark Fork is swift, deep, broad, and green, and it's easy to imagine trout as big as footballs.

Steadying the boat while I jointed my 5-weight and tied on a Joe's Hopper, I said to Brian, "Give an old man a break—you take the oars first."

"Sure," he said. "Always happy to oblige." We pushed off, and the river sucked us along with strength and authority. The feel of it brought the blood up. As we swirled past the huge cement pillars that hold up the spans of I-90 that cross the river, I made a few desultory casts behind the pilings. Nothing.

A pro athlete in top summer condition, Brian backstroked the boat easily, holding us in the current at likely places. Shortly, we came to an old snag washed up against the shore. I let go the hopper. *Slussshhhuuup!* The fight was on.

This was a very strong fish. A rainbow and a hot runner. Spirited. It dove and jumped and surged and fought. Honorably. Pooped out and bringing it alongside, I quickly spanned it without taking it from the water—my hand span is nine inches, and it took two spider moves to get from tail to nose. After flicking the fly out and reviving the gift, I bragged the measurement to Brian. "Eighteen."

"Come on," he said. "Sixteen."

"Eighteen. It's my hand."

"Well, I suppose you are getting too old to lie about a fish."

"Thanks," I said. "I needed that." On my insistence, we swapped ends and I took over the rowing. Brian would have let me take another trout, but he was, after all, due back in New York soon and needed to lay up a memory or two before summer ended.

That's when we ran out of fish.

Fishing stories usually go on and on about how great the fishing was. Ain't necessarily so. The truth is, sometimes you don't catch fish—no matter how important the moment, no matter how perfect the setup, no matter how much skill you possess, no matter *anything*. That is why fishermen fish.

But it was okay. We'd catch fish tomorrow. Besides, I've often thought that perhaps the best memories are the ones you make doing something chancy and a little bit crazy, and for the first time. It seems so. So as the river pulled us along and around and down through the places we'd never been before, catching trout became incidental to the journey.

After a time, the river before us split on either side of a large island, as if to ask the question "Whither goest thou?" We chose right, but for no more esoteric reason than that we were already headed right.

We whipped down through a chute and came out on what appeared to be the best rainbow water of the day. I rowed in and beached up.

Brian said, "Why don't you row back across and we'll hit both sides?" I said okay, and he shoved me off.

But as pretty as that water was, it was almost dead. Or at least dead to us. I brought up a couple of small fish, but hooked neither shadow nor desire. Brian's luck was no better. A herd of white cattle grazed in a sloping green pasture above us, and we could hear the steady chug of a pump pumping river water to irrigate one last cut of alfalfa. To the east that great cobalt-blue Montana sky had begun to dim and darken, and whatever the great rainbows were going to do, they were going to have to do now, or we'd all be finished: day, fish, fishermen.

Finally I shouted across the river, "What say we cut our losses?" I got a nod, and so rowed quickly back across the tail of the pool and nosed toward the shore. Then we shot off down the river in search of the highway and a takeout. That's when I heard the sound of fast water—out of sight, but there nonetheless.

Too old to drown stupidly, I'd at least asked the kid at the gas station about rapids downstream. "There ain't nothin' to be afraid of," he'd said. But as I saw the rapids and white water approaching, I suddenly remembered back to when I was seventeen. Hardly a paragon of sound judgment, and looking to avoid responsibility, I said to Brian, "Want to row?"

"Naw," he said. "Just don't dunk us."

"Then check your life preserver." I'd never been in charge of running a rapids before. But remembering how the guides had done it, I stood up in the stern as we hit the fast water, took firm hold of the eight-foot oars—and promptly lifted them clean out of the open-top locks, thus rendering us powerless, rudderless, and helpless. Gaining speed, we headed into a jagged row of boulders the size of Volkswagens. Brian, God bless him, kept casting.

I suppose there never was any real danger, and with a bit of single-oar work, I managed to keep us out of harm's way. But for a moment there, I felt something sparky and dangerous. Even vital. It made me feel a little younger. Or at least a little foolish. Or both. I'm not sure which, or that it matters—either way it felt good and I was rather proud of myself.

The quickening didn't last long; the river swept us out through a narrows and into a long calm pool. Drifting the pool around the next bend, we could not see the road running hip and thigh with the river, and although we moved swiftly, we were not so swift as the night. To hurry us home, Brian took the oars.

Watching a pair of teal streak over the darkening river in search of an eddy for a night's lodging, I said, "It's a little spooky. Beautiful, but spooky. What if we can't catch a ride?"

"Relax," said Brian, rowing in firm, measured strokes. "We just have to find the highway."

And we did. Around the very next bend. Beaching up, we cased the rods, secured the gear, took the boat by the gunwales and dragged it up a steep beach, through a stubble field, and along the little rut of a road until we came to a gate. From there, it was a relatively short drag to a black and empty highway.

"How many cars before we get a lift?" I puffed, wiping beads of sweat from my forehead. "One," said Brian.

"One?! It's after dark. I'll bet it takes ten. I know human nature."

"One. I know Montanans."

I lost. Not five minutes later a lone, downsized pickup came roaring through the canyon, headlights glaring. He zipped past, then hit the brakes and backed all the way up.

"Catch any?" asked a blondish young man wearing a baseball cap and a big smile. He had a high-caliber scoped rifle slung in a gunrack behind him.

"Not many," we said.

He smiled again. "I didn't get a bear either. Let's throw that boat in the back," he said. "Save you a trip."

It did.

There wasn't room in the cab for three, and so, having lost the wager on human nature, I offered to ride in the back with the boat and gear. Taking off my hat to keep it from blowing away, I unbuttoned my shirt and settled back to gaze up at that big, wide, marvelous, star-filled Montana night sky as we rushed along under it. The warm night air whipped over the cab and cooled my skin. It was a good ride. The perfect ending to a good and different journey.

Fishing in Dream Time

"Where have you been?!"

"Fishing."

"No, I mean *where* have you been? People have been calling all day!"

"Fishing . . . you know, for trout."

"Do you know what day it is?"

"Of course, it's Monday. I go back to work tomorrow."

"Boy are you in trouble!" said Ann, shaking her head in disbelief. "You've missed all kinds of meetings and appointments. People have been calling all day. I was about to call the search and rescue people myself. Don't you know it's Tuesday?"

"Nawww," I said. "It can't be Tuesday. If it was Tuesday, I'd be back at work, so it's only Monday."

"A hundred dollars says it's Tuesday."

I stared into those jade-green eyes I know so well.

"Bet!" she dared, extending her hand.

"Show me today's paper."

"Bet first!"

ß

I once lost a hundred bucks on a horse named Lightning; didn't like it much. Losing a C-note to Ann wouldn't be much fun either, but at least there was an outside chance she might spend the dough on me, what with my birthday and Christmas around the corner. She might even buy me a new watch to tell me what day it is, although I probably wouldn't look at it when I'm fishing in dream time.

Dream time isn't like normal time. In dream time watches don't count. Minutes don't count. Hours hardly matter. Only fading light and hunger tell you a day is ending.

In dream time you can time-travel. Sometimes you travel forward through time, sometimes backward. Sometimes you just stand still and cast while the arrow of time zips past you.

You can't travel in dream time in the heart of civilization anymore. The timekeepers won't let you. Newspapers won't let you. The time criers on radio and TV won't let you. If you punch in and punch out of work, you know time has you pinned down. Same drill if an appointment book runs you. A work schedule loaded up for six months is like lifting the heavy end of the board—you can feel it in your lower back. And who among us doesn't wear a wristwatch to make sure time doesn't sneak off on us?

Having lost a day fishing in dream time, I did a little research on time; found out we're pretty much addicted to it. We go eyeball to eyeball with digital clocks stuck in everything from VCRs to toaster ovens to dashboards. Americans bought forty-seven million clocks in 1993 alone, and the average family owns six. In the less than three hundred years since the invention of the clock, we've divided time so finely that the most common complaint in America is "I don't have enough time." Relief cannot be found even on the face of a Rolex.

Computers track our lives in nanoseconds. A nanosecond is one billionth of a second. It is very hard to slip into dream time when your life is divvied up into billionths. I think the scientist who invented the nanosecond has a lot to answer for.

Aboriginal fishing man didn't have nanoseconds, let alone clocks. Time travel was easy. He had the moon, the length of a day, spring floods, the return of the first salmon into the riffle below camp, and geese headed south or north. Inside nature's clocks you could roam around a bit. You still can. But you have to go fishing without a clock first.

To enter dream time you have to narrow your focus, concentrate, and not be distracted. For time to pick up speed or slow down or stand still, you have to cut out all the external interrupters: ticking clocks, TV specials, newspapers, tolling bells, trains, and blaring this and screaming that.

Quite unconsciously, the mind tracks time by the events going on around it; the more activity, the more time the mind senses is passing, which is why you can spend ten years in Manhattan in a couple of hours.

Somewhere on this fishing trip my partner, Ron, and I wandered into dream time. While there we did a bit of time-traveling. I think we fell into it through a hole in that big Montana river. Like the black holes that distort time in deep space, trout rivers have holes, too. The bigger and wilder the river, the more holes it has.

You may not always know when you've stepped into a hole, into dream time, and started time-traveling, but you know when you come out again. Glancing at your watch, you say, "Whew! Where did the time go!"

After several days of fishing and camping in dream time, Ron said, "Why don't we drive into town and have supper? I could use a piece of pie."

"Sure," I said. "Why not."

So we drove down out of the mountains and into a town so little you could lag a penny from one end of Main Street to the other. The wide spot had a gas pump, a small restaurant and bar, and a grocery store they would open for you on request. The town was in a hole too, so deep a hole that the most recent newspaper available was a week old.

"Is this the latest paper you have?" I asked the waitress.

"A week isn't bad," she said, without apology. "Did you guys want ketchup with your steaks?"

At the time I felt no disorientation, no panic that we'd somehow fished so long in the hole that we'd traveled backward from this week to last week. After all, you go fishing in the wild to get away from things like newspapers, even old newspapers. After the pie, we tipped heavily and headed back to camp.

I'm not sure where we lost the day. But thinking about it later, Saturday night must have been Sunday night. On Saturday night in the only bar for seventy-five miles there should have been more cowboys and loggers bellied up to the mahogany, more noise, maybe even a fistfight. So we must have traveled through time earlier in the week.

The fishing flywheel takes a bit of effort and practice to get going, but after the first couple of days things begins to spin easier and easier until all you have to do is open your eyes in the morning, swing your feet to the floor, wader up, and get on down to the river. Then you're into it.

Finally one evening Ron said, "We're running low on food. Maybe we ought to think about heading home."

I was ready. After the morning hatch, we pulled out.

ß

"I'm in trouble, huh?" I asked the green-eyed lady as I wrote the check for the hundred smackers.

Ann neatly folded the check in half, tucked it away, and handed me a note pad. "Here are the people expecting a call today." Then she grinned. "Not that I mind, but could you tell me again how you can lose a whole day fishing?"

Searching wildly for a comeback, I feigned a study of the list. "Maybe I didn't *lose* a day, my dear," I finally countered. "Maybe I *found* one."

I knew an old man who threatened to go fishing each spring. For fifteen years he repeated the threat. He was angry when he said, "By god, I'm going to wet a line this spring for sure! Nothing is going to stop me!"

But something always did.

He died with his line still dry.

Casting Lessons

I'm not much of a flycaster. But I'm working to get better. I think too many anglers assume that if you've fished a lot, casting well comes cheap and easy. It doesn't. Nothing beautiful comes cheap and easy, even if it looks like it did.

Years ago I corresponded for a time with a famous watercolorist. He'd done a beautiful painting on assignment to illustrate a piece I'd written for a national magazine. Without ever laying eyes on my son and me, he'd captured the scene, and us, perfectly, including a mountain clearing, a herd of elk, the color of our hair, our faces in profile, everything. In awe of his capacity to *see* a scene from the written word, I called him to extend my congratulations and say thank you.

We chatted. He invited me over. An older gentleman apparently unaccustomed to the clarity of the modern telephone, he thought I lived nearby. We were actually a continent apart. "Too bad," he said, "I just brewed a fresh pot of tea."

Out of curiosity, I asked him how long it took him to paint the painting in question.

"Oh," he said, "about fifteen minutes."

I knew what galleries charged for his work: nothing less than $5,000, and usually $20,000 and up. I'd worked hours and hours on the story, and I think I said something like, "Gee . . ."

"I'd like you to have the original," he said. "You can have it for five hundred. I sometimes do this with good writers, and I like your work."

I think I stammered, "Sure," and reached for my checkbook.

"You know we watercolorists work fast," the famous painter continued. "We don't really have much time before the paint dries. The trick is having a good idea like the one your story supplied. That, and getting ready to paint." Then he chuckled. "Of course it takes about fifty years to get ready."

Same goes for casting flies.

When I was a young man I thought that hooking a wild steelhead on a fly just might be better than sex; now that I am an old man, I am sure of it.

Tenbatsu Cures a Case of Angler's Rash

Before this essay is finished I will explain who Tenbatsu is. Given how much this impish little Japanese god gets around, I'm surprised more people don't know him.

First, what is angler's rash?

Angler's rash (a.k.a. AR) is a very bad itch that can only be scratched by fishing. There is no known cure. Afflicted fishermen break out in AR in the damnedest places: on Montana trout streams, Alaska's Kenai Peninsula, the Baja coast; on the Au Sable River and Lakes Superior, Fontana, and Crowley; on Louisiana bayous, farm ponds, and impoundments across the fruited plain; on every manner of river, creek, fiord, and lake; and on the ocean deep. Not everyone who ever fishes contracts the rash, but those who do suffer a lifelong chronic condition.

I caught angler's rash from an eight-inch Rogue River rainbow trout when I was seven years old. I can still remember the zing that trout, dime-bright and slick as slippery, shot through my body the instant I touched it. The charge raced up through my fingertips, fanned my heart, and seared something deep in my brain. Not unlike an alien invasion, whatever virus got hold of me took over body and soul. I have not been the same since.

For most of my youth the rash was out of control and I suffered greatly, including at the hands of parents who did not consider skipping school to search for a cure among the bluegills at Miller's Pond medically indicated.

Unlike acne and awkwardness, I did not outgrow AR. The less I fished, the worse it got. As I grew older and tried to discipline myself to work first, fish second, the rash would go into remission. But it always came back.

By middle age I'd be sitting in a meeting in some office building or other on a fine spring day and find myself daydreaming about fishing Montana or Mexico or North Carolina. The itch would start. I'd pinch myself and try to refocus my attention on the important matter at hand. For a time I thought I could substitute a notebook for a fly book.

I told myself fishing could wait. I figured that if fishing really needed doing someone would bust through the door of some damned meeting or other and shout, "Hey, enough of this already! There's trout feeding not twenty minutes from this hotel. Grab your rods!"

But no one ever did.

Until I did.

But first I had to learn something.

Observing the rash over the years, I learned that it had a certain seasonality to it: dormant in winter, outbreaks in spring. Near good bass water on summer nights the croaking of frogs could bring on a major attack. Proper names like the Bitteroot, the San Juan, and Christmas Island ignited unbearable itches. The rash would repose quietly for a couple of months; then, without half thinking, I'd be driving a river road and find myself studying smooth water for the ring of a rise. Seeing one, I couldn't sleep for the tingling.

One evening in southern Spain, on an otherwise uneventful holiday in 1976, I got a good view of the surf busting up in the tidal pools from a restaurant window overlooking the Mediterranean. Suddenly I was mad to fish. Tossing and turning that night, I spent the next day scratching up a rod and reel and bait. I didn't feel right again until my first cast hit water.

A temporary palliative measure for severe outbreaks of the rash was simple: Just go fishing. Just go ahead and wade and boat and float and cast and troll and hook 'em and land 'em and love 'em until, like a man sleepy from gluttony, you could head back to fishing camp, toss off a nightcap, and sleep like a stone.

I noticed that when I fished long and hard until well past dark, and didn't quit until the last fish was hung, my sleep was perfect and round and untormented. Worries and bullshit never entered in. All my dreams were of splashy takes and righteous hook sets. After a full week of fishing the rash would go into a dormant phase, perhaps for as long as three weeks.

But it always came back.

Now past the middle of my life, and with more fishing seasons behind me than ahead of me, I've found at least a partial remedy for angler's rash. His name is Tenbatsu. Tenbatsu helps you find time to take the cure.

Tenbatsu is an ancient, smirky little Japanese god who, just for the hell of it, likes to lean down from heaven and smack people upside the head. A bolt of lightning here, a business reversal there, a divorce you never saw coming—Tenbatsu's specialty is surprise misfortune.

On a lark Tenbatsu can send a runaway logging truck through the trout hole you're fishing and take you out of your waders and into the next life. Tenbatsu doesn't care if you're a good man or a bad man.

He doesn't care if you're busy fishing or busy making love or money. He doesn't care if you're thoughtful, caring, kind, moral, go to church or skip church, catch and release or kill them all. He doesn't explain his reasons for picking on you or the guy next to you and, being a god, he doesn't have to. So even though you're taking care of business and living a proper life, that doesn't mean Tenbatsu can't reach down and, say, hand you a heart attack.

Once you understand that Tenbatsu never sleeps, doesn't accept prayers or bribes, and doesn't give a fig for St. Christopher, things like fishing begin to work their way up the "to do" list. When you watch Tenbatsu having fun (drowned fishermen, runaway buses, TWA's Flight 800, etc.), the fishing cure becomes first order, not second order.

Believing in Tenbatsu resets your priorities. Where my business travel dress-check mantra had always been the classic "spectacles, testicles, wallet, and watch," I added "rod and reel and collapsible creel."

I resolved that there was no good business trip without fishing mixed in.

I determined that the only excuse for saying no to a fishing invitation is your own funeral—a funeral Tenbatsu may have already planned.

I fish enough now to have the disorder under fair control. I can ease the itch with a mess of crappie, or a good bass, or a silver salmon, or even fifteen minutes on the river that runs near my office. I can swab fly floatant on it for topical relief. Tying flies helps, and so does dressing lines and patching waders, and cruising tackle shops. But if I go more than a week or two without wetting a line I can feel that tingle come back. It's the same tingle I caught from that Rouge River rainbow trout that infected me more than fifty years ago. The tingle lies deep within me. It's a great little tingle. Thank God it's incurable.

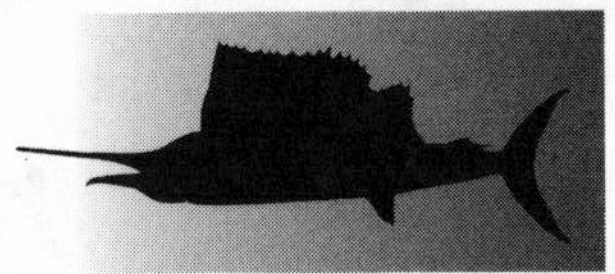

Journal Entry:

Selway River, Idaho

The road up the river is a bumpy bastard. Logging trucks make it that way. They pour out of these hills and brake in the curves and the big tires jump and pound the gravel to washboards. But it's okay. The alternative is pavement, and pavement means people.

Rained today. All day. But that's okay, too. A good rain keeps the mosquitos and people down.

Drove to the end of the road this morning. The river keeps going, up into the wilderness. Except for elk hunters, not many go beyond the end of the road.

Looking upriver at first light through a falling gray rain you could see misty clouds hanging in dark evergreens that walked right down out of the mountains to the river's edge. If you forgot about the parking lot and campgrounds and garbage cans and roads and highways and cities and the milling billions of humans downriver for a moment, you could be right back in that time and space when all the rivers were as wonderfully wild as this one.

Stepping into the Selway to cast was like stepping back in time. I could see the wilderness as it had once been, feel it pull against my legs, smell it in the rain, hear it in the riffles, and touch it with my hands.

This is how it had *all* been, once.

Knee-deep in the river, I just stood for a few moments before starting a cast, not knowing whether to shout for joy at being in what little remains of it, or to weep for all the wilderness that's been forever lost.

So I did both.

Then I wiped the tears from my eyes, pulled some line from the fly reel, and made a cast.

Travel Fishing

To feel at home, stay at home. A foreign country is not designed to make one comfortable. It's designed to make its own people comfortable.

—Clifton Fadiman

A few years back an old fishing editor and friend called to ask whether I would give a little thought to writing a short essay on the psychology of travel fishing. I promised I'd give his notion a little thought; I'd have given it a lot of thought if his request had come with a check. But it didn't. So here's a little thought on the psychology of travel fishing.

When traveling to far places to fish, people ask, "What should I take along?"

This is the wrong question.

The right question is, "What should I leave behind?"

Too many traveling Americans try to take America with them. This requires an oversized bag, not for your gear, but for your national ego. Sure, take the right fishing tackle, but leave the rest at home. The more you leave at home, the lighter you will travel and the more you will learn about how the rest of the world lives. You might even learn something about yourself.

Here are ten all-American things to leave at home:

Your need to be on time

Your need to feel superior

Your need to set goals and control outcomes

Your habit of working too hard at having fun

Your habit of thinking about money

Your need to impress strangers

Your need to catch the first/most/biggest fish

Your food habits

Your expectations for fast service

Your TV guide and remote control

Now here are ten things you might consider taking along:

Your sense of wonder

Your sense of adventure

Your angler's ethics

Your sense of sportsmanship

Your willingness to learn from strangers

Your love of nature

Plenty of tip change

A few trade goods for the locals and fishing guides

A good story or two about America to share

Your sense of humor

Back on U.S. soil from fishing in far places, you can once again pick up our national ego, hug your dog, and know what Dorothy meant when she cried, "Oh, Toto, there's no place like home!"

Bystander's Luck

My good friend Tad Hasebe breezed into my office the other day to brag about how his seven-year-old son, Bryant (who'd never held a fishing rod until last Sunday) had hooked and landed a six-pound largemouth bass.

"From Bead Lake?" (You can count all the bass in Bead Lake on one hand.)

"Yep," said Tad.

"He was fishing for minnows?"

"Yes, but . . ."

"With salmon eggs?"

Tad stepped back. "How'd you guess?"

"Didn't guess," I said. "The only way a bass that big could come out of Bead Lake was if a little kid like Bryant wasn't fishing for him, was using the wrong tackle at the wrong time of the day, and was in the wrong place. And, of course, it helps if he didn't want to be fishing."

Tad sagged against my desk. "That's uncanny! He wanted to go to a soccer game!" Tad shook his head and stumbled out of my office, amazed as usual at my spooky ability to know a fishing yarn before I've heard it.

I'm always surprised by people like Tad, people who've been around the pond a few times. You'd think they'd understand a few of the fundamentals of fishing by now. You'd think, for example, that they would be familiar with the different kinds of luck that attend people who go fishing. For the reader who needs a refresher, the categories are as follows: good luck, fair luck, bad luck, rotten luck, #$%&!!! luck, beginner's luck, old-timer's luck (I'm looking forward to this one), and, of course, bystander's luck.

The reason that Tad's boy was able to catch such a nice bass was simple: He had two of the best kinds of luck working for him, beginner's and bystander's. This is, by the way, the most potent combination of luck known to man, and if you happen to be anywhere near these two forces when they are about to converge, you should by all means get a camera crew assembled.

Everyone knows about beginner's luck: It lasts approximately a year, convinces the novice that fishing is easy, and then, when he or she is just beginning to learn how to brag, *shazaaam!*, it's gone, never to return. A veteran fisherman understands this phenomenon and never complains when a beginner catches a prize fish. (He may whine a little, but you'll never hear him complain.)

Bystander's luck is something else again. In case the reader is not familiar with bystander's luck, here's how it works.

A bystander is a casual spectator, a trifler, someone who doesn't fish or particularly care to, but who, in the course of things, takes a rod that is thrust at him and then proceeds to land the best fish ever to come out of whatever water he happens to be dabbling in. If no one on a fifty-acre lake has had a bite all day, you can count on a bystander to flip a bare hook into the water and catch a fish, generally on his first cast.

Hardly a fisherman alive can tolerate a bystander who catches a great fish. The customary response for an old fisherman who sees a bystander land a trophy from his favorite water is to smile, say congratulations, and then wander off somewhere to find something blunt but sturdy on which to bang his head.

Sometimes, however, the lucky bystander may come to an end most foul. "Golly!" cried a fellow one morning as half a dozen of us experienced anglers gathered round to admire a twenty-four-pound hen steelhead he had just pulled from the Snake River. "This is my first time fishing. I'm really a golfer. I didn't know steelheading was so easy!"

By barking threats and waving my rod in an intimidating manner, I was able to drive off a quickly forming lynch mob and escort the young man to the safety of his vehicle. "Take my advice," I said, "clear outta here fast. Some of these guys haven't had a bump in two years."

"What's a bump?" he asked, eyes wide with innocence.

I personally had made twenty-seven trips to the river that year without a single bump and was sorely tempted to do something rash. Familiar with bystander's luck and exercising perfect self-control, however, I did what I could for the young fellow—but he got away before I could get my hands around his Adam's apple. I did have time, though, to get back to the therapy session and to secure my spot at the boulder upon which the others were banging their heads.

My first encounter with the phenomenal luck of bystanders occurred while I was just a small boy. I still remember it well. The beneficiary in this instance was my older brother, John, with whom I had a warm and loving relationship at the time—provided that you overlooked the moments when I plotted to kill him. John was bigger, stronger, and uglier than I and could take me in a fair fight. And there was always something wrong with him. For example, he would rather go see a Roy Rogers movie on a Saturday morning than go to the river to fish, which to my mind made him a very sick little boy with a lousy prognosis.

"Let's go fishing," I'd say on a bright summer morning.

"Naw, let's go to the movies."

"Mom!" I'd call out. "Come take John's temperature!"

Since the house rule was that neither of us could go to the river alone, I had to figure ways to get John to go fishing with me. Blackmail worked best, but on the morning in question I didn't have anything good on him and had to resort to an outright bribe of fifty cents. Thanks to John, I was never able to save enough money for my own bicycle and was the only boy in our neighborhood who rode a pogo stick to high school.

We set out for the river that Iowa morning loaded down with our rods, worms, apples, and high hopes. Since John didn't want to go in the first place, I carried everything. Shortly after arriving at our favorite backwater, we had the bobbers dancing.

"Ah," John said after twenty minutes, "this is boring. We should have gone to a movie." (This sort of comment made while reeling in a fish correctly identifies 99 percent of all bystanders.) "I'm going downstream to look for caves and arrowheads."

I waved him off and stuck to business. At the rate I was going, I figured I'd empty that stretch of the Boone River of catfish before lunch.

Half an hour later, John came trotting up the bank. "Geez!" he wheezed. "I just saw a monster fish. Come quick!"

We took off at a brisk pace, John letting the willows go so as to smack me in the face—a practice he had developed to a fine art—and arrived at the spot where he'd spied the big fish.

"Right there," John said, pointing the tip of his rod. "I saw his shadow."

We quickly strung up the first two volunteers to surface in our Prince Albert worm can and set them adrift in the current, letting them swirl with the water, around and down and under a large boulder. Nothing.

John tried a third cast and then gave it up. He moved down to a little sandbar, flipped his worm into the slack water, propped up his rod, and then stretched out on the sand, leaving me, the only true-blue fisherman, to cast for the ghost fish.

I'd been at it for several minutes when I heard John holler and saw him make a dive for his rod. He hauled up hard—so hard that the piddling chub that had chased his worm flew up out of the water and landed halfway to the beach. I chuckled and was working hard on a good wisecrack when his rod suddenly doubled over.

"I got him! I got him!" The handle on his reel started buzzing, backed itself off the stud, and flew into the air. His line started downstream and John, down on his haunches, dug his heels into the sand. "He's pullin' me in!" he cried. "Help!"

Now it isn't all that often that a youngster is presented with this sort of perfect solution to the big brother problem, especially one so rich in irony, so far-fetched that everyone would have to believe it, and so deliciously simple in design as to make all my other schemes seem rinky-dink by comparison. All I had to do to become Dad's oldest boy was to stand by, smirk, and polish up a plausible account of John's disappearance.

On the other hand, as appealing as the vision of John wading ashore some days later near New Orleans was, I did have to have him around so I could get to the river to go fishing. Then, too, whatever it was that was causing him to skid down the bank had triggered my curiosity.

First, we took turns pulling and hauling and then, as the fight wore on, we fell into some rare teamwork and soon had the line going our way. John practiced his profanity while I, still an innocent, took mental notes on what forms of speech seemed to get the most leverage. Slowly, a fish about as long as a Louisville Slugger came in, on its side, sliding head first.

"Grab his neck!" John cried.

I did as he instructed, but with considerable difficulty. (Only later did I learn that fish don't have necks.) But somehow we beached the leviathan and then, as brothers are wont to do, fell to disagreement on a couple of points: what sort of fish it was and, more important, whose fish it was.

As I had studied piscatorial matters at some length, I argued that it was a stray Atlantic salmon. John held with its being some sort of pike. Considering that I had saved his worthless life, I said it was as much my fish as his. He took a different view and put me in a half nelson. Too puny to defend my fair share, I was forced to settle for 20 percent.

Later, Grandpa determined the fish to be a northern pike. "Biggest one to come out of the river in years! I guess that makes you the fisherman in the family, John."

Being a resilient child, I wrote off Grandpa's remark as merely careless and quickly got over the raging jealousy that filled my being.

I did, however, learn a couple of things. Whatever it is that accounts for the extraordinary good luck of bystanders, it is safe to say that the phenomenon is at least as reliable as beginner's luck, and certainly a good deal more aggravating. The other thing I learned is that when an older brother hooks a fish large enough to drag him down to the Gulf of Mexico, a younger brother should stand clear and let him take all the glory.

Plan B

For reasons I will explain in a moment, I keep a copy of my passport in an unpolished brass clip on my office desk. The deep-blue U.S. passport with the bad picture inside sits just behind my phone, where patients can't see it, but I can. The passport is there to remind me of something very important: Plan B.

Nietzsche said that of all life's possible conditions, we humans could endure any how if we knew why. I, too, believe we can endure any how if we know why. But I also believe that life is not an endurance test. People endure bad jobs, bad marriages, and even bad fishing, but their existence is painfully grim.

The Buddha's observation that life is suffering notwithstanding, why be grim just because you know why?

If life is only about enduring, and suffering, and toughing it out with a stiff upper lip to mark your grimness, what's the point?

I ask my miserable, grim patients grinding their way through Plan A this question all the time. From the looks on their faces, you'd think no one had ever asked them that question before.

Plan A is the life you are living right now. From opening your eyes tomorrow morning to shutting them tomorrow night, everything you do in between is Plan A. Like the rest of us, you've probably been neck-deep in Plan A for years or decades, or maybe your whole life.

Most people live Plan A without half thinking. Plan A can be drawn up for you by thoughtful parents who fund your college education, or by a strict uncle's expectations, or by a high school English teacher who thought you could write, or by a pal who invited you to apply for a job with the police department or to go fishing with him in Alaska, or by a knock at the door, an unexpected phone call, or by getting an F in organic chemistry that led you into acting instead of astrophysics.

You can choose the life you think you want to live, but chance deals most of the cards. And as much as we independent, free-willed, designer-career Americans would like to believe otherwise, most of us end up living Plan A for reasons a lot more obscure, petty, and meaningless than we can ever admit to ourselves or explain to others.

"If Plan A isn't working," I ask my patients, "then what's your Plan B?"

"Plan what?" they ask.

"Plan B," I say. "You know, what will you do with your life if the plan you're working on now doesn't work out?"

Most patients don't even know they are living a plan, however fortuitously designed and unsatisfactory—even if that plan is literally killing them.

Suffering it out in Plan A, most people never even pencil in a Plan B. They never give a second thought to whole new solutions to the problems of living: how to make money, whom to fall in love with, what to do if you get suddenly poor or suddenly rich, where to find meaning, reward, pleasure, or even how to find true joy or great trout fishing.

All the human-problem-solving research says that when we are faced with a bigger problem most of us reach for a bigger hammer, not a different tool. And when you're a hammer, every problem looks like a nail. So when Plan A stops working, most of us just try to hammer harder, which makes us miserable and grim, and can savage our physical, psychological, and spiritual well-being.

So what's a Plan B?

A Plan B is anything different from whatever you are doing now. Plan B is an alternative, old or new. Plan B could be grabbing a brass ring passing before you today, even as you read this. Plan B may be a dream you tied a ribbon around when you were young and put up on the Someday Shelf, saying, "Someday, I'll live that dream."

When you were young you were a dream chaser; you believed anything was possible. But somewhere along the line someone—some teacher, some institution, some note on a report card or probation report or psychiatric evaluation—beat the dream out of you. Someone believed in you less than you did, and the sad fact is that you signed off on their appraisal and discarded your dream. At that moment you began Plan A.

People have asked me, "What's your Plan B?"

Here it is.

For years my Plan B was to move to Spain and write. I wouldn't make much money, but I'd be out of Plan A. The passport on my office desk has a visa stamp from Spain. My older brother and his wife had been living in Spain for some time, so in 1976 Ann and I went to Spain to kick the tires on a developing Plan B. We ate the food. We drank the wine. We met the people. We checked out the villages and priced the rent. I fished and caught fish. I speak a little Spanish and could learn more. With the few American dimes we'd saved, we could live well enough in Spain. We'd get by. We love the music, the literature, the climate, the history, and the tradition and beauty of the land. And there is fly-fishing in the mountains. I told a writer friend about my Plan B; he thought it was so good that he and his wife quit their jobs, moved to Spain, and stayed three years.

The writing life in Spain is only one Plan B, and it was mine for twenty years. I have another Plan B now. There are millions of Plan B's.

Ann and I have worked up many Plan B's. We've thought them through, run the numbers, and explored the dream territory over long conversations and even on the ground in places close by and far away. There is a great freedom of spirit to be found in the imagination of alternatives and coming to understand that life should not be left to chance, but seized by choice. To rewrite the philosopher, we humans can endure any how when we have a Plan B.

Each Monday morning when I drive down Sunset Hill toward my office to begin another day, I ask myself, "Is this what I truly wish to do today? This week? This month? With the rest of my life?"

If my answer is yes (and it has been yes for a long, long time), then I continue down the hill, find a parking place, and spend myself passionately working Plan A.

But come that Monday morning when the answer to the question is no, then on that very day I will stop at the office long enough to tidy things up, turn in my resignation, pluck the blue passport from the brass clip, and return home to fire up Plan B. Plan B is waiting there, rods packed and engine running.

Without Plan B I'm pretty sure I could not have loved living Plan A, full out, full measure, full bore.

You don't have a Plan B?

Get one.

Big Boat, No Fish

When the book *The Millionaire Next Door* hit the *New York Times* best-seller list I happened to be between fishing trips; stranded in a mall at low tide over a lunch hour, I wriggled into a Barnes & Noble, found the title, relaxed into one of their inviting chairs, and gave it a fast read, thus saving myself $22.95—a trick even the cheapest millionaires had overlooked.

I am not a millionaire. Far from it. But I'm happy to report that I have many of the same habits as millionaires. I drive three-year-old quality cars until the wheels fall off. I buy three-year-old boats and fish them for decades. I don't spend hard-earned money on a flashy lifestyle. I live below my means and invest heavily. Except for a mortgage, I don't carry any debt or pay interest on credit cards. And if for some reason I couldn't work, I could go fishing for several years on the dough I've put to work in mutual funds and other investments.

Although considerably less than my wife alleges, the amount of money I spend on fishing trips and tackle is not inconsiderable. With my other obligations met, why shouldn't I? If you don't spend your money on the things you love, what are you going to spend it on? A fancy casket?

As a fisherman I may not need a lot of things in this life to be happy, but I do need to be at the right place at the right time with the right gear, just in case happiness comes swimming along.

The right place is where the fish are running, the right stuff is quality gear. I may drive to a far steelhead river in my 1988 Chevy four-by-four with 130,000 miles on it, but the rod I fish will match the fish I'm after for grace, beauty, and power. And if this sounds like some hokey post hoc justification for spending big bucks on my passion—well, it is. I mean, what's the point of carrying around one of these big, bulky brains if it can't help you rationalize your passions?

Besides, "big bucks" is a relative term. To enjoy money, you've got to have perspective on it. You have to know what it means to you, or how little it ought to mean to you. I've worked on the following rationale for years, and I give it to you freely.

Consider that most people live 28,000 days or so. Most of those days are wasted at school and work, or watching TV or learning to become a receptor site for the Internet on your home computer. Divide 28,000 days into $1,200, the price of a top-quality fly rod and reel, and the cost of the outfit works out to less than half a nickel a day (4.29 cents). Using long division again, a $3,000 weeklong bonefishing trip to Christmas Island costs you just about one dime a day (10.71 cents). In sum, you can have both a new rod and reel *and* the bonefishing trip for exactly fifteen cents per day.

If you can't see the wisdom in this logic, you are obviously not a fisherman.

The Bible says, "Money is a good servant, but a poor master." To be a good servant money should buy you fishing gear, take you fishing, tip the guide, and bring you home smiling. If money can't serve you in this fashion, what the hell good is it?

Most important, money-the-servant should buy you the *time* to go fishing. I know way too many wanna-be, would-be, could-be, should-be, oughtta-be fishermen who have plenty of money and who own tons of expensive tackle and big boats, but who never go fishing. They've got the money, but they don't got the time, so they don't got the fishing. Money has become their bitch master, and the bitch master's got them.

For just one year, I'd like to have a nickel for every unfished fishing rod in America. America's garages are filled with unfished fishing rods, new reels still in the boxes they came in, barely used boats and motors, and waders that will go, someday, onto a garage-sale table bearing the sign "Like new, worn once!"

The trouble is that too many of us have confused *owning a* thing with *doing the* thing. If I own a fine fly rod and reel, that must make me a fine fly-fisher. If I own a big bass boat, that must make me an expert bass fisherman. And so on.

Our selves are not made up just of what we do or think or feel, but also of what we own. And sometimes what we own becomes too much of who we think we are.

Despite my love of fine fishing gear, I could still enjoy fishing with cheap gear, and for years and years I did. Fine gear is value added to the fundamental joy of angling, but not essential. I guess I worry that somewhere along our long march to materialism some of us have mixed up money and ownership with happiness and joy, and have come to believe that without the former we cannot have the latter.

In the end, it's all about choices. With only 28,000 days to live, and only so much time to make the money to support a happy and joyful life, how we choose to spend our money determines how we choose to spend our lives.

In *The Millionaire Next Door* there's an anecdote in which a quiet, low-profile Texas millionaire says of people who spend their money on appearances, "Big hat, no cattle."

For the fisherman who spends his fishing time making money to buy bigger boats he never fishes from, we might turn a similar phrase: "Big boat, no fish."

The joy of fishing is not only about catching fish, but about being in places where fish are caught.

The Contour of Luck

Jim was the younger brother and he was coming home from a war. I remembered bits and pieces of our childhood together, but man to man we'd missed a lot. In an hour he'd be standing in my house.

As boys we'd hiked together in the high mountains, our father leading us up, growing us up under heavy pack boards. We'd fooled trout together. In all our lives there had been no better times.

I tried to remember. Was the last time we'd fished together the summer of 1963, before Kennedy was killed? I wasn't sure. Our older brother, John, was away serving in Germany, and I was just home from a tour of duty in the Orient and once again in college. The last time we fished together I thought myself a man and Jim, fourteen or so, only a kid. I probably treated him like a kid, but the memories are not clear. In an hour I would see what war had worked on my little brother.

I never took much time to understand the war in Vietnam, or why my brothers and father were against it. In our family, the line between religion and fly-fishing was clear, but the line between blood and politics was nonexistent. If Jim and John and Dad and Mom were against the war, the war was wrong. I sided with them blindly. Blood is thicker than politics.

The war was hard on all of us—those fighting it and those watching it on the evening news. Like Americans everywhere, we prayed our brother and son did not lie still in one of those long metal boxes headed home.

As a family we've always been lucky, in love, fishing, and battle. My great-grandfather got home safely from the Civil War. My father got home safely from World War II. And my younger brother was coming home safe from Vietnam. Some uncles and friends were not so lucky, but luck has followed us, contoured itself around us.

Jim objected to killing humans. Formally. He offered to carry the wounded or a radio, just not a rifle. Because he'd questioned the morality of America's war there, a bitter drill instructor assured him he would not return from 'Nam alive. But once in-country, a sympathetic lieutenant granted his request to be a radio man. The lieutenant was killed by a sniper while talking on the field phone Jim carried for him.

His luck held, he survived horrendous casualties in his company, and now he was home again. I met him at the bus station. Decorated, quiet, tired, and very much in need of a good night's sleep, he'd been out of combat only a few days. "Don't come into the room in the morning," he advised on turning in. "I've been sleeping in the jungle with a pistol for a pillow."

I honored his instructions.

In the morning, over coffee, I could see Jim had grown all the way up, and then some. He wasn't fourteen anymore, or even twenty-three. His soul seemed closer to forty. He had a touch of gray at his temples, and little crow's-feet around the eyes. Still, his eyes were clear; any uncertainty about life seemed far behind him. It was good just to be there with him, drinking coffee and talking about fishing again.

"Ready to catch some bass?"

"Sure." He smiled, shoving back his chair.

Because I believed that men who survive war are reluctant to talk about it, I expected Jim to avoid the subject. When he didn't, I was glad. He didn't say much, but his words were Zen paintings, filled with beauty and blood and death. He described jumping from a helicopter into a hot landing zone. Just ahead of him a boy from New Jersey had jumped. Jim noticed a grenade pin dangling on a door latch where the soldier was standing. Jim waited out the count, and the boy from New Jersey blew up. "Later I picked up the blood-stained pictures of his wife and child from a bush. He was a nice guy, but his luck ran out. 'Nam was like that."

After breakfast we loaded the fishing gear into my old Volvo and headed across the wheat fields toward the river. Spring was in the hills, green and fresh and bright. Jim said he'd missed fishing, maybe more than anything else. He'd been tempted more than once to toss a grenade into a highland stream to see if there were trout holding in the pools.

"Do you remember Ducy Lakes Basin," he asked as we sped down Wawawai Canyon to the Snake River and the smallmouth bass I hoped were hungry.

"Yes."

"I remembered it all the time," Jim said. "In the nights on watch in the jungle. I practiced remembering. The high mountains. The slender streams. The cushion of meadow underfoot, and the little golden trout lying tight against the grassy banks, and the campfire talk. Those memories helped get me home."

The smallmouth were waiting for us.

We climbed down over the rocks to the surging Snake and I rigged Jim's spinning rod with a quarter-ounce black marabou jig and showed him where to cast to the top of an eddy behind a rocky point.

On the very first cast, luck held him one more time.

Solo Breakout

Every so often I feel the urge to strike off cross-country to far parts. Far fishing parts. One day I am fine and normal and keeping all my commitments like a well-regulated citizen, and the next day I'm in my old Chevy pickup barreling down a highway to no place in particular. The urge to see new country, new water, comes to me in the form of a small, violent voice. "Break out, man! Break out before it's too late!"

Years ago I worked with a recovering alcoholic who had inherited a million dollars. He had a breakout problem, too. He said that when he drank he used to "break out in spots."

"What kind of spots?" I asked.

"Oh," he said grinning, "Sitka, Alaska. Singapore. Hell, one time I sobered up on safari in Kenya dressed like a great white hunter and carrying a Holland and Holland elephant rifle. That was some hangover."

I don't need strong drink to break out. Aspen leaves unfurling in spring can do it. The first tinge of gold in a stand of birches can do it. A summer heat wave, a fishing story in a magazine—it doesn't take much.

A breakout begins with the impulse, then a rough idea of direction, and commences, usually, before dawn the next morning. By dawn I'm loaded up with some fresh meat, water, a little whisky, and plenty of rods and flies and hope. With a drop of the shifter into drive, I'm gone.

I like to hit the road with the thin red line of dawn in front of me. Going west from my home, it is only three hundred miles to the Pacific Ocean, which is hardly enough room for a decent breakout, so I head east or north toward the Rockies and Idaho, Montana, Wyoming, or maybe British Columbia or Alberta. They say Daniel Boone needed "elbow room," and I'm told he and I are blood-related somewhere in the distant past. So maybe I inherited the too-crowded-too-civilized-let's-ramble gene. I don't want a destination or a reservation; the whole point of breakout is not to go from Point A to Point B, but to go from Point A to Point ?.

This peculiar behavior does not get me into trouble at home. After almost four decades together, there is nothing much left I can do to raise any real alarm in the woman I love. "Have a good time," Ann says when I announce a breakout. "But call if you're near a phone. It's much easier for the search and rescue people if they have some idea about which state you're most likely lost in."

But I've never been lost. Let me correct that; I've never been so lost I needed professional help to get home again. Getting home may have taken an unusual amount of time, but I was never lost. Part of the adventure of a breakout is to risk getting high centered somewhere on the backroads of America, or at least the backroads of your mind.

Loaded with life's three essentials (food, water, and trout flies), I enjoy running without maps and prefer orienting by the sun and stars, high peaks and river valleys. Wherever I end up, I like to think dead reckoning got me there, not road signs. I like to imagine that with a little luck I might end up on some long-lost mountain stream tucked back in the hills that no one has fished since the 1870s.

Going alone is essential. But even if I didn't want to go alone, I don't know anyone whose life is so uncomplicated that he can just say, "Screw it!" grab his waders and rods, and join me. And even if there were such a person, I'm not sure I'd want to share the quiet thinking time breakouts afford. Besides, after you've run off a dozen or so solos you get jealous of your singularity and a little weird, like the grizzled old prospector who has been in the hills so long his mule is talking back to him.

On breakouts I avoid formal campgrounds, live simply, bring my own firewood and water, cook over small fires, sleep in the back of my truck, and do not stand on ceremony. I fish when I want, eat when I want, sleep when I want. Here's a note from an old journal:

> *Location: Upper Bitterroot River, Montana. Early summer 1991. Solo. Camped in a county gravel pit. Other occupants: none. Had a drink, enjoyed a steak, prepped coffee for a.m., read a little Edward Abbey, and then worked quarter mile of the river before it was too dark to see the fly. Water was high and a bit off color. Sundown brought a sharp chill. Catch: two small rainbows on a no.12 Adams, both released. Moving on in the a.m. Where?*

You see how it goes. No appointed rounds. No commitments. No timetables. No schedules. No debate with someone else about next moves. On a solo there is no duty but to self and pleasure. If the fishing is good, stay on; if it's poor, move on.

Over the next mountain range.

Up a big valley.

Into the mouth of a far blue canyon.

The first day or two of a breakout are not easy. After being held captive so many weeks and months and years by the chains of our appointment books, the unencumbered life feels unnatural, uncomfortable, even reckless. This unfettered surge of freedom is not found in the dreams of the damned, but in the reality of a tank of gas and an open road.

On a breakout, dusty roads are welcome roads, no signs are good signs, and far places are promising places. To get free you keep going and going until life returns to its more natural rhythms, until you are once again in sync with the sun's metronome of dawn till dark, dark till dawn, and you are broken free from the tick-tock of a man-made clock.

Years ago on a breakout to a place in the West, I introduced myself to a rancher as he left the field he was haying. The field lay like a welcome mat at the mouth of a deep canyon. I asked the rancher, a friendly man, about the stream that emptied from the hills behind his ranch and cut along his fields. Did it hold fish?

"Yep," he said, "but mostly small ones." He advised I fish a famous river another fifteen miles down the valley.

"Small but plenty?" I asked,

"Yep. Nobody's fished the creek in years. You're welcome if you like."

"Could I camp there?"

"Sure," said the old rancher with a smile. "By the old line shack at the base of the canyon. But watch your fire. I don't want my winter range goin' up in smoke."

Late on a summer afternoon I followed a dirt road up into the green hills and found the stream quick and promising and trouty. New country, unfished water—my chest filled with anticipation. I set a quick camp and hiked a half mile into the shadows of the canyon, wondering to myself, "Has anyone fished here since 1870?"

The stream was filled with small wild trout that took the dry fly eagerly and danced and danced and danced until the sun went down. After supper, as the fire burned to ashes, I could see the lights of ranches twinkling down the valley under the stars. I would sleep well tonight, and tomorrow I would be on the road again.

Or maybe not.

I've been asked many times whether I ever prescribe fishing as therapy; only a quack would not.

Wrestling with Ernest Hemingway

As a young man I wanted to grow up to be just like Ernest Hemingway. I wanted to hunt like him. I wanted to fish like him. I wanted to write Nick Adams stories like him. If he hadn't written it first, I like to think I could have written *The Old Man and the Sea* myself one day. God knows I tried.

To learn to write I used to copy Hemingway's prose style, word for word, line for line. Until his deconstruction in the 1960s at the hands of a bunch of psychoanalysts with too little honest work to do, I was never shy about my admiration for the man.

Then came the 1970s. Kill all the old lions. Stop the testosterone poisoning. The new man was to be soft and caring and thoughtful and tender. We should all aspire to be Alan Alda.

For a time, I thought I might try to be Alan Alda. For a time I too came to believe that old Ernest was a psychological cripple, a braggart, a macho man who exaggerated his way through life, if not to intimidate other males, then at least to sell his novels. I thought that maybe Dorothy Parker's dig was true when she cut him with, "Even when he's deep, he's shallow."

But I'm older now, maybe even wiser. What I didn't understand about Ernesto when I was young was that for all his strutting and gunning and fly-fishing and crashing airplanes and fist fighting and storytelling and lovemaking, he knew, clearly knew, how to live life.

Full out.

Ernest Hemingway lived a life most suckers can't even imagine. Compared to the little men who took him down after his death and whose names we've already forgotten, Ernest Hemingway and his stories will go on and on and on.

Only one thing bothers me.

There's a story told that, on his fiftieth birthday in Havana, he claimed to have shot ten rounds of pigeons, fished marlin all afternoon, finished off a case of fine champagne with some pals, and, somewhere in between all these manly endeavors, made love three times.

Now, Ernest, you know I love you, but I'm not buying three times. I'll give you twice, because of your birthday, but not three times.

You might as well fish a little while; you'll be dead forever.

Paul's Pulsing Pullet Pike-Pulverizing Practitioner

Several years ago a bunch of Northwest outdoor writers were invited by the Alberta government fto fish the province for a few days, enjoy ourselves, and get a feel for the country. According to the tourist industry folks who set up the all-expenses-paid gig, we'd fly around in the governor's plane, catch a bunch of fish, learn about Alberta and its many treasures, and later write favorably about our experiences. Which is exactly what we did.

Sound fun?

Think again.

Fishing writing is serious business, even dangerous. Difficult choices have to be made about where to fish. Rods and reels must be carefully packed against breakage in bush planes. Flies for several species have to be tied in preparation, and notebooks and cameras must be checked and rechecked for blank paper and fresh film. The angler-writer must also guard against the dreaded repetition hook-set wrist syndrome and against potential back injuries from fighting outsized fish. Lapping up too many free toddies at open bars, overdosing on fishing lies, and too much sun extend the list of risks. Most important, grins must be carefully secreted away in duffel bags lest an IRS agent looking to prove fishing writing isn't real work catches you smiling. Make no mistake, this work is not for the fainthearted, nor for those without a good tax lawyer.

Among the invited on this perilous mission was Barry Thornton, a Canadian expert on steelhead and saltwater fly-fishing for salmon, and an old pal of mine. Barry and I were the only fly-fishers on the trip, and, for a change, we decided against trout and chose a northern pike trip. Neither of us had fished pike with the fly. Having some fun at our expense, and because we had brought only little bitsy flies to fish "great big mean pike," another Canadian writer tabbed us "the fly guys."

Before the trip an experienced pike fisher told me that all I needed to take northern pike on the fly was a gob of bright chicken feathers tied to a big hook. So I tied gobs of bright chicken feathers to big hooks and called it good.

"These are pretty awful," said Barry, on inspecting my inventions. We were making ready to take a small boat out onto Island Lake, a large, rarely fished, wild, and remote piece of water on the Great Shield. "Think they'll catch pike?"

"Don't know," I said.

The flies caught pike. Like gangbusters. Barry and I caught pike the first morning, all day, that evening and every day all day for the remainder of our three-day stay. Compared to the spin-casters fishing the same lake with plugs, spoons, and spinners, we "fly guys" caught the first, most, and biggest, and the only two genuine trophies of the trip, both almost four feet long.

The fly that earned its name on that trip is a cluster of eight four-to-five-inch-long orange-and-white chicken feathers laced with crystal flash and cinched onto a no. 2 salmon hook. The fly has no head or eye or anything special, but does pulsate wonderfully underwater.

It is the ugliest fly in the world, unless you are a pike. Barry dubbed it "Paul's Pulsing Pullet Pike-Pulverizing Practitioner," and it's my kind of fly: big, gaudy, unforgettable, and so technically undemanding that neither manual dexterity nor sobriety are required to tie it.

After all the "fly guy" teasing, it was good to win all the bets and make the "spin guys" eat crap and die. With the new fly named, our trophies acknowledged, and all kudos fairly won, I felt myself edging ever so close to the sick temptation of righteousness, the one that lures the angler into that fetid fraternity of elitism. I even caught myself practicing a sneer.

But I fought back. Heroically.

The next day we were back in Calgary. Our chief tormentor, a fellow from the Northwest Territories, pulled me to one side. "Say," he whispered in Canadian, "you wouldn't mind giving me one of those Pulverizers, eh?"

I gave him three.

Fly-fishermen make new fly-fishermen out of bait-and-spin fishermen not by preaching to them, but by example. And of course by outfishing them so badly those little tears of envy begin to ooze from the corners of their eyes.

A Lesson from Mr. Bone

It is good to be beaten by a fish once in a while. You don't want to make a habit of it, but it is good to get taken down a notch or two from time to time. Losing a good fish can humble you, and we could all use a little humility. Still, I am happy to be of an age that, when a good fish beats me, I can smile and tip my hat to the winner.

Which is not to say I hope to be beaten. Not at all. I never plan to lose a fish, unless I know it is foul-hooked, in which case I immediately point the rod at the fish and break the tippet. "Why did you do that?" asked a guide after I'd hooked a nice silver salmon in the belly while stripping a fly through a pool loaded with fish. "Bad connection," I replied.

Getting beat in a fair fight by a good fish means you underestimated the fish, or were not fishing well. You cannot attribute your loss to bad luck, only to shoddy preparation and poor skills. Luck has nothing to do with it.

I remember clearly losing a very big bonefish, from which fish I learned an important lesson about knots. It was on Christmas Island and my guide that day was Simon Corrie.

"Big bone!" Simon whispered loudly, pointing to that magical blue-green band of water where the sea meets the white-sand flat. "Cast quickly! One o'clock. Forty feet!"

I saw the big green torpedo and made the short cast, leaving several coils of fly line in the water near my feet. The fly settled and the bone knifed toward it. It was a very good fish, the biggest I'd seen all week. It picked up the fly and turned. I struck.

I had been hoping for a big bonefish all week. This one was it. As it bolted toward deep water in a long sizzling run, I tried to drop my left hand out of the way of the extra line whipping up from the water and flying out through the guides.

Too late. I felt the line coil and wrap around my fingers and cinch down with great force. Bowing to the fish and laying the rod over sideways in an attempt to turn my raging opponent, I shifted the rod under my right arm and grabbed for the line cutting into my fingers. The pulling fish cinched the loops tighter around my flesh, turning my hand into a grotesque knot and jamming my fingertips into the guide. Like Ahab, I was hopelessly entangled.

The bone broke free.

I reeled in the slack line, thankful I hadn't broken a finger or the rod. The fly, tippet, and leader were gone. The braided leader loop I had glued Chinese-finger-cuff fashion to the end of the fly line had been pulled off by the fish, stripping the fly line clean of its exterior coating and leaving only a few strands of internal cord. Such is the power of a big bonefish.

I know the game. I know the rules. I know better than to bring a bad knot to a bonefish fight. I know how to throw my free hand out and away from my body to avoid getting it caught in running fly line. I know that to land a trophy you must bring all your skills and knowledge to the challenge.

Fortunately for anglers, excitement can erase knowledge and skill; otherwise we'd land all the big fish all the time, in which case we would learn nothing of ourselves.

I was not happy to lose the big bonefish, but I was glad for my pounding heart. If you must lose a great fish, lose it in passion.

"How big?" I asked Simon, as he tied fresh leader and tippet to my line with a nail knot. I had leaned over to grab my knees in an effort to ease that little stabbing pain you get across your lower back after a major shot of adrenaline.

"Ten pounds. Maybe eleven." He grinned. "Yes, a big bone. Mr. Bone, he taught you something?"

"Yes," I said. "He taught me something."

I never saw another ten-pounder.

The only thing better than fishing with new friends is fishing with old ones.

My Secret Fertilizer

Despite my occasional detractors, I have always tried to do right by Mother Earth. I have, to the best of my ability, tried to do those things which are consonant with the highest principles of conservation. Waste not, want not—that is my philosophy. As a fisherman, I try to use every part of every fish I catch and kill to eat. If, for example, I happen to catch a catfish while crappie fishing, I fillet it out and bring it home to eat. Ann, due to prejudice, will not eat catfish. And so, when I have filleted out a catfish and brought it home, it becomes a crappie. Deep-fried crappie is one of Ann's favorite dishes.

Shortly after recycling was invented (circa 1972), I stumbled upon a plan whereby filleted fish carcasses could be dedicated to high purpose, namely, fertilizing garden crops. The business of planting a fish carcass under a kernel of corn is as old as agriculture itself, and in the spring of 1973 I was as busy as a farmer-fisherman could be, running to and from my favorite lake, removing nutrients from one ecosystem with rod and reel and injecting them into another ecosystem with spade and sweat—sans the choice cuts. But then, by the end of May, a problem developed. "What are you going to do with all those fish guts?" asked Ann, after the boys and I had made a particularly good raid on the local perch population. "The garden is in."

"Not to worry," I said, "I'm recycling them."

"That's fine," said Ann, "but the garbage man doesn't come till Thursday. They'll smell to high heaven by Thursday."

"Tut-tut," I said.

At the time, we lived in a tight little suburban neighborhood peopled by professors and schoolteachers and businessmen and a retired air force major. As human ecosystems go, we tolerated each other rather well. And so, thought I, who would care if I started a fish fertilizer factory? Fish emulsion fertilizer, as green thumbs will tell you, is the finest fertilizer known to man. A cupful can work a wonderful magic on most anything that grows.

My recycling plan was a study in simplicity. Briefly put, I would trim out the best cuts for the humans in my house, toss the carcasses into a fifty-five-gallon barrel, add a splash of water, age the mixture, and then work it into my soil and grow tomatoes as big as basketballs. The cycling of protein would be complete, and we at the top of the food chain would grow rich and strong. A plan of genius proportion; nothing would be wasted.

Along about the end of June, I was out on our deck broiling hamburgers when Ann stepped out to deliver the salt and pepper. A slight breeze was blowing from the backyard toward the house.

"Good grief!" she cried, pinching her nose with one hand and waving the other toward the garden. "Something has died out there. Find it and bury it."

(I do not, I will confess, have a sensitive nose. It takes a very ripe fish to register on my olfactory bulb at all. Ann, bless her, is just the opposite. She could age fish professionally.)

"I'll go see," I said.

"Do it quick." Ann escaped into the house.

Actually, it didn't take all that long to locate the source of the odor.

The barrel was jet black and we'd had a full week of sunshine, with temperatures in the low eighties. There were probably two hundred fish carcasses breaking down nicely within, and just as I had foreseen in my conservationist's dream, the whole stew was working wonderfully. The gray, fetid process of decomposition may not excite everyone, but I—once the wave of acute nausea had passed—enjoyed a stellar vision of strawberries the size of golf balls. I did notice, however, that the bouquet which ushered out as I lifted the lid had a certain robustness. When I was breathing steadily again, I returned to the house.

"It was only the fish," I said, tossing down a glass of lemonade to quell the rising tide of nausea sponsored by the pungent fragrance emanating from the fertilizer factory.

"The fish?"

I then explained my little recycling experiment—how, a year from now, we would be dining on carrots as big as baseball bats.

"You mean . . . ?"

"The garden was full," I said. "And have you priced fish emulsion lately?"

Ann is not much of a conservationist. She would, for example, prefer to run radish tops down the garbage disposal rather than carry them out to the compost pile. On the other hand, she is very good about things social and maintains the best of relationships with our neighbors—who, she pointed out, would probably file suit when they discovered what I was up to.

We debated the merits of my fish fertilizer factory for some minutes, and just as I had predicted, Ann came around quite nicely to the clear, elegant logic of ecology in action and the indisputable virtues of my invention.

"Now," she said, "get rid of that barrel immediately!"

"Too late," I said. "The thing must weigh four hundred pounds. I'll dislocate a disk if I try to move it."

"Better a disk than a jaw," said Ann.

"Okay, okay," I said. And then, knowing how right and ethical and responsible I was being with my recycling project, I moved the barrel behind the storage shed where Ann couldn't see it from the kitchen window.

By mid-July the factory was in full swing. The prime energy source came up every morning and drove the thermometer into the nineties. A little water, a few more fish heads, and the odd condiment from the refrigerator were all blended together by a quick stirring with an old hoe handle. (I say "quick" stirring because while thus employed, the effect was a temporary loss of consciousness.) Still, visions of ten-foot corn danced in my head.

Then one day in September, I noticed Major Regan—he lives downwind from my garden—standing on his deck carefully glassing my backyard with a pair of binoculars. I was reminded of Jimmy Stewart in the Hitchcock thriller *Rear Window,* wherein he plays a wheelchair-bound photographer who, with little else to do, spends his time peeping into the lives of his neighbors with a pair of binoculars. Gradually, it dawns on him that a murder has taken place, and the corpse is buried in a flower bed. Major Regan, when I passed him on the street, studied me with the same quizzical expression Jimmy Stewart employed so well in *Rear Window.*

About a week later Ann and I hosted a neighborhood potluck, and everyone within shouting distance showed up. Just to be safe, I sealed the factory's lid with masking tape to prevent any radiation leaks. Everyone was polite and jovial and quite, I must say, flattering about my tomatoes' reponse to the elixir.

"How do you get them to grow so big?" they asked.

"A secret fertilizer," I said.

"Yes," said Major Regan, his eyes narrowing. "I've been meaning to ask you about that. What, exactly, do you use?"

I hemmed and hawed. "Oh, just some stuff I recycle myself."

An old intelligence officer, I could see the major was not satisfied and for a moment scanned the guests to rule out any missing persons. Unsatisfied still, he wandered away toward the garden, looking, I presumed, for a fresh grave under my strawberry patch.

Then, just as dessert was served, tragedy struck. A couple of teenagers discovered the conversion plant and, goofing around with it, partially tipped it over, causing several gallons of my elixir to gush down the garden path and under the picnic table where our guests were passing round the cakes and pies. The effect on the garden party was not unlike that of the little problem at Three Mile Island, only more immediate.

"Eeeek!"

"My heavens!"

"Help!"

When the shouting died down, those who had not fainted dead away grabbed their serving dishes in one hand, their noses in the other, and began moving smartly toward the exits. As I told Ann afterward, I was certainly impressed at how social behavior holds up in times of panic. Here were twenty or so perfectly motivated people on the edge of hysteria, and yet, true to their conditioning, they all stopped long enough to say thank you and what a nice party it had been—although, I hasten to add, several of those good-byes were hastily thrown over the shoulder as the company sped away.

When the last guest had tired of lingering (about twenty seconds longer than the next-to-last guest), Ann and I sat down to have one of those little person-to-person chats couples must have from time to time if they hope to enjoy an enduring relationship. Ever cautious, I stationed myself between Ann and the cutlery.

"Why don't I just kill you?" Ann began.

"Because you love me."

This, unfortunately, was a poor rejoinder. However, due to a certain practiced quickness, I was able to duck a left hook and envelop her in my loving arms. She struggled while I promised to clean up the spill, terminate the project, and make amends to our friends and neighbors. Then, gradually relaxing, she smiled her forgiveness smile and I loosened my grip.

"That would be nice," she said, stomping on my instep and crushing an arch as she moved away.

In the end, everything worked out quite well. Since I did not have the heart to haul my fish fertilizer to the dump, I ladled it into gallon milk cartons and, in the name of reparations, offered it to all those neighbors whose sensibilities I had, through no fault of my own, offended. By comparison, Bible salesmen are better received, and I was forced to conclude the majority of gardeners have no sense of humus. Major Regan, apparently disappointed at not getting a murder conviction, did not even invite me in for coffee.

And so, always the able learner, I have changed my conservation practices. Now, after the boys and I have filleted our catch at the lake, and where it is permitted, we return that which is not edible to the seagulls, raccoons, and crawfish, who, according to my studies, quickly recycle the remains in nature's own way. But we still use all the fish we catch. Especially catfish. Ann would be greatly disappointed if we didn't have deep-fried crappie once in a while.

Even Fishermen Get the Blues

"Trouble sleeping?" I asked.

"Yes."

"Food taste like cardboard?"

"How'd you guess?"

"Lost weight in the last three months?"

"Twenty pounds."

"Care about sex?"

"Not much."

"Feel like crying?"

"No . . . well, maybe sometimes, but I don't actually cry."

"No," I said, "of course not. Tired all the time?"

"Yep."

"The chief says you quit the baseball team and don't go fishing anymore. That right, you don't fish anymore?"

"You got it."

"Ever felt this down before?"

"Nope."

"Any thoughts of death or suicide?"

"Yeah, but I wouldn't do it. I got a wife and kids."

Knowing better than to tell this fisherman he was clinically depressed, and also knowing that the patient's idea about a diagnosis is at least as important as the professional's, I said, "I wonder if you could tell me in your own words what you think is wrong with you?"

"Well," the forty-three-year-old police officer responded, chin down and tears forming at the corners of his eyes, "I think my give-a-shitter's broke."

"Good," I said. "Then we have a diagnosis. I think your give-a-shitter's broke, too. Fortunately, we have excellent treatments for broken give-a-shitters."

I got the grim little smile I was after, confirming our therapeutic alliance and the first step toward treatment and recovery.

This patient had a broken give-a-shitter. A lawyer who tried to kill himself by driving his BMW into a brick wall told me, "I'm just a little bitter about how things have turned out." A clinically depressed surgeon snapped at me, "I'm not depressed, for Christ's sake, I'm just tired!"

Women sometimes make the same error in self-diagnosis. I recently saw an executive who, after making it through five months of a major depressive episode without medications, said, "True, I got a little apathetic back there, but I never got depressed."

In our culture, big boys don't cry. Men don't get depressed, women do. Depression is not a guy thing. We guys may become brooding, cynical, gloomy, glum, moody, morose, pessimistic, irritable, embittered, withdrawn, somber, sullen, pissed off, and suicidal—but we do not get depressed, thank you very much. When dying of despair on the inside, we don't reach for a Prozac, we reach for a pistol. Even the newspapers protect us after our suicides: "No one knew why he was despondent."

Let me spare you the full depression lecture, and make a short cast here.

Clinical depression is a life-threatening illness, by whatever name you wish to call the cluster of symptoms that make up the diagnosis. A recent edition of the *Harvard Mental Health Letter* reported that moderate depression was associated with a 60 percent greater likelihood of high blood pressure and a 50 percent greater likelihood of a heart attack. Following surgery, depressed people don't get well as fast as others. Fifteen percent of those with a diagnosis of depression who remain untreated eventually kill themselves, and depression accounts for at least 60 percent of suicides worldwide. Untreated depression can negatively affect your social, psychological, physical, emotional, and spiritual well-being—which means it can seriously cut into your fishing time.

Dr. King had a dream. I have one too. Here's mine.

I dream that someday we will rise above our ignorance about mental illness. I dream that someday we will be as understanding of those with brain disorders as we are of those with diabetes or heart disease. I dream that someday we will, as a people, lift this terrible, life-threatening stigma from those around us and treat them as kindly as we would wish to be treated.

I need your help.

Open your mind. Learn something about depression and other mental illnesses.

Know someone in trouble? Reach out and help. Get them a screening interview. If you think you're depressed, get help. Don't wait; your life may be at stake.

The good news is that treatment for depression works wonderfully well. The bad news is that only one third of the millions of Americans suffering from it every year will ever get properly diagnosed and properly treated.

Result? Hundreds of thousands of lost fishing days, unnecessary divorces, broken families, lost jobs, and untold numbers of premature deaths and disabilities due to depression-fostered disease, illness, and suicide. Despite fishing's healing powers, even fishermen get the blues. When a fisherman stops fishing, it's time to get help. Pronto.

Help me with my dream. The sooner we overcome our medieval beliefs about mental illness, the sooner we can claim to live in an enlightened society.

Not long ago I saw my first truly enlightened patient in more than thirty years of practice. Maybe he was from the twenty-first century.

After stating his name and the nature of his phone call, he began, "I saw a brochure on depression. There are nine symptoms, right?"

"Yes," I said.

"Well," he replied. "I've got eight of them.

We set up an appointment.

My new patient had correctly diagnosed his own depression, which had resulted from a series of enormous stressors. A bright, able, well-read Boeing engineer who considered his health more important than any male pride, he responded well to treatment. At our last session he said, "I came to you because you're the expert on depression. When you need a consultation on metal fatigue, you can come to me."

This is how my dream plays out in the world of the future we can make together. We learn about depression, we confirm our self-diagnosis with an expert, and we get timely treatment. End result? More joy, happiness, and fishing.

If this engineer is representative of the kind of people Boeing hires to build the jets we all fly in, I think we can follow the copilot's advice to "relax and enjoy the flight."

I know I do.

A Therapy Lesson

I have a son, Brian, who is six feet eight inches tall, played three years in the N.B.A. for the New York Knicks, has the fingers of a gorilla, and yet can tie the most dainty, perfect, no. 18 Parachute Adams trout flies you ever saw.

This is not right.

Tying delicate trout flies should be left to small people with nimble fingers—dentists, watchmakers, and retired brain surgeons, not N.B.A. forwards. It is a constant shock to my system to watch this man who can palm a basketball in each hand hunch over a small vise and whip out itsy-bitsy trout flies. Like Rosie Greer's needlepoint, it's unnatural.

As his biological father, and representing half his gene pool, I ought to have at least half as much skill.

But I don't. In fact, about the only trout flies I tie with ease are Woolly Buggers in size 2X double long, which, as it turns out, gorillas have also been taught to tie.

Although small fly–challenged, I still tie flies to catch fish. I have my reasons. One reason is I tie flies for personal therapy.

Compared to other flytiers, I'll confess right off that I'm a slob. A hacker. A butcher. I have four thumbs and six fingers. Or is it the other way around? No matter.

If I give the word "clumsy" new meaning, at least I'm not orderly. My tying bench looks as though a twister passed through a chicken ranch and dumped the debris on a Christmas tree. Thanks to all this chaos, and since I can seldom find what I need when I need it for a particular pattern, I invent a lot of flies. A few have even caught fish. I showed one of my new trout patterns to a purist friend of mine. He slapped me.

Mind you, I've been tying flies since I was a boy, and for a time as a teenager made a few dimes tying crappie flies for a local sporting goods store. My father called tying flies for money honest work; I called it tedious.

One day, after tying about the ten thousandth identical red-and-white crappie fly, I experienced a great vision: trade tying crappie flies for study time, go to college, earn big bucks, and buy flies from high school dropouts. With only a few detours, I have followed this vision closely.

Now I tie flies for only three reasons: I can't find what I need at the fly shop; occasionally I lapse back into being the Cheapest Man in the World; and I know I need therapy.

The third reason is the most important. I tie flies so that I can, at least for a while, feel a degree of perfect control in my life. While I'm at the tying bench I'm the boss, the ruler of the known universe, the man in charge, the . . . well, you get the picture.

Tying flies takes you out of whatever you do for a living and puts you in the driver's seat again, thereby reducing felt stress. Stress is caused by high-demand, low-control environments. The classic high-demand, low-control work environment is the one in which Lucy and Ethel took what they thought was going to be a sweet job wrapping candy in a chocolate factory on *I Love Lucy*.

It seemed a wonderful job: good company, light work, free candy. Then the conveyor belt speeded up.

And speeded up.

And speeded up.

You remember the scene. Wrapping candy as fast as they could, they couldn't keep up. They stuffed their pockets, they stuffed their mouths, and still the candy kept coming, and they couldn't keep up. Mayhem. From heaven to hell in only a few frames.

Lots of Americans are trapped in the chocolate factory. Mail sorters. Grocery checkout clerks. Air traffic controllers. Police officers. 911 operators. Sometimes the chocolate factory is of our own making, sometimes not. Sometimes we don't even know we're working in the chocolate factory until our blood pressure shoots through the roof and we drop dead.

Tying flies takes you out of the chocolate factory.

Tying flies demands nothing.

Tying flies gives you perfect control.

Where there is perfect control and no demands to perform, respond, meet standards, return calls, reach goals, beat deadlines, avoid penalties, or otherwise spend your vital forces trying to get ahead of whatever is gaining on you, there you will find peace.

And contentment.

And satisfaction.

And lower blood pressure.

Tying flies is a low-demand, high-control environment. According to the latest health research, low-demand, high-control environments lead to better health status and a longer life.

A longer life means more fishing time.

Three hundred years ago the father of fishing, Izaak Walton, lived ninety years in a time when most people never made it to fifty. To get there, he tied his own flies.

Little Bass from Never-Freezing-Water

My favorite bass lake has another name now, but when the first Europeans came to the country I call home in the mid-1800s the local Indians called it Never-Freezing-Water. And for good reason. Over even the longest and coldest winter the lake never freezes. Big water, cold water, sacred water, strange water, deep water, mythical water—any black bass that grows to five pounds in Never-Freezing-Water is so old it's on social security and should be helped across the street.

Mind you, I live so far north I can cast a bass plug to the Canadian border. Even when our bass waters are warm they're cold, and cold waters grow small bass.

How small?

We're talking mostly twelve-inchers, with a two- or three-pounder thrown in once in a while to keep you coming back. A few fivers are caught, but rarely. Anybody who claims to have caught a ten-pound black bass this far north is required by law to have his medications checked.

I can imagine some southern bass-fishing soul mate reading this and muttering to himself, "Those po' Yankee bastards. They got too much money and not even enough bass. No wonder they're all so depressed and irritatin'."

Only an idiot kills a big black bass for the table this far north, although that is precisely why they were imported in the first place. Riding in rain barrels lashed to the sides of covered wagons, both black and smallmouth bass were brought to the Northwest by hungry pioneers. Advertised as a new eating fish for the West, fun and easy to catch, bass were planted to provide cheap protein for the lean years. Having traveled this Northwest country and explored its wet places for more than thirty years, I know it is still possible to find largemouth bass in remote ponds and small lakes near old homesteads in the great outbacks of eastern Oregon and Washington.

"Don't even think about it!" said an old widow as she opened the screen door.

"Think about what?" I replied, caught off guard by her gruff manner. I'd spotted a small lake deep in a coulee a half mile behind her remote ranch house and thought to ask if it held fish.

"You want to catch the big bass, don't you?" she said, and glared.

"Bass?"

"Don't play the fool, mister. The answer is no. Now good day!" And she shut the door in my face.

I think about that little old lady guarding that little old bass lake a lot; it's just possible it hasn't been fished since the Great Depression. I've been back to visit her a couple of times, hat in hand. She's warmed up some but hasn't changed her mind.

So mostly I fish the little bass of Never-Freezing-Water. It's a big, sprawling, dangerous lake whose shore has never felt the rough hand of the developer. Still wild and raw, it's the way I prefer my out-of-doors. Home to crappie, largemouth, pumpkin seed sunfish, native suckers, rainbow and brown trout, it's the kind of water over which you can spread your passions, or your ashes.

Once in a while in the spring you can be in the right place at the right time on the water that never freezes, and catch lots of little bass. They don't pull hard, but they think they can. They're all attitude. Old enough to start wearing purple now, I figure that when it comes to fishes or people, it's not size of the body that counts, but the size of the heart.

Lyndon Johnson was a master politician who knew how to make friends and influence people. While campaigning for his first term in Congress, he made it a practice to run his car with a half-empty tank so that he could buy a few dollars' worth of gas from every little station owner in the vast, sparsely populated country of West Texas, where votes were few and far between. Stopping often for gas, he took the opportunity to get acquainted, to politic, and to build goodwill.

We fishermen need goodwill in the sparsely populated places, too. Perhaps we could all take a lesson from the president.

It may be easier and cheaper to buy food, gas, and tackle in the cities, but the small-town people need and appreciate a fisherman's business. For the few pennies you save shopping at home, you can buy a lot of good public relations in the backcountry, not only for anglers, but for the fishes. Then, when the river and the town and the fishes and the habitat need help, the local votes will be there to protect them.

Guides

"They're here," said our guide, Dennis Dickson.

"Further out?" I asked.

"No. You're casting right over them. But your mend isn't getting the fly down. Try casting further upstream and throwing a bigger mend, or even two. You have to get the fly down, right on their noses."

Exasperated on my first November Skagit River chum salmon trip, I hadn't touched a fish in two hours of steady casting. And I wasn't getting any smarter. Like some patients I've had over the years, I was paying good money to ignore the advice I was paying for.

It helps to be stubborn and prideful. With enough pride you remain stupid your whole life. What could a fishing guide teach me, a fishermen for fifty years? Shoot, when someone once asked me what was the last fishing book I had read, I replied, "I don't read fishing books, young man, I write them."

Totally frustrated and growing testy, I waded out of the river to warm my feet and handed Dennis the rod. "Show me they're here," I said. He did. On the second cast. The big chum slashed down the river in a strong run. Dennis offered me the rod. I refused, but *now* I was ready to listen.

Once you accept the fact that you might need a little help in life, and that that help has a price you can afford, the edges of the world begin to look a little softer. At some times, in some places, on this river or that lake or headed up one trail in life or another, each of us can use a little help, a mentor, a priest, a midwife, a therapist, a fishing guide, or an old hand who, like John Wayne, accepts us as honest pilgrims lost in strange parts and in need of a sheltering sky, a cup of coffee, a friendly tip, a show-how, a where-to, and a point in the right direction.

There is nothing wrong with traveling solo and learning everything the hard way to grow character and self-reliance, but there also comes a time when it is good to accept a little help, even paid help—if not to gain something we want, then at least to keep what we've got.

This is a lesson women seem know without having to learn it, and it is a lesson some men never learn. I have seen many old men in need of a simple surgery and a little nursing care shoot themselves rather than have to rely on the kindness of strangers, paid or volunteer. Far too many gentleman believe not only "Death before dishonor," but "Death before dependency."

In the beginning I found it hard to hire fishing guides. I thought nothing of hiring a doctor, or a mechanic, or some other specialist when I needed one, but a fishing guide? Why would a guy who taught others to fish hire a guide? Why would I pay good money to be dependent?

This is an especially silly position for a mature person to take when you consider that I've made part of my living as a psychotherapist, which is only another kind of fishing guide. I suppose it has something to do with being male and therefore bone stubborn.

Fishing guides, rabbis, monks, coaches, teachers, pastors, and psychotherapists are all pretty much in the same business. All must acquire specific knowledge, serve an apprenticeship, and develop a good bedside manner. Helping others becomes both creed and honorable duty. Whereas a fishing guide mentors you through difficult and challenging waters in search of fish, the others mentor you though difficult and challenging times in search of peace and meaning.

You need only pay a guide fairly for his or her time, and your learning curve will climb steeply. If, like Socrates, you accept right off that you are ignorant and know nothing, and if you keep your mouth shut, your learning curve will positively skyrocket.

After he'd released the big salmon, I accepted the rod from Dennis with fresh humility. The student's failure, not the coach's: I had listened to his instructions all morning without *listening*. Despite his telling me repeatedly to cast more upstream and mend earlier, or even twice, I had continued to stick to my old habits and fished too high in the water column, passing the fly over the fish. We therapists call this refusal of help resistance. I believe fishing guides call it dumb.

But now I was a student again.

Now I listened.

And, yes, I started catching salmon: big, strong, handsome chums that, badly underrated by anglers, never quit the fight and come into the shallows straight up with their shoulders squared. I caught so many chums that, hell, I could even show you how.

Fly-fishing had better watch itself, lest it become the epicenter of pretension.

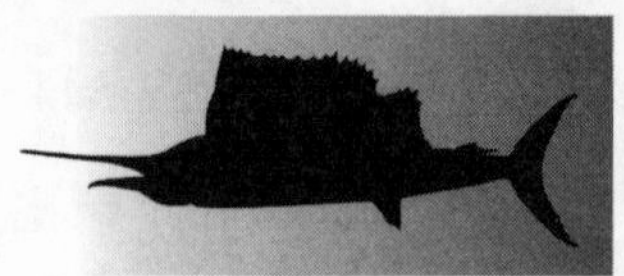

Journal Entry:
Christmas Island

Day one, 5:20 A.M. Coffee time. The anticipation is finally over, it's time to go fishing. It's actually November 19. You cross the international date line flying from Honolulu to Christmas Island, and you cross it again going back to Honolulu. So if you're here on New Year's Eve of the year 2000 and leave for Honolulu in the morning, you get two New Millennium's Eve parties, which is two too many for me.

If you're fishing Christmas on the morning of January 1 in the year 2000, you'll be among the first human beings to see the first sunrise of the twenty-first century; Christmas is where the sunlight first strikes land. New century, first sunrise, first hookup, first bonefish . . . What could be better than that?

Evening note. Christmas is a weird place. You meet nice people. You meet people you met last time. You meet new people. We flew in late yesterday, put our things away, rigged our rods, grabbed a snack, and got out on the flats. On the runway was a Gulfstream jet with "JN-1" painted on the fuselage. Turns out "JN-1" stands for Jack Nicklaus. He'd flown in from Hong Kong for a day of fishing and to rest his pilots. He had drinks with us and flew out again after dinner. He caught eleven bones. Not bad for a guy with a marginal golf swing. I shook his hand. Found it was a lot smaller than a giant's hand ought to be. Very amiable fellow.

ß

Day two. Three-quarter moon tonight. Today was a good day of fishing. Jack Nicklaus caught eleven bonefish yesterday, I caught fourteen today. I think. Unlike the requirements of golf, sometimes I track the numbers, sometime I don't. Our guide today, Simon Corrie, guided Mr. Nicklaus yesterday. Simon said Nicklaus likes to fish by himself and is a "good caster." Imagine that.

Clouds over the flats today, so sighting fish was tough, especially for me. Despite bonking a few bones on the head with flies, lining them, spooking them with poor casts, bad hooking, break-offs, and other assorted sins, I still landed more fish today than Jack Nicklaus did yesterday. Imagine that.

Day three. Am sitting on the beach by the hotel after sundown. A breeze is blowing in from the Pacific. One of those big, beautiful banks of fluffy Pacific clouds is sweeping in front of an almost full moon.

The moon and bonefish go together, like a tide and a title.

Soon the big bones will be running on Paris Flat. Everyone waits for the highest tide of the month and the run of the big fish. We'll be wading deep and casting heavy lead-eyed Crazy Charlies to them. The fish will run twenty-five inches, maybe thirty, maybe even a record. Anticipation upon anticipation.

Saw plenty of fish today, hooked a bunch, broke off five in a row on sharp coral when they cleared the flat and dove for deep water. The rods were arching all day. Nothing prettier than to look across the flats and see your friend, fast to a fish, with his dark rod arched in the blue-green sky of the equator. Here your heart sings.

You're lucky in life if you get just one day like the one I had today. A day like today gives you a glimpse over the rim of whatever rut you're trudging in. A day like today poses a real threat to whatever version of a First World, money-grubbing, fast-track neurosis you happen to be suffering from. A day like today is much more than medicine for the mind, it's a tonic for the spirit.

Tomorrow we fish the big bones. They say to push your tippet weight up to 15 pounds, to bring extra backing and extra lines and extra rods. Maybe it's all hype. Maybe it's all part of fish talk. Or maybe it's all true. The only thing better than fishing is anticipating fishing. Tomorrow . . . tomorrow.

Done properly, angling is not so much a sport as a way of life.

Fool's Hill

My mother had a saying when I was growing up: "Now don't go climbing Fool's Hill." But I climbed Fool's Hill anyway, enough times to leave a footpath. Even today I'm occasionally drawn to a Fool's Hill that doesn't look steep enough to really wind me.

The main reason I wore a rut up Fool's Hill was that I grew up in a Southern California subculture where it wasn't cool to ask questions. Only dorks asked questions. The more questions you asked, the dorkier you were.

Among other footpaths I've left up various hills are those worn while, for years and years, I preferred to remain lost (but cool) in strange cities. Cool guys know it is better to be lost six hours than to ask for directions and have to shave six seconds off your pride. Really cool people can stay lost their whole lives.

Then one evening, many, many years ago, a fisherman walked into my camp.

"Could you show me a triple surgeon's knot?" the stranger asked. Obviously a dork, he'd come over to my campfire carrying a couple of lengths of heavy leader.

"Sure," I said, "I'd be happy to." The cool rules say it is okay to help a dork, just so long as you never let a dork help you.

Because I was cool and had never asked anyone how, I learned to tie the triple surgeon's knot from a drawing in a sports magazine. As a result, and for about a quarter of a century, I tied the triple surgeon's knot wrong. Over the decades, thousands of freedom-loving fish pulled the knot apart as a result of my stubbornly wearing a trench up that particular Fool's Hill.

But about a year before the stranger asked me for instruction, a doctor friend of mine showed me how to tie the triple surgeon knot correctly. Being cool, of course I didn't ask him to show me how; he just offered. The cool rules say you can accept a gift like this, but you have to act as if you already knew how to do it, which performance I was able to pull off with a short nod of the head and a soft "Oh."

There is a reason for that flat spot on your forehead; it's for slapping yourself with the palm of your hand after discovering how stupid you've been. I have a very large flat spot on my forehead, made ever larger over the years by all the palm slapping. Finally learning the correct way to tie the triple surgeon's knot triggered an especially powerful urge to swat the flat spot—which urge I managed to contain until late in the evening when the lights were off and no one could see me.

"What was that?!" a voice called across a darkened tent.

"Big mosquito," I replied. "Very big."

Cool people can never admit they've been wrong, either.

I asked the stranger to sit down next to me, and slowly showed him how to tie the knot. Three demonstrations, half a minute of coaching, and he had it.

"Thanks," he said, smiling broadly. "I've always wanted to learn that knot. I didn't catch a lot of fish this trip, but now I've learned something I'll never forget. Thank you again." And off he went into the night to sleep that deep, learned sleep of the dorks.

I learned something, too. And not a minute too soon.

Near to the Madding Crowd

"Where are you going?"

"Out."

"For how long?"

"An hour. Maybe more."

"Lunch?"

"Probably."

"Sure."

Rita, the secretary who keeps track of us office slaves, smirked. "I'll expect you at two. Any particular lie you'd like me to use?"

"No," I said, "I'll leave that up to you." I checked my watch.

Time: 11:55.

You think that when you leave home, you leave your mother. Not so. They teach guilt induction at secretarial school. Rita, God bless her, got an A in the course. "Have a nice lunch," she said, as if I were on my way to commit an indiscretion that would land me on page one of some scandal sheet.

How did Rita guess I had a hot date? Was it my grin? Was the glance at my watch a bit too furtive?

Well, I certainly was hoping to get a little action. After all, a little action is good for a fellow my age. But why tell Rita whom I was planning to meet? Let her imagination dream up a really juicy rumor about how a middle-aged relic like me spent a long lunch hour.

Driving across the city, I convinced myself that a man needs to do something crazy once in a while—otherwise life turns into tofu. Making four green lights in a row, I slipped into the empty parking lot. Time: 12:02.

No one was there. Good. No witnesses. Above me, up in the city, I could see the madding crowd. Trucks and cars crawled across the bridges that span the river high above. Steam rose from heating pipes protruding from tall buildings. I could hear horns, a siren.

But here, near the river, two hundred feet below the city, it was quiet. Not perfectly quiet, but a veritable tomb compared to my favorite restaurants. Out of the car, I slipped off my coat and pulled on a warm jacket. It was November, cold but clear. A little breeze worked up the river valley. The spot was perfect. Cold, but perfect.

Even from the parking lot I could see that the water was clear. It would be cold, too, but not too cold. You can't make water too cold for trout to feed. I tugged at my tie, then left it more or less in place. For the first time in my life, I would fish in a cotton buttoned-down shirt and a silk tie. Pretty fancy. God help me if I fall in.

I put my 5-weight rod together quickly, strung the line, slipped a pea-sized yellow corky steelhead floater on the leader, and snugged it into place with a broken toothpick, allowing about four feet of leader to hang beneath the corky. Then I tied on a no. 8 Hare's Ear fly, a good all-round winter nymph. If my date showed, she wouldn't refuse.

I wasn't sure whether she (or he) would show. I'd heard about the trout in the river from several reliable sources. I'd even fished the river twenty years earlier and taken some nice fish. But back then it was so polluted no one fished it seriously, and the story went around that if you ate a trout from the river, you went directly to the hospital.

But now things were different. Now the river was clean. The dumpers had stopped killing it. It was coming back. It needed picking up (truck tires, shower sandals, beer cans, and such), but it was coming back. And so were the fish—browns and rainbows mostly.

I popped on a warm hat and started down the rocks. The hole I'd cased earlier was all mine. I liked that, too—250,000 people up in the city above me, half of them waiting to get seated in a crowded restaurant, and I'm alone, scrambling toward a wide, deep hole below a riffle.

The water was swifter than I had bargained for, and I made a mental note to bring a wading staff next time. Teetering a bit and proceeding on a yellow light, I waded through and around the big, round, slick boulders that lay between me and the lie. With the water sweeping by just above the knees, I made my first cast.

I hadn't weighted the Hare's Ear, and as the yellow strike indicator swept through the near side of the pool, I doubted I had gotten deep enough. Another couple of casts and I would add some lead. Casting badly, I realized that my clumsiness was due to a mild state of first-fish frenzy. First-fish frenzy has ruined my concentration ever since I hooked that first trout so many years ago. That's why I go fishing. Time: 12:18.

On the third cast, it happened. Sometimes the take of a nymph by a trout is so subtle as to defy detection. There may be only the slightest pause in the current-carried line or strike indicator. In trying to teach others how to read such a take, I have often given the following sage instruction: "If it looks funny, *set the hook!*"

There was no mistaking this take. Partway into the drift, the yellow corky jabbed down and upcurrent. Viciously. Experienced trouter that I am, I blinked, sucked air, pondered, paused, and, some part of a second later (after recovering from the shock of an actual strike during my lunch hour), I lifted the tip of my fly rod.

It was enough. The trout surged against the rod, arching it wonderfully. Gaining little quarter, it burst through the surface and into the sky. The trout jumped again. And again. And again. And again.

After a couple of good runs and a short tussle in the slack water, I quickly powered the fish to my knees. Measuring it with the spread of my thumb and middle finger, I made the rainbow out to be sixteen or seventeen inches. I removed the hook, rested the trout, and then watched it swim back into the hole. "We'll lunch again," I said. "No, no—my treat." Time: 12:23.

In the following minutes, the yellow corky dove three more times. I missed all three strikes. The next dozen casts produced nothing. Checking my fly, I noticed the tinsel had been chewed through, some thread was trailing behind the hook, and the herl was working loose. I switched to a Muddler Minnow, weighted it heavily, and moved the corky up the leader.

Bingo! Again the take was unmistakable.

This, too, was a heavy fish. It turned immediately into the current and ran. It felt like a small steelhead. Line started off the spool, and I prayed the fish would get me into the backing.

The second rainbow "taped" eighteen or so inches and, like the first, was deep-bodied, strong, and splendid. I immediately set it free. Both fish wore a bright-red streak as wide as a strip of 35mm film on their sides.

Time: 12:57. Time to go.

As tempting as it was to stay on and keep casting, the guilt buttons my parents installed in my childhood were still quite operational—despite my attempts to dismantle them over the years.

Retreating from the river and unstringing my rod, I looked around to see if anyone had been watching. No one was in sight. I had just had a slightly dangerous, delightful dalliance with not one but *two* lusty beauties. Positively bracing!

"My, but our cheeks are red," Rita said with a knowing smile as I blew into the office at 1:15. "Have a nice lunch?"

"Forgot to eat," I said. "Too busy."

"Forgot to eat, eh? Well, you forgot to tighten your tie, too." Giving me the once-over, Rita searched for additional data to crank into the rumor mill. "I didn't expect you back until two."

"It didn't take as long as I thought," I said. "You know how it is with guys when they get older."

Rita's eyes bulged ever so slightly.

With just a touch of swagger, I sidled up to her desk in the reception area and leaned over so the others couldn't hear me. "You know, Rita," I said, "a little action on the side is good for a guy my age. It makes you feel young again. In fact, it felt so good I think I'll be doing it once a week from now on. Maybe twice a week. You wouldn't mind covering for me if I run a little late, would you? Course you wouldn't. And let's keep this little affair between just the two of us, eh? What say?"

Then I reached over and gently lifted Rita's jaw until her mouth closed.

If fishing were just a sport, there would not be more books written about it than about any other sport.

Getting to the Truth

My friend Paul Wert makes his living as a forensic psychologist. He spends a lot of time trying to figure out who is and who ain't telling the truth in such matters as murders, rapes, child custody fights, domestic violence cases, sexual predator allegations, and other disappointing areas of human behavior. Because he spends most of his professional life in and around the legal system, he says the last place anyone ought to look for the whole truth and nothing but the truth is in a courtroom.

But then he's not a serious fisherman seeking the truth from other anglers.

Extracting the whole truth and nothing but the truth from a fisherman is at least as difficult as trying to extract it from a psychopath, especially if that whole truth concerns someone's favorite fishing spot.

I know this to be true because once or twice I have not told the whole truth myself. Several years ago when a fellow asked me where I'd caught a brace of wonderful steelhead trout, I told him, "In the Snake River." This was the truth, but not quite the whole truth. The Snake River is fifteen hundred miles long.

All fishermen scan, search, spy, probe, inquire, query, interrogate, quiz, and otherwise pester other fishermen for fishing intelligence.

Without good fishing intelligence, catching fish is a whole lot harder than it needs to be. But getting the precise location of and directions to the shoals, reefs, streams, submerged lake structures, rivers, pools, runs, hidden stock tanks, and other fishy places requires special investigatory talents, even low and underhanded methods.

I have my own ways of worming new fishing spots out of other fishermen, but am not particularly clever at it. I usually have to give up one of my spots to get a new one, and sometimes get the fuzzy end of the lolly for my trouble.

A student of human behavior, I have run across a few admirable truth-detecting techniques that do not require physical torture. So far as I know, none of these truth-extracting methods is specifically illegal. One comes from dentistry, one from medicine, and the other comes from the legal profession.

My dentist knows I am a fisherman and also knows how to extract the truth without half trying. He begins every procedure with the following three steps: (1) "How are you? How have you been?" (2) He asks his assistant for the syringe and holds it up for me to see. This is followed by (3) "Where have you been fishing lately?" I never lie to my dentist.

A lawyer friend of mine extorts fishing information from people he meets in his practice. To protect his anonymity and professional reputation, I'll just call him Jerry Cartright. During the deposition of a plaintiff suing one of his clients, Jerry might proceed as follows:

"It says here that because of this whiplash injury you no longer enjoy fishing because holding a fly rod causes you severe pain in the neck and shoulders. Is that correct?"

"Yes."

"Is that while you are casting, or while fighting a fish?"

"Both," replies the plaintiff.

"And how big a fish does it take to cause you pain?"

The plaintiff looks to his lawyer, "Do I have to answer this question?" His lawyer shrugs his shoulders and nods.

"Any size fish, but the big ones hurt the most."

"Trout?"

"Yes, big rainbow trout."

"I see," says Jerry. "And where, exactly, do you catch these big, pain-inducing rainbow trout?"

Before the plaintiff can consider his answer, Jerry adds, "Now remember, sir, you are under oath . . ."

But the prize for getting the truth out of a fisherman must go to a heart surgeon of my casual acquaintance. After establishing that his fisherman patient has some hot spots tucked away somewhere, the surgeon begins the procedure:

"Now, Mr. Jones," he says, fully gowned and speaking through a surgical mask with a scalpel raised in his right hand, "the anesthesiologist is here to administer that pleasant gas we spoke of, the one that will put you to sleep. You won't feel a thing until it's all over. Then we'll chat."

With eyes as big as saucers, the patient nods his understanding. The surgeon continues, "Oh, and do you recall my asking you about that bass pond on your farm?"

With the anesthesiologist poised to slip on the mask, the patient tries to smile through the tubes in his mouth.

"Well, I'd sure like to come and fish it sometime."

The patient begins to nod furiously.

Turning to a backup nurse, the surgeon says, "Please make a note of the patient's invitation to come bass fishing."

Using a professional relationship to garner fishing invitations is an ethical violation for mental health professionals. As a young psychologist just starting out I was assigned a patient recently admitted to the hospital. In our first therapy session I learned that his father owned a large ranch that hosted some very fine private trout fishing, and, said my patient, wouldn't I like to come by and try it someday? After the session, I raced to my chief psychologist—who was also a fisherman—and announced the happy news. He told me, sternly, "Don't even think about it."

To make sure I understood his meaning, he lowered his voice and repeated, "Don't even think about it."

Which only made me think about it.

But only for three or four years.

I am a great admirer of spectator sports, especially on television; it keeps the riffraff off the trout streams.

Jim's Hole

Except to Jim and me, Jim's Hole does not exist. You won't find it on any map. You won't find a sign to it on the clear bright river where Jim's Hole fills the canyon from wall to wall in one long pool; a pool with a wide tailout whose far side runs smoothly against a slick, sheer rock wall, creating perfect holding water for wild cutthroat trout. Jim's Hole is Jim's Hole because Jim and I say it is.

For all I know, you know Jim's Hole as Pete's Riffle or Harry's Run or, since Bing Crosby once fly-fished this river in a bygone time, Bing's Hole. This sweet spot in a North Idaho river no doubt had a Nez Perce name before Bing, you and I, and whoever came before us or will come after us ever saw it. Humans never really own the earth, they just rent pieces of it with their names.

To name a place is to know where it is and how to find it again. To name a place is to believe you possess it, if not forever, then at least for a little while. Perhaps this is why we give our lovers pet names and our children our own names, and name our favorite fishing waters. To name something helps us pretend we have rights and power and privilege in a world where, in reality, we have damn little of any of these.

Because names are so important to us, one of the first things a respectful therapist learns is to ask a new patient, "How do you like to be called?" The patient's answer must be honored. To lighten up what might be a tense first interview, I often open with the following gambit. "So, you'd like me to call you Bill?" The patient nods. "Good," I say with a smile. "Then you can call me Dr. Quinnett." This always produces a laugh and helps mitigate the sometimes uncomfortable power differential built into the business of psychotherapy.

Because words hurt, calling someone a bad name is a form of aggression. Like bark on a tree, some names stick and can never be removed, which is why we hated our nicknames when we were kids. Because my older brother was thin, he was nicknamed Bones. And because I was also thin and less than a year younger, I was temporarily nicknamed Little Bones. But the last kid to call me Little Bones got a punch in the nose and from then on I was called Paul.

If we hated our childhood nicknames, we are grateful to outgrow them and leave them behind. In my work with patients I will often ask whether, as children, they were tagged with a nickname. Many of them were. In some cases, they lived their lives not only to escape the name, but to expunge it. To know someone's name and pronounce it correctly is a sign of respect.

If you want to know how important names are to people, purposely call a child or friend or lover by the wrong name. The first time you will be forgiven, the second time you will be corrected, and the third time you will be punished.

Wendell Berry said that it is hard to know who you are if you don't know where you're from. Our lives are made meaningful by names of the places we live. Georgians on their deathbeds are reported to say that, when they die, they don't want to go to heaven, but to Atlanta. In our psychology of self we need these name-tethers, these ties and hooks to the good earth from which we sprang. We need a handrail back to a sense of place, of family, of race and religion and rightness. Without these, are we not hard-pressed to explain ourselves? Without these, do we not risk becoming space junk?

A friend's daughter and son-in-law were killed in a tragic automobile accident. As the terrible grief was waning, my friend suddenly began to name things on his small farm. He named his John Deere tractor Herbie. He named a stray tabby cat Old Yeller. He named a grove of aspens near the back of his place where his daughter used to play "the church." It was as if by renaming old things and places, he could somehow replace his losses.

Naming a favorite fishing riffle or pool or run takes but one person to think up the name and say it aloud, and another person to begin to use it. The name may show up on a map someday, but mostly the name lives among the people who were present on the day the naming occurred. Certainly, it would be hard to improve on Hangman's Valley, Mary's Tit, or Bloody Dick Creek—all genuine place-names in the West, where I fish.

"This hole is *mine!*" Jim shouted the day he hooked his tenth wild trout in a row. "From now on, this water will be known as Jim's Hole."

I didn't think to argue with him. I wouldn't want it any other way.

The Care and Feeding of Greenhorns

When I was a boy of eight or so my father tried to go trout fishing without me. "I'm sorry, Paul," he said, "but you're too little to go on this fishing trip. We'll be gone overnight." An accomplished whiner, I went to work on the old man. Ten minutes later he feigned a sigh. "Okay. If you pull all the weeds from the rose garden, I guess that would make you old enough to go." An hour later the rose garden was ready to be photographed for *Better Homes and Gardens*.

Every fishing camp needs a kid. An eager apprentice. A beginner, a neophyte, a tenderfoot. John Wayne called them pilgrims. I like "greenhorn."

Greenhorns can be of any age or sex, but young is better than old, and strong is better than weak. If your greenhorn is a slow learner, this is hardly a handicap. A powerful desire to fish is the only requirement, and a certain gullibility for tall tales is preferred—thus enabling old hands to add three or four pounds to their brook trout without causing so much as a raised eyebrow or triggering a preemptory challenge.

Greenhorns add immensely to the quality of the outdoor experience. If someone around camp is not learning, then someone else is not teaching. Besides, if you are not teaching a greenhorn, it means you're doing too much of the heavy lifting, and weeding your own roses.

A good fishing camp requires at least one greenhorn. Two are better. Pitching tents, felling snags, splitting and stacking firewood, cooking, cleaning—all of these are critical learning experiences for greenhorns. After you carefully show a greenhorn how to fillet the first of fifty perch caught on a chilly spring day—and explain that an old hand could fillet the lot of them in under an hour—the greenhorn will shove you out of the way with something like, "Here, let me at 'em!" Just watching a greenhorn thus employed can warm you all the way through.

Sure, buy your greenhorn a rod and reel, but the enlightened shopper will remember the greenhorn's birthday with things like axes, ice augers, fishing knives, pack boards, leather work gloves, foot-driven air pumps, whetstones, and other such essential gear as make up a complete educational package, while simultaneously ensuring the old hand's camp comforts.

In case you've been wondering what to do with a teenager lately, teenagers make the very best greenhorns. The only problem with them is they have a nasty habit of growing all the way up and, eventually, becoming old hands themselves—at which time their utility plummets sharply.

"Dad," said the last of my three greenhorns one morning a few years back, "I notice that you have a habit of fussing with something on the boat while I clean all the fish. Am I right?"

Having recently turned seventeen, this particular greenhorn had just savvied up about the learning-to-filet-fish ploy, which meant I was going to have to start cleaning my own catch again. On the other hand, he was still falling for the why-don't-you-drive-the-pickup greenhorn gambit, and so could be counted on to motor us smartly home while I napped.

If you care for and feed a greenhorn, one day that greenhorn may care for and feed you. A master woodsman and master child psychologist, my dad knew all about greenhorns.

"You can carry all the firewood if you want to, greenhorn," he'd say at fishing camp, "but it takes a big boy with lots of muscles."

Or "I wouldn't let you clean these fish, except that one day you'll probably want your own knife and may need to learn how to use it."

Or his perfect "I'm sorry, Paul, but you're too little to go on this fishing trip. We'll be gone overnight."

I don't know about others, but I'm counting on my children one day to produce greenhorn grandchildren. With any luck at all, I'll never have to filet another perch.

Wondering if you qualify as an old hand?

Sure you do.

An old hand is nothing more than a greenhorn of either sex who has spent a little time in the out-of-doors. "See one, do one, teach one"—that's the Old Hand Motto.

Don't have a greenhorn of your own?

Sure you do.

Remember, when it comes to greenhorn specifications, sex, age, race, and blood relation don't matter. With millions of kids in this country dying to get into the Great Outdoors to fish or camp or hike or hunt, the greenhorn supply is unlimited. There are probably several in your neighborhood alone, and if not, the Big Brothers and Big Sisters in your town have a waiting list.

They're expecting your call.

God Helps Those Fishermen Who . . .

A highly religious bass fisherman named John badly wanted to catch the next world-record black bass. A man of great faith, he began to pray, "Oh, God, please let me catch the next world-record largemouth bass. It would mean so much to my family and me. It would mean fame and riches and glory. Oh, God, please, please, please let this faithful son catch the next world-record largemouth bass."

Every night the fisherman prayed for an hour.

Over and over and over again he pleaded with God to let him catch the big bass.

A month passed. Two months passed. John kept praying.

After six months he increased his supplications to two hours a night.

Then three hours. Then four.

Adding to his evening vespers, John began to pray after breakfast for an hour.

Then two hours.

A year passed. John prayed on.

At the end of the second year, John was praying most of the day and half the night.

He barely took time to eat. His wife threatened to leave and take the children. His pastor scolded him. But still he persisted.

With his life in tatters at the end of the third year, John was awakened in the night by a booming voice, a voice with touch of irritation in it.

"John, this is God. Do you hear me?!"

John nodded. "Yes, God, I hear you."

"John, meet me half way. Go fishing."

Poets and fishermen have two things in common: They trust nature and take inspiration from her.

All Fishermen Go to Heaven

There are several confirmed reports that all fishermen go to heaven. And why shouldn't they, being pure of heart, good-natured, and generally nice people? If there is a heaven, then surely it is crowded with anglers.

But I've heard one disheartening story. It comes from a man who, after nearly drowning in the Big Hole River while chasing trout, had one of those near-death experiences.

"You're a little early," St. Peter said to the man as he arrived at the Pearly Gates, rod in hand and soaking wet.

"You're telling me!" said the fisherman. "It's the middle of the salmon fly hatch! Talk about inconsiderate. I was fast to good trout when I tumbled in!"

"Well," St. Peter said with a grin, "take it easy. We don't call the shots on deaths like yours. As one of our students put it, 'Stupid is as stupid does.' Now let me show you around."

St. Peter guided the fisherman through the golden streets and wondrous palaces and fountains. Along the way they saw angels strolling around wearing long white robes and beatific smiles.

Then, from one huge building, came cries and moaning and wailing and a great gnashing of teeth. St. Peter opened the door. Inside were thousands of men and women, each one chained hand and foot to a great ball of lead.

"What's this?!" asked the alarmed angler.

"A sad bunch, these fishermen," said St. Peter. "If we don't keep them chained up like this, they keep running off every weekend to go fishing back down on Earth."

A true fisherman does not believe in luck, except as she smiles outrageously on the other guy.

AOG

People sometimes wonder—hell, I sometimes wonder—where I find the time to do all I do and still go fishing. I do a lot. In a typical year I maintain a busy family life, fly thousands of miles, speak, write a couple of dozen articles, columns, and stories, knock out half a book, see patients, conduct national workshops, run a small clinic, and spend no fewer than eighty full or part days in the Great Outdoors. The days roll into weeks into months into years and, pretty soon, I'll be dead and no one will much give a damn.

And that's fine.

In the meantime, I enjoy a full and merry life.

A full and merry life is what I'm after, with the emphasis on merry. Charlie Chaplin was right when he said, "A day without a laugh is a day wasted." I would only add that a day without a little reading, a little learning, a little earning, a little writing, a little loving, a little giving, a good meal, or a fish caught is also a day wasted.

Because it is abhorrent to me, I never waste time. Not wasting time is an old, old habit, a habit that goes all the way back to my days as a paper boy, or even earlier, when as a kid I picked boysenberries for twenty-five cents a flat. If you were a slow picker in the berry patch you made no dough, or got fired. I got in a berry fight with a kid named Jesus Sanchez and, for the first and last time in my life, got canned from a job. "Pablo got fired! Pablo got fired!" the voices sang out over the berry field in a teasing but good-natured refrain as I walked, head bowed in shame, from the field.

Berry picking lesson? The world doesn't need slow pokes and goof-offs. If you don't know that boysenberries need to be picked *in their time*, quickly before the sun is hot, the world will find someone who does. Berry picking taught me discipline, but chickens taught me efficiency.

At age fourteen I went to work on a small family-owned chicken ranch, a job I had inherited from my brother. I was the hired hand. No job is nastier than baby-sitting chickens, and I say this with all apologies to the essayist E. B. White, who wrote some delightful pastoral observations about the joys of raising these stupid, obnoxious, faithless, jumpy, bloodthirsty, filthy, illegitimate feckless beasties whose main purpose for being, in my seasoned view, is to provide eggs for omelets, meat for the pot, and bright feathers for the construction of trout, salmon, and saltwater flies.

I have good reasons for my attitude toward chickens—indelible, emotional reasons that, in more than forty years, have abated not one whit. After all, I spent the best three years of my young life shoveling chicken shit, spreading chicken shit, breathing chicken shit, picking chicken shit off chicken eggs, smelling like chicken shit, and going to school with chicken shit on my shoes. This is to say nothing of being pecked bloody by chickens, raked and scratched by chickens, and repeatedly humiliated by the witless sons-of-bitches when, after I opened a coop door and failed to be recognized, dozens of the startled, moronic creatures would burst into the air and fill the coop with chicken-shit dust so fine it stuck to the insides of your nose. Unless you had a cold, in which case you couldn't breath through your nose, and were forced to eat chicken shit, which subsequently deposited a quite characteristic brown ring around your mouth not unlike the stain from a Snickers bar, only less yummy. Poultry are poison. Worldwide, they outnumber us four to one. Colonel Sanders's founding of Kentucky Fried Chicken may have been a slasher nightmare to chickens, but to me the colonel was a deity at the head of a relief column. On the basis of this vast personal fowl experience, I can say with considerable authority that the only good chicken is sizzling on a barbecue.

Still, I owe chickens a great debt. Because I came to hate them so, and wanted nothing more than to be done with them before six o'clock each evening, chickens taught me to work with a terrible efficiency. The sooner I finished feeding and watering and gathering the eggs each afternoon after school, the sooner I got to go fishing on Miller's Pond, a little bass and bluegill stock tank a half mile from the ranch.

With fishing as a positive motivator and chickens as a powerfully negative one, I grew muscles strong enough to toss fifty-pound sacks of grain like feather pillows, to push two sacks of feed in the wheelbarrow at the same time, and to spade great piles of chicken shit so fast I looked like a boy shoveling snakes in a Buster Keaton movie. I learned to carry water one way, mash the other. I shaved minutes off the schedule by doing two things at once, and sometimes three. I learned never to waste a step, a motion, or a minute. I learned that the only way to work is to work until you sweat, and for three years I never stopped sweating. Since no one had yet claimed the title, I became the World's Most Efficient Chicken Rancher.

When I inherited the after-school chicken job it took four hours to complete the day's tasks. In eighteen months I had the chicken chores down to one hour and thirty-three minutes flat. I was getting $1.25 an hour, but since the boss was never there, I nicked him the full four hours, thus tripling my hourly rate. An exploiter of child labor, the owner once worked me 297 days in a row, including every Saturday and Sunday. So I kicked him in the shins by making $3.75 an hour. He got good, thorough, responsible work and I, in my boy's mind, got even. In the end, the chicken ranch greased the wheels of my work ethic.

Jump ahead a few years.

AOG stands for "ahead of the game." I was trained by the U.S. Army to take Morse code. The *dit*s and *da*s came into your ears through earphones and were supposed to go out your fingertips and onto a typewriter keyboard. *Dit-da* (one short, one long) stands for A, *da-dit-dit-dit* (one long, three shorts) stands for B, and so on down through the alphabet and numbers. These you had to memorize, listen to, and type. If you learned this ear-brain-finger game faster than your classmates, you moved to the top of the class; you were ahead of the game.

Once you earned your AOG badge for the week, you could skip class, go to the library and read military history, or hang around the snack bar and smoke cigarettes. It was hardly the equivalent reward of a trip to Miller's Pond for a mess of bluegill, but it was still better than having your brain addled by the staccato pounding of Morse code.

Not unlike a chicken ranch, there is an awful lot of chicken shit in the army; it took me about a week to figure out where some of it was piled. I could already type, and memorizing code bore a strong resemblance to chicken ranching. So, on a bus ride to Boston on my first weekend pass, I began to teach myself Morse code. Looking out a bus window, I read the next billboard in code: *da-da-dit*, *dit-da*, *dit-da-dit*, *dit-da-dit-dit*, *da-dit-dit-dit*, *da-da-da*, *dit-da-dit*, *da-da-da*: "Marlboro." Then I read the next one. And the next one.

Then restaurant menus. Then street signs. *Da-dit-dit-dit, da-da-da, dit-dit-dit, da, da-da-da, da-dit*—and, just like that, I had "Boston" in my pocket.

The next week I was AOG.

And the week after that.

And every week thereafter until the end of the six-month training program. Not only did I learn a lot of military history, I graduated at the top of my class and had the choice of any available spy base in the world. I was no smarter than anyone else in my class; I just knew how to shovel chicken shit faster than the rest.

The army taught me another important lesson about efficiency and making time work for you: Never wait for someone else to teach you what you will have to learn anyway. Teach yourself. You may start slow, but you will finish strong.

It seems lots of people want to get ahead of the game these days, but too many of them wait for someone else to show them how, or to lead them to the head of the line, or they expect someone to hold their hand while they take baby steps. It doesn't work that way. Life is not a sheltered workshop.

This is not to say mentoring isn't important; it just isn't enough. You don't have to be a bloody genius to get ahead of whatever game you're in, but you do have to show up every day, skip the berry fights with Jesus, and be willing to work harder *and smarter* than the next guy. You may work for The Man to earn your daily bread, but it's nobody's fault but your own if all you take home from a job is money.

With few exceptions I've been ahead of whatever games I've been blessed to play in life. As a boy I was fortunate enough to have hardworking parents to model the nature and meaning of work for me, and to teach me that hard work is not a curse but a blessing. Hard work gives life purpose. Hard work teaches worth, and gives us the opportunity to give back to our communities.

Thanks to the taste of chicken shit, I taught myself to be efficient and to get things done in a hurry. Sure, I break a few things, muff jobs, lose the details of one project while starting on another, and screw up plenty. But at least I make my mistakes quickly; I mean, if you're going to foul something up, why do it slowly? When you save a second here, redeem a minute there, salvage an hour over there—hell, pretty soon you've got a whole week off to go fishing.

Unfortunately, the brain never forgets a painful experience. Thus, the fisherman must suffer again and again the sharp disappointment of breaking off a great fish.

Love Story

I heard this story from a Japanese fishing friend. The story is an old one and comes from the journal of a Japanese fisherman who loved his father.

The man who kept the journal learned that his father was dying and returned from his job in the city to his father's country farm to visit him. He found his father very ill and old and frail, and he could see that death stood near his bed. He asked what he could do for this man he loved.

Too weak to climb the high mountains to the streams of his youth, the old man asked his son to take him one last time to the brook where the wild trout held fast in the clear pools beneath the tall pines.

Having dressed his father warmly and locked the old man's thin legs safely in his arms, the young man could feel his father's arms around his neck as he carried him upon his back up the steep trail into the green mountains. Under this burden of great consequence, the son's legs were made strong.

On that perfect day together they fished and laughed and the dying old man caught the last few trout of his life. They boiled water from the brook and made green tea and drank it from small cups, and broiled the small fish over hot coals and ate them. The old man relished every bite.

Home again that evening, the old man was greatly comforted and at peace for the first time in a long time. His son put him to bed. That night the old fisherman slept so soundly that when morning came, he did not bother to wake up again.

Student

To catch a trout on a fly is to know how nature works and to become a part of her, if only for a time. If you will pace yourself and not go bungling into the stream fishing last year's fly, the trout will teach you how to catch them.

But you must sit down, be patient, and learn to watch and listen carefully.

You must study the water—its shadows and dimples and bulges and swirls, the forms of splashes above and the shimmer of flashes below. You may even see trout at work in their killing ground.

You must observe the insects and how the trout are taking them. You must see if the prey are wriggling toward shore along underwater pebbles, or poking their snouts up through the surface film trying to emerge, or falling from trees to smack the stream, or if the trout's target is already in the air, silently landing on your shoulders to dry its wings. Perhaps the duns have spent themselves in mating and are lying, dying and dead, flat-winged on the water. The bugs may be so tiny you cannot see them floating helplessly by in the dark current, or they may blare their presence in the ratcheting roar of grasshoppers warming their engines for precarious flight from a sun-warmed rock. Study these things, and the trout will teach you much.

Or, if you are mad to fish and impatient like me, go ahead, crash into the stream with the same old no. 14 Adams you fished last time out and begin casting with a fury. Odds are, you will catch trout.

But if you are denied, do not compound your ignorance with blind persistence; rather, cool your passion and sit upon the grassy bank beside the pool and rest your rod and high ambitions. Undertake a careful study of the water and the air and the sounds in the world around you. Look inward and outward at the same time; the trout will teach you much more than how to catch them.

If there is no good fishing in bad company, there is no bad fishing in good company.

Be Gentle with the Fishes

Be gentle with the fishes. They were not put in the streams and lakes and rivers and seas to be abused. If you eat them, kill them quickly and surely—as you would like to be killed.

If you release them, release them quickly and without rough handling, as you would like to be released.

Because we are all made of stardust and are traveling as one through time and space and the cosmos, we cannot afford to treat our fellow passengers without compassion.

Besides, what if God is a fish?

Where Have All the Fathers Gone?

On a recent solo fishing trip to a North Idaho wild cutthroat trout river I saw a boy fishing by himself. He happened to be casting to water I had hoped to fish myself, but since he was already knee-deep in the honey hole, I hiked downstream and began to work a pool I'd done very well in over the years. A short time later, the boy appeared at my elbow.

"Doing any good?" he asked.

"Not much. They're playing zipper mouth today. Maybe later."

"I haven't caught anything either, but then I'm new at this."

I nodded and kept casting a no. 16 gray caddis to a small trout rising against the far bank. I was being ignored by the fish, but not the boy.

"How do you cast like that?" he asked, an admiring tone in his voice. "I can't seem to get any distance. My line just sort of piles up in front of me."

Presenting their insoluble problems, beggars come in many forms. Some want bus money home, some want food, some want drink, and some seek instruction. This boy wanted instruction. Perhaps more. I reminded myself of the old tale where the Oriental potentate challenges the young beggar to discern which of his eyes is made of glass before he will give him a coin. The young man quickly says, "That's easy, sire. I chose the left one!" And the potentate responds, "That's amazing! How could you tell so quickly?" The young man replies, "It was easy, sire, I chose the eye with compassion in it."

So I turned to my young beggar and said, "Show me your cast."

The young angler wore sandals, a baseball cap, and glasses and had long, stringy hair. He looked more like a computer nerd than a fisherman, but his cast wasn't half bad and his enthusiasm was genuine. He was making just one small mistake—moving the rod too fast and failing to load the line properly—for which I offered a remedial tip. The boy was a quick study. "Gee!" he said on seeing his cast sail out over the water, "How long have you been doing this?"

I can spot a needy student as well as the next geezer. The boy wanted me to check his rod and line. It was okay. He opened his fly box with the comment, "I don't know what to use. I just catch something in the air with my hand and try to find a fly that matches it. I've only caught one trout on a fly . . . a little brookie in a lake. I'd sure like to catch one of these, but I don't know how."

I try to keep a little compassion visible in my real eye, so I took some time with the lad, taught him a bit about the river and about what kind of flies cutthroats prefer, and gave him a couple of no-miss patterns from my own box. I showed him how, when they're feeding in the film, you can sometimes get takes on bright little emergers swept down and across the holding water. The lad sucked it all in like a hungry fingerling.

When it was time for me to go and I started back across the river, the boy followed me, step for step.

"I think I'll go, too," he said, splashing behind me, "maybe try another place." Then he added, "I wish my father would go fishing with me. He used to fly-fish. He could teach me so much. We could have some fun together. I even bought him a new reel last Christmas in hopes it would get him fishing again. But all he does is work."

We climbed the riverbank to our rigs and put our rods away. For an uncomfortable moment we stood looking at each other. I didn't have anything worth saying, but wished like hell I had his father in my office for about thirty minutes.

"Thanks a lot," the boy said, finally, extending his hand in a formal handshake. "I hope to see you again sometime. You could teach me a lot."

"Good luck," I said, taking his hand. "You've got a good cast and a good start. You'll figure it out soon enough."

On the drive home a thought kept returning to me: To be an orphan, your father doesn't have to die.

Back in the office on Monday the mail included a handwritten note from a professional woman, together with a troubling poem about death and suicide written by her eleven-year-old son. Included in the envelope were two color snapshots of her son, one in which the boy was wading a small stream, and one in which he was being shown how to release a trout by what appeared to be a professional fishing guide. In neither photo did the boy look happy.

The mother's note read, "I've read your books. I know you could help my son. His father won't have anything to do with him. As you can see from his poetry, he needs help. Could you please come and take him fishing?"

I couldn't. But I called her and made a referral to a good child psychologist in her community. It wasn't much, but it was the best I could do.

A few days later I stopped to say hello to a young fishing guide whose father had died a few years ago. We discussed business, told a few fishing yarns, and planned a trip for the early fall. As I left the young man joked, "I need an older guy to fish with. I think I'll adopt you as my father."

"I'd be honored," I said, meaning it.

Except for a few years when I was a teenager and wouldn't listen to him, I always had my father to count on. Lean on. Seek advice from. Go fishing with. When I needed help building a new home, he was there to keep the contractor honest and help shingle the roof. Having him was like having a great offensive line in front of you; you could run with impunity, knowing a big guy was knocking down the opposition and making holes for you to sprint through. Because he was always there for me, for too long I assumed every boy and every young man had a father to lean on and learn from. How wrong I was.

One night my father and I were sitting around a campfire in the mountains. We'd spent the day prospecting for garnets in the Clearwater River country of northern Idaho. We'd finished dinner and were talking late into the night about his experiences in World War II, and life and death and fly-fishing. As the flames died down he said, "When your father dies, you know there's no one else between you and the Ditch. My father died when I was nine, but that day comes for every man, and there's nothing you can do about it. Except to know it's coming and enjoy life between then and now."

The Ditch is irretrievable and unstoppable death; everything else is willful abandonment. For a child, death is the easier of the two for a child to accept. After the funeral at least you can adopt a new father—that is, if you can find one.

A child psychologist I work with came out of his office after a difficult session with a suicidal young boy the other day. The boy's father had just announced that he was moving to another state and wouldn't be coming back. The boy's tear stains were still visible on his cheeks as he left the waiting room. My friend stepped into my office. No longer professionally obliged to contain his anger, he asked, "How'd you like to form a vigilante committee of therapists? After work we could put on ski masks, find these sons of bitches pretending to be fathers and beat the shit out of them."

Wherever it is that all the lost fathers have gone this side of the Ditch, I pray they will find their way back. And soon. Their children are looking for them.

If the only thing between you and death when you tread into deep water is your wits, you'd better use a wading staff.

Space Aliens, Where Are You?

On a beautiful afternoon along North Idaho's Clearwater River, my cousin Steve and I were casting Green Butt Skunks to steelhead trout when, out of an orange-colored sky, a pod of three jet skiers appeared from around the bend in the river below us.

I enjoy jet skiers on steelhead rivers as much as the next angler and only hope that legislation to downgrade killing one of them from a felony to a misdemeanor will soon be introduced here in the Northwest, where, unless I am much mistaken, the bill will enjoy broad voter support among fishermen. Until such a law is passed, however, I suggest we all call a psychic hotline and ask the channelers or parapsychologists or whoever answers the phones to pass along targeting instructions to space aliens in search of sexual experimentation victims. Just tell them, "It's simple to find them, just follow the noise." Lord knows you can hear two-cycle thunder from deep space.

As the rubber-clad, sun-glassed trio advanced on us and our steelhead like a scene from *Waterworld,* I remarked to cousin Steve, "These guys won't turn back until they've buzzed our fish."

"You're a pessimist," said Steve.

"You're an optimist," I said. "Bet you dinner they keep coming."

"Nobody's that rude," Steve assured me.

The bet was down; the trio continued upriver toward us.

I smiled to myself. My fishing might be ruined, but at least I was going to get a free steak dinner. I wished it weren't so, but betting against civil behavior these days is easy money. The recent appearance of a spate of books decrying the loss of civility among Americans should alarm us all. Especially fishermen. Absent good manners on our waterways, the world of angling is headed toward the equivalent of freeway shootings. In some places, this slide into barbarism has already begun.

Increasingly, fishing is less about catching fish than finding a bit of solitude. Anglers are willing to pay dear for a little space and time away from the madding crowd, because in an overcrowded world sanctuary is all. With recreational America riding a noisy machine into the twenty-first century, we anglers have much to lose if the current trends continue.

In case you haven't noticed, noise is up, silence down. Sound pollution is so prevalent in modern America we hardly notice we're shouting at each other to carry on normal conversation. More, the research on the psychology of overcrowding has not produced cheerful results. As crowds increase, manners decline. When everyone is a stranger, why treat anyone as family?

I laid out a cast, mended once, and watched the yellow line curl and sink my fly into a slip of green current at the far edge of the lie. Now quite audible, the buzz of the jet skis rose on the afternoon like the roar of angry insects. As they approached to within one hundred yards of my dreamed-of trout, I still could not make out the expressions of the riders, but I hoped they would soon make out mine: that of a grizzly bear with an abscessed tooth.

"Want to throw a fine cigar into that bet?" I shouted to Steve over the din.

He shook his head, and stripped in his cast.

"Right over the fish!" I shouted. "Right over the fish!"

We in the Northwest enjoy a great deal of public fishing water. Experienced, civil steelheaders know they are supposed to cast, take two steps downstream, cast again, take two steps, cast again, and so on until they are through the tail of the pool. This custom allows other anglers waiting at the top of the run access to the richest slot water. Properly done with nods, smiles, and a smattering of small talk, this anglers' dance of mutual understanding and respect has become an admirable tradition. To position oneself on the best spot on the best run and refuse to move along is not only rude, but unsportsmanlike.

Some fishermen don't know stream etiquette; or they do know it and treat fellow fishermen badly anyway. Perhaps they secretly own jet skis, and suffer a deeply flawed character. Sometimes bad manners are simply ignorance on display. Sometimes bad manners are intentional and mean-spirited. At the root of many bad manners lies greed. That etiquette exists suggests civilization is possible; without etiquette, barbarism must rule.

If you don't know you're supposed to fish a steelhead lie awhile and then move on so the next angler can get to the same water, it isn't like someone is going to report you to the politeness police. But as a fisherman matures, he or she has an obligation to learn the requisite etiquette. Likewise, crowding the other guy to hurry him up is impolite. Casting into another angler's water is wrong. Drifting your boat through a shore fisherman's spot and spooking his fish is poor form. If you have to get downstream, and absolutely can't avoid the water he's fishing, at least shout an apology. Sportfishing rises or falls on its ethics, its rules, and its sensibilities.

Don't know what is civil on the trout stream? Observe. Ask. Read.

Different places have different customs, and customs, to the degree they work to enhance the quality of fishing for everyone, become our standards for angling etiquette. In light of what is happening on our highways these days, we should never underestimate the importance of quick forgiveness, understanding, good manners, and civil behavior; they keep us from killing one another. Besides, being treated rudely can spoil your whole day. Even worse—though few of us will admit it—treating others rudely can spoil *our* whole day, and maybe even our sense of who we are and want to be.

The jet skiers roared into our water.

They say a bad man does what a good man thinks. If so, it is a good thing I am not a bad man, because I was dreaming of my Swedish-made .308 deer rifle that. . . . And it's a good thing you can't be arrested for fantasies.

Fundamentally, I think what my fellow fisherman wants is what I want when I'm on the bright waters: to be given some elbow room, to be left alone as much as possible, to be allowed to enjoy the great quiet of the Great Outdoors, to be treated with respect, and to be given equal access to the best water when more than one of us wants to fish it. This may be too much to ask of jet skiers, but it is not too much to ask of ourselves.

P.S. I won the dinner, but was saddened by the aliens' no-show.

The February Trout

I know a little out-of-the-way trout stream exactly fifty miles from home where, if you really need to catch a trout in February, the fishing gods will let you catch one.

Not two. Not three. Not fifteen. But one. Unless you've been an exceptionally good person for a whole year, and then they may let you catch a couple more. These are beautiful, wild rainbow trout, and a single wild trout in February is a great gift indeed.

One trout is okay . . . better than okay.

Especially in February.

But to catch a rainbow in this little stream in February, you need to know what the gods demand.

The gods that govern this little trout stream are odd. They don't respond to prayers. It's as if they believe praying is a cheap substitute for living a good and honorable life. "Keep your words," they say. "Show us good acts." Perhaps these gods are from Missouri. Certainly they demand good behavior, not for a day or a week or even a month, but for a whole year at a time.

So I never pray to the fishing gods of this little stream. Long ago I stopped asking them to trust me. However I came to understand their nature, I think they know what I know about me. And I wouldn't want to anger them. After all, to fish their stream in winter you must wake them up, and awakened from their moral slumbers, they could be cranky. I just fish the little stream quietly, reverently, and if they grant me the one rainbow, I am happy.

One trout in February is enough, isn't it?

Even if you have to drive a hundred miles to catch it?

Of course it is.

At least for me it is. With winter's white blanket smooth upon the ground, and sheet ice in the eddies, a single February trout is quite enough. I am delighted with one. I am fulfilled with one. I am grateful for one. Even at the steep price.

The price these gods demand for a February trout is an old-fashioned one. They insist on right actions, kindness, and honorable behavior. Above all, they absolutely insist we humans be kind to one another. It is an anthem with them.

They want us to be thoughtful of others and to help our neighbors without being asked. They don't want us to honk our horns unless we really have to. They expect us to smile at strangers and wave to farmers. They demand that we sit on our anger in heavy traffic and not aggravate our fellow travelers with word or sign or deed.

To catch the February trout, these gods require that we let the other guy go first, smile at old people, and speak to them if we can. They expect us to donate a little money to help people down on their luck, volunteer some of our time in good causes, and stand up to the bad guys. They want us to vote, write thank-you notes, and learn to live and let live. They demand that we take care of the earth so that the rest of the humans, and all the creatures we share the ride with, have a nice place to picnic and enjoy a summer afternoon.

These fishing gods don't expect us to sacrifice a virgin or slaughter a firstborn son to catch the February trout, but we do have to tip well, and not kick dogs or be hard-asses. And we absolutely must be nice to the people that make the world work: the receptionists, the waiters, the bus boys, the secretaries, the people who pump gas and fix flats, serve food, wear name tags, and have no titles or prestige or big money, and yet greet us with a smile and a helpful heart every single time.

Mistreat these people, and—though it is not my place—even I hope you never catch the February trout.

I have been fishing this little out-of-the-way trout stream for many years now. Sometimes in summer, more often in winter. When Super Bowl Sunday rolls around, even if it is snowing, I return to the little stream in late morning, arriving around kickoff time, uncase my rod, string it, tie on Griffith's Gnat, and hike into the sagebrushed canyon filled with snow to a long, dark, curving pool where the February trout waits.

On my journey to the pool I review what kind of human being I have been in the past year. It is as honest an accounting as I know how to make. Feeling okay with myself but never cocky, I loose the hook from its wire holder, check the barb, burn the memory from the coiled leader between my fingertips, and lay out the first supplication in a quartering upstream cast.

This is my theory of how to catch the February trout. It is a rotten theory, but so far it's working.

Journal Entry:

Campbell River, Vancouver Island

You could see them. Well, not exactly see them, but from time to time you could see where one slashed through a school of herring near the surface, causing the herring to dash and sail out of the boiling water in a mad rush to escape death. Afterward, you could see the herring scales from the kills glittering in the water like diamond flakes as they sank down to the depths. The salmon were feeding; your heart leapt.

The beginning of the great salmon run up Roderick Haig-Brown's Campbell River on Vancouver Island, British Columbia, was in full swing this morning. The cohos and kings were returning. Fishers were everywhere to meet them. And yet, in the midst of this cast of thousands, no salmon were being caught. Everywhere the nets were dry.

I tried to count the boats. There were too many. In constant motion, they crossed and recrossed each other's wakes until the only way to guess their number was to quadrant off a piece of the horizon, count the boats in that quadrant quickly, and then multiply by four. There were maybe two hundred sport fishers in the flotilla working the broad estuary.

"I can't guess the problem," said the guide, changing our lures again. "But sometimes the fish just won't bite."

I waved away his excuse making, as did my companions. All experienced fishermen, we understood.

The afternoon wore on. Still no nets flashed and no salmon were caught. Strangely, I began to take some small pleasure in this fact. Here were millions and millions of dollars' worth of boats and tackle and guide fees at work in the estuary, and yet the salmon swam under us and past us and beyond us to the river's mouth, ignoring our offerings while taking one last herring in a final feast before mating and dying.

I mused to myself that while man has mastered the day and the hour of the salmon's return, and even the very stream a given salmon will climb to spawn, there remain these wonderful limits to our knowledge and skill, these knotted mysteries we have yet to untie. So long as we angle for sport alone, it is good that the fishes can still humble us.

Then I saw the eagle.

Even from far below, I could see the white head as the bird circled above the fleet, soaring on the thermals, watching, watching.

Others saw it too.

"A bald eagle," said the guide. "Another fisherman come to reap the harvest."

People in the boats near us craned their necks, pointing upward. Some stopped fishing to watch.

The eagle turned slowly in the sky.

The eagle turned slowly in the sky.

Then, suddenly, it folded its wings and dove.

Then it rose up again, a bright-silver salmon shivering in its talons.

From across the vast fleet, a great cheer went up.

Fishing Laws

While resting on a desert island after a day of bonefishing a coconut fell from the tree I was sitting under and hit me on the head. As with Isaac Newton before me, the blow produced a new understanding of how the world works. In my case, the blow triggered new insights into the laws that govern the universe of fishing. Here are the first five laws:

First Law of Fishing: The best fishing tends to be yesterday.

Second Law of Fishing: The very best fishing tends to be last week.

Third Law of Fishing: The biggest fish of the day tends to be caught by the person who didn't want to go fishing in the first place.

Fourth Law of Fishing: The biggest fish of the year tends to be caught by a beginner, unless the beginner is a child, in which case it will be the biggest fish of the decade.

Fifth Law of Fishing: Fish don't know the laws of fishing.

Rubbing the knot on my head while polishing off a gin and tonic produced a baker's dozen of fish-specific laws. In no order of importance, here they are:

Trout tend to be easy to catch until you really need to catch one.

Largemouth bass tend to prefer plugs when you are using spinner baits, and spinner baits when you are using plugs.

Whatever color rubber worm you are using, smallmouth tend to prefer the other color.

Trophy king salmon generally strike after you've set your rod down to take a shot of coffee.

When you are casting from a skiff for bonefish, fly lines tend to migrate under the angler's feet. When a school of small bonefish are being cast to, the fly line will be found under one foot; when it is a school of large bonefish, the line will be found under both feet.

When finally spotted, large permit tend to be swimming away.

The smallest fish in any school tends to be the first one to your fly.

Catfish are stupid and can be caught pretty much anytime, anyplace. The exception to this law is when you are really hungry for a mess of catfish, in which case they cannot be caught at all.

Steelhead tend to be caught by high school dropouts.

Walleyes tend to be under the other fisherman's boat.

Underrated until accidentally caught, carp tend to catch fishermen.

Marlin tend to be seen but not hooked.

Migrating striped bass tend to have just migrated.

And now, so have I.

Never get into an argument with an ignorant fisherman;
you have nothing to gain, and he has nothing to lose.

Fishermen Always Round Up

Last evening I caught a 23-inch, 6-pound brown trout from a nearby lake. The big boy took a black Woolly Bugger fly with a special twist of orange chenille through the body. On a 5-weight rod, it was some tussle.

Would you believe it if I said a 22½-inch, 5½-pound brown trout?

How about 21 inches of trout with the tail barely touching the 22-inch mark?

Since I didn't have a scale, the fish could have weighed only 5 pounds. I mean, the brute was thrashing around something fierce before I released it, so we're not talking hard scientific measurements here.

So I rounded up a bit.

So what?

Rounding up was invented by fishermen.

Rounding off figures is a widely accepted method of simplifying life. When you round up or down, you can skip the fractions and pennies. The only moral question about rounding numbers is, when do you round up, and when do you round down?

I was always taught that to round up to the nearest inch or foot or dollar or pound, you need to be a bit over the halfway mark on your way up, not a bit under. If you're a bit under halfway, then you must round down. Because you've been honest with yourself and others, everything will work out in the end.

Fishermen don't go along with this; fishermen always round up.

Some people live for numbers: statisticians, sports enthusiasts, members of the International Game Fishing Association, competitive anglers.

Men are nuttier about numbers than women, which is why fishing with women is less combative than fishing with men. To control wanton rounding up in everything from professional fishing tournaments to professional football—and to keep themselves from killing each other off—men first had to invent numbers, then stopwatches, scales, tape measures, judges, fines, and punishments. Just to keep the rules of war straight, everyone now has to use the metric system.

People who are fussy about numbers make me nervous. Except for a few accountant friends, most accountants don't seem as happy as they should be. Unlike fishermen, who always round up, half the time accountants must round down. I think rounding down is hard on people.

I asked my personal accountant—a man who doesn't take himself or the IRS very seriously, and who rounds up or down with equal ease—what the difference was between an accountant who must keep very neat and orderly figures for a living and, say, an economist like Alan Greenspan.

"Oh," said Jim, "that's easy. An accountant is just an economist with the personality removed."

Except when it comes to counting out your limit, staying within required slot limit lengths, competitive fishing for big money, and setting new world fishing records, most fishermen are going to keep rounding up.

And they should. After all, rounding up means that, on average, you catch bigger fish.

When you catch and release your fish, rounding up gets easier and easier. Routinely rounding up is your main defense against people with small, mean minds. For example, when you round up and release your fish, no one can call you to account for a trout that was twenty-two inches long when you landed it and twenty-three inches long when you released it. Only an IRS agent with a grinch attitude and a ruler would make you round the same trout all the way down to twenty-one inches.

Rounding up may be mildly inflationary, but it is always fun.

Rounding up simplifies life.

Rounding up is relaxing.

Take it from a doctor, rounding up is good for your mental health.

Gonzo Fishing

"I'll be at your place at five sharp. If you're not waiting on the porch with your rod and tackle, I'm leaving. Nothing personal, it's just that fishing waits for no man, and I don't either."

That preface to a fishing trip thirty years ago was how I was introduced to gonzo fishing. The man who said it meant every word. Older than me by twenty years, Woody was a World War II combat veteran with only one lung (the other had been permanently deflated by an 8mm German round on the beaches of Anzio), and he knew the value of time and daylight. Woody never fooled around when it came to fishing. I knew that if I wasn't standing in the street with my gear when he pulled up, he wouldn't bother to touch the brakes.

Woody didn't care about being liked or lovable; he cared about catching fish. He was the kind of fisherman you could learn reams from just by shutting up and watching. He showed me how to catch my first walleye and how really simple it was to catch steelhead in a hot run. "You have to fish them hard," he explained. "After about twenty years they start to come easy."

Fish hard.

Fish long.

Fish when the fish don't bite.

Fish when they do bite.

If they're not biting, keep fishing until they start.

Catching fish is as much about persistence as about skill and timing. Gonzo fishermen, like the Energizer bunny, just keep fishing and fishing and fishing and fishing and fishing . . .

Woody's gone now, but I try to carry on the Code. If the bite is early, I'm on the water early; if it's late, I'm the last one off the water. If a guy says, "It's supposed to rain, maybe we ought to wait a few days," it's the last time I ask him to go fishing. And I don't wait twice for people who forgot to set the alarm.

The other day I had to make a trip to Southern California. I called ahead to a fly-fishing club to see if someone could put me into some fish. Any fish. You don't risk your life on a trip to Los Angeles in June unless you can catch a fish or two. A guy named Greg called back. "Like largemouth?" he asked.

"Yep."

"Mind fishing at night?"

"Nope."

"Mind fishing from two in the morning till dawn?"

"Nope."

"From a float tube, with huge catfish snapping at your toes?"

"Whatever it takes," I affirmed.

"Good," he said. "Then bring your waders and eight-weight rod, because I've got some very good bass for you. I'll take care of the tube and fins."

I didn't know Greg from Adam. But his questions told me all I needed to know. He practiced the Gonzo Code. Even if we didn't find bass, we'd find friendship. We found both.

The first year I made it to Christmas Island for bonefish I went with my friend Rick and his lifelong friend, Nick. As we loaded up the first morning, a fourth guy was assigned to our group. The gods were smiling. All of us practiced the Code.

We were the first out of bed. First at breakfast. Lunches packed, we were first on the road to the beach or boat, then first into the water. Wade, cast, wade, cast, wade, cast, set hook, fight bone; wade, wade, wade, cast, cast, cast, fight bone, wade, wade, wade, cast, cast, cast, take a hurried shot at a small trevalley, wade, cast, ignore sun, ignore lunch, ignore drinking water until lips stick together, wade, cast, wade, cast, wade, wade, wade, cast, cast, cast. . . . Imagine this litany continuing until the sun starts down and there is no longer enough light to make out bonefish shadows on white sand.

We paid the guides overtime to get all the fishing light we could, and came in well after sundown with the headlights blazing. Dinner was cold. Normal anglers were sipping brandies. Between dinner and bed we got out the vices and tied fresh Crazy Charlie flies for the morrow. Some guys walked by our bungalow one evening while we were tying. "That's them," one explained to his companions, "those crazy, gonzo fishermen."

About a half a lifetime ago I was drinking Sapporo beer with an army pal, Merle, from Mississippi in a bar overlooking the Sea of Japan. We'd spent the day bait-fishing from a wooden boat with an old Japanese gentlemen, and without much luck. We were sunburned, thirsty, and young, and after finding a little tavern, we were pounding them down at a good clip.

In quite good English, the bartender asked, "Why you Americans drink so fast?"

Merle fixed the bartender with a level stare and drawled, " 'Cause we're only goin' be here two years."

Gonzo anglers also know time is short. We don't want to waste any daylight or moonlight or pitch-dark nights waiting for some otherwise nice fisherman to fix to get ready to plan to make a commitment someday to arrange for a time to get on down to the water, after breakfast of course, and make a goddamn cast.

That's just the way we are.

When listening to someone tell a favorite fishing story, never pass up the opportunity to keep quiet and pay perfect attention—unless, of course, you don't want friends.

Silver in the Rain

It had rained Wednesday through Friday. But for months it had been raining off and on from thick gray skies—the kind of steady, relentless rain that people, when you mention Washington State, think we have too much of. They are partly right. Washington, however, is not just Seattle or Olympia or Port Townsend. Washington is Spokane and Ritzville and Pullman. For the record, the points east are drier by far.

The rain was as much on my mind as on my windshield as I rolled up Sunset Hill on a Friday afternoon, my radio tuned to an all-news channel. (Fishermen, like farmers, play close attention to jet streams.) The weatherman was sorry, but the rain would be with us through the weekend. From eastern Washington through northern Idaho and western Montana, everyone was going to stay wet. Still, I had been dreaming all day of getting out to Silver Lake for an hour or two of fishing.

They say the older you get, the more weather-sensitive you become. Cold gets to you. Wind gets to you. Heat gets to you. They say your thermostat wears out after about forty years. When I was hitting the home stretch of freeway, it seemed true; I *had* stopped fishing in bad weather four, maybe five, years ago. Looking at my face in the rearview mirror, I wondered, "Is this what over the hill looks like?"

As I came up the stairs, Ann asked, "You're not going out in this?"

"Don't know," I said. "But if I don't go fishing soon, I'm dead meat. Where are the kids?"

"All out for the evening. And I'd rather you didn't go by yourself, especially in this weather."

I dropped into an easy chair and opened the newspaper: evil tidings, dastardly deeds, frivolous lawsuits, smoke hanging over a dozen battlefields, famine, scandal in the White House, whole countries threatening to default on loans to the same banks where I keep my few shekels; murder, pillage, terrorism, and an editorial on the "possible" negative effects of a radioactive leak in our neighborhood. I needed to go fishing.

"It's raining. And cold. Don't be silly," Ann said.

"I want to go fishing."

"It'll be dark in a couple of hours, and it's only forty-two degrees."

"I want to go fishing."

"Lie down for a minute; it'll pass."

I tossed the paper onto the coffee table. "Let me put it this way: I *have* to go fishing! If I don't go fishing, I will go stark, raving mad."

Ann smiled her patient smile. "You don't have all that far to go, dear."

All my old trouting pals would, I knew, pass on a last-minute invitation to rush down to Silver Lake to lay a fly on the water, especially late on a Friday night with the rain falling, however lightly, out of an unforgiving sky. Then I remembered Jim, a man I had just met. Jim, a physics professor who lives down the road, had said when we had talked fishing one evening at a dinner party, "Call me anytime you get the urge." I certainly had the urge.

"Jim, this is Paul. Want to go fishing?"

"When?"

"Now."

"Now?"

"I know this is short notice, but I have to go fishing."

"It's raining."

"I know."

The line went silent for a minute, during which time I imagined he was consulting with his wife over how to handle a bizarre phone call. In a moment he was back on the line. "Five minutes?"

"You got it," I said.

I grabbed my fishing vest off the back of my desk chair and my rod case from the corner of the family room where I stack it, and hurried out to the rig, shouting something to Ann about how wonderful it was to find another fisherman so close to home, to which she replied, "God help us!"

"This is insane, you know," I said to Jim as we wheeled out of his place. "You have to be certifiable to go out in this kind of weather."

"Crazy people . . . fly fishermen . . . what's the difference?"

Driving down the road to Silver, we kicked things around: graphite rods, early mayflies, chironomids in the spring, sinking-tip lines, big trips to Yellowstone country. Men go at friendship slowly. But now, as we barreled down a wet road with the windshield wipers beating and trout on our minds, it seemed as if we had been lifelong friends.

Silver Lake, as I had anticipated, was ours: no boats, no shore fishermen, no people. Falling steadily, the rain drizzled down, dimpling the lake. Like a well-practiced team, we readied the boat for launching, and with a single try, I managed to put the trailer wheels squarely down the ramp.

"Nymphs in the film," I said, shutting down the motor smack-dab in the middle of a dozen subsurface swirls.

"What do you recommend?"

"A midge. Black or green. I doubt if it matters."

As Jim tied a fly to his leader, he remarked that he had not caught a trout yet this season or even tried to.

We greased the tippets down to the last six inches and cinched on some little grams of ingenuity that best resembled what was emerging. Anchored down, we fell naturally to casting stations.

The first fish was mine. A strong jumper, it hopped around and cleared water three or four times, wiping out most of the distemper I'd built up over the past several days. Twelve inches of silver, the color of a new dime, and with bright-red stripes running down its flanks, it came over on its side after an honest fight.

"You eat 'em?" I asked.

"Rarely," said Jim.

I slipped the fly out of the rainbow's jaw and watched it tail down.

I caught two more before insisting Jim try one of my no. 14 black midges. He did. Two casts later, he was fast to fish.

The rain kept up, and the sky darkened. Somewhere, up above the weather, the sun was shutting down business for the day. Jim had good rain gear, but no gloves. I had a pair of fingerless rag-wool gloves but no rubber pants, and the rain, running off my slicker, soaked quickly into my jeans.

"I never thought about gloves," said Jim, blowing into his cupped hands.

"Had enough?" I asked.

"Not quite."

You never really know a fisherman until you're out in foul weather with him, or rather, you never know how truly crazy he is about fishing until his hands turn blue. And Jim's hands were turning blue.

"Shall we take a few home?" I said after a while. "This is a put'n'take lake, and fish are good for your heart."

"They're better for your soul," said Jim, "so why not?"

With the last minutes of light failing and the rain pelting down and the cold creeping in under the skin, we hauled them in, hand over fist, killing them quickly with a rap of the head against the gunwales. Then, when it was too dark to see a fly and with the rain running down our necks, we finally admitted we'd had enough fun.

"You know," said Jim on the drive home, "I'm really glad you called. That was fun. I needed to get out more than I realized."

"Maybe next time it won't be raining," I said.

Jim smiled. "I don't care if it is. Call me anytime."

"The same goes here," I said.

"I never freeze trout," he said. "I either eat them fresh or I don't take them home. Shall we get the ladies together and cook these up for supper?"

"You bet," I said. "Your house or mine?"

Journal Entry: Kelly Creek

August 16, 1997. Camped on the fork of Kelly Creek and the North Fork of the Clearwater River in northern Idaho. Fished Black Canyon and the lower end of Kelly from about ten in the morning until the last dog was hanged.

Am alone and writing this in front of a campfire. I invited two people on this trip, but life got in the way for both of them. My mother says life is what happens while you're making plans to live it. Tonight, life is this campfire and the soft roar of the North Fork rushing toward the sea.

On my way to Bozeman, Montana, in the morning to give a luncheon talk at Wild Trout Symposium VI, sponsored by the American Fisheries Society. Planned to fish my way over and back. It's against the law to drive through Idaho and Montana on business alone; if they catch you without waders and a fly rod in your vehicle, you can be cited for failure to yield to good sense.

The symposium papers to be presented by the scientists over the next few days will cover all sorts of issues related to helping preserve wild trouts, especially the natives. There are not all that many native trouts left, and those that are left have a fight on their hands. You can't save a wild native trout without a wild trout watershed, and it had better be pretty much the sort of watershed that that trout evolved in, otherwise we're all just sitting around watching another extinction parade. With all but 5 percent of the national forests already logged, nobody but a fool believes we have a single watershed left that needs cutting.

On the road down Hoodoo Pass to the North Fork this morning I noticed a nicely placed sign. I stopped, got out, and looked around. The sign read, "Timber harvest built these roads. Drive safely and enjoy yourself." Signed, "The Clearwater Resource Coalition."

I don't know who the Clearwater Resource Coalition is, but except for a guilty conscience, why would anybody waste good money on a sign to tell you who built the road you're driving on? I took a minute and turned full around, scanning the mountains.

The sign stands in a high meadow near a spring-fed tributary of the Clearwater River. The view is spectacular, wild and beautiful. But the view does not include a single clear-cut, or timber road, or slash pile, or mud slide, and not one rusted choker chain, beer can, or empty oil container the loggers leave behind them when the dirty work is done. Downriver at the murder scene you can see all these things, but not from the sign that tells you whom to thank for the road and the view.

I wanted pretty badly to pull up the sign with my portable winch, toss it in the back of the pickup, and haul it downriver to the blowouts below some of the world's biggest clear-cuts, where last winter whole roads washed into the spawning grounds of Idaho's remnant wild steelhead and silted them in forever. I'd find a spot for the coalition's sign that offered a little different view of reality, and put it up again. After all, people ought to know whom to thank.

To understand such grand deception, you have to go out in the woods, get on the ground, and see the truth for yourself. The tranquil, bird-singing, elk-bugling, technicolor timber company TV ads about being such good stewards of the forests don't get it quite right—although they serve as a reasonably good emetic if you need to throw up.

Time to hit the sack.

The first fish today was a small endangered bull trout, which I quickly released without touching. The next trout rose to an elk-hair caddis, took strongly, and jumped four times. Full of spirit, the large par marks made it a wild steelhead smolt. The next fish was a wild Westslope cutthroat that rose to a Griffith's Gnat. Heavy and almost nineteen inches long, if you round up a bit.

Three fish. Three wild trouts. A North Idaho grand slam. I wonder, will I be the last fisherman in Black Canyon to be so blessed?

The Perils of Philosophy

Fishing and philosophy go together. Each gives the other balance and perspective. Thanks to Izaak Walton, fishermen are expected to be philosophers. People believe we anglers plumb the depths of philosophy regularly, practically on every cast. We even encourage this sort thinking in people who don't fish. It's nice to be thought of as insightful, wise, and able to spell Nietzsche on the first try.

"All those long days of silence, surely you must get something out of fishing besides catching fish?" nonfishermen ask.

"Isn't it inspiring?" they query. "Do you think about Kant or Plato while you cast for winter steelhead?"

You smile wisely and say, "Yes, yes I do." Then, if you own a briar pipe, you take a puff and gaze thoughtfully into space. A truthful answer from a winter steelheader would be, "Actually, no, I don't think of Kant or Plato, I think about numb feet and why in hell some genius hasn't invented a really warm pair of fishing waders."

I've been known to occasionally mitigate a taxing and fishless day by later waxing philosophical at some local pub or other—especially if some admirer is buying the drinks. Being both a lot Scottish (my middle name is Guthrie) and a little Irish, I like to point out that while the Irish kept philosophy alive through the Dark Ages by copying the great works of the Western world, we Scots were busy fishing and making whisky. I'm told the reason God created Scotch whisky in the first place was to prevent us Scots from conquering the world, which we could have done on any given Monday morning if we had invented a weapon of war more effective than a large rock, instead of so damn many trout flies.

Philosophy is deep water.

Dangerous water.

One minute you're wading knee-deep in the stream of ordinary existence; the next minute you've stepped off the ledge into the Meaning-of-Life Hole and are thrashing wildly to keep your waders from filling up. Uncoupled by the hypnotic rhythm of casting from the usual *click-click-click* of a life divided into nanoseconds, the angling mind can slip its customary moorings and find itself adrift in the treacherous waters of philosophy.

For example, the other evening I was out fishing by myself when I had a small philosophical accident. It was the middle of August and the bite was slow. Dog days. Hot. All the sane people were inside breathing conditioned air. But being a fisherman and quite certifiable, I was out dredging the depths of a fly-fishing-only lake with a full-sink line and a dragonfly nymph. Better one evening of trout fishing than a thousand TV reruns.

Big trout don't give a damn for summer reruns, or e-mail, or any of the junk we humans manage to clutter our lives with. Big trout go deep in August, deep enough for easy living on torpid midge larvae, slow-moving dragonfly nymphs, and the odd damsel in distress. Taking a big trout from deep water is good medicine any time of year, but especially in late summer.

But lolling and drifting deep for trout on a late summer's eve can prove perilous.

On a slow summer evening you can lie on your back in the bottom of an open boat as the sun goes down and stare up at the emerging visible universe, and, because no ringing phone can interrupt your reveries, you may find yourself observing the death of an ancient star and wondering about the life span of our solar system, about the meaning of quarks, and about whether, in the end, life and death and fishing are all pretty much the same thing.

If you are not philosophically inclined, however, you may stare up at the very same sky and see the *Mir* space station, space junk, or even commuter shuttles in orbit. These things are all quite big enough to see with the naked eye. To correct the misperception that all anglers are well-informed philosophers, I am reminded of sitting at a campground fire early one November evening when an older fisherman dropped by for a chat. The stars were very bright that night, and America was shooting everything but the kitchen sink into space after the embarrassment of *Sputnik*.

As the old gentleman and I talked about the weather, the starry sky, and fly patterns for late-fall brown trout, I glanced up into the night and, as luck would have it, spotted an orbiting satellite.

"You've seen these satellites?" I asked.

"Heard about 'em," said the old man. "Never seen one."

"Well," I said, "now's your chance." I tried to point out the bit of moving light to the old fellow.

It took him some time to find the target, but when he did he jutted a finger into the sky and exclaimed, "By God, they sure put one helluva headlight on those sons of bitches, now don't they!"

"Ah, yes . . . yes, they do," I replied, resizing the generation gap.

The old-timer and I did not wax much more philosophical that evening, but fell instead to talk of rods and creels and Hardy-made reels. By bedtime we'd agreed that a November brown trout is a sucker for a Woolly Bugger, and a sucker is any fisherman who hangs up his rod before November.

On that August evening, what tempted me into the deep waters of philosophy was a setting sun striking a single white cloud in a clear-blue sky. I hadn't caught a fish or felt a strike in better than an hour, so I lay down in the bottom of the boat to rest my back and watched the sun set the cloud on fire. Except for a pair of great blue herons that reside at the end of the bay I fish, I was alone on the lake with my thoughts.

From my singular position on the bottom of a fishing boat floating on a little lake on the North American continent, it suddenly struck me that I was the only human being in the entire world, in the entire history of the world, in the entire history of life on planet Earth, who could see and reflect upon the single white cloud directly above me as it turned the most glorious shades of pink, yellow, amber, crimson, and gold. Such a unique diversity of light and color and shape would come but once in the history of time.

I was it. I was the only intelligent witness to this miracle of light. Wading briskly now toward the ledge at Meaning-of-Life Hole, I wondered whether this was the same glorious gift God imagined and intended for mankind when He rejoiced, in Genesis: "Let there be light!"

Then, I wondered if . . .

But my next thought was finished by a powerful strike—which would have been wonderful except that the take caused me to rise up suddenly from the bottom of the boat, bang my head on a boat seat, and yank so hard on the fly rod that I broke off the big trout; which wouldn't have been so bad if I hadn't simultaneously pulled a muscle in my lower back; which wouldn't have been so bad if, while all this was going on, I hadn't run the boat into a rocky shoreline, which hapless, numbskull stunt broke off the tip of my backup dry-fly rod.

As I said, philosophy is a perilous business, and fishermen should avoid going there if at all possible—especially those prone to wool gathering and cockpit trouble.

But if they can't help themselves, at least we Scots have invented a cure for philosophical injuries; it's called single malt whisky. Most any quality brand will do, but Macallan's caters especially to anglers.

Not bright enough to avoid dangerous territory altogether, at least I'd remembered to bear Scottish arms for medicinal purposes. Finding a flask in my tackle bag, I quickly took a wee drop to ease the pain, reeled in, and started down the dusky lake for home.

A great passion for art, for music, for wine, for fishing, for life, for whatever, is vastly underrated—especially by people who do not get out of bed until ten in the morning.

Postcards from the Ladies

Not long ago I received a card from my old friend Joan Whitlock, a lifelong angler who runs a fly-fishing speaker's bureau out of Tulsa, Oklahoma. I'd sent Joan a bit of smoked salmon for the holidays. In part, her thank-you/holiday card read: "Just returned from the Baja where 170-plus women attended the Second International Festival of Fly-fishing Women. I was so lonely on the stream forty years ago, you cannot imagine how good that felt."

Not a week later I received in the mail the inaugural copy of *Women's Reel News*, the first national news publication for women who fish. In addition to reporting on the festival, the cover letter contained downloaded data from a 1996 National Sporting Goods Association survey: thirteen million women now fish the nation's lakes and rivers, and over three million fish in salt water. Women represent approximately a third of all sport fishermen.

Or maybe it shouldn't be fisher*men* anymore; just fishers.

Personally, I don't much care what you call me, just call me to go fishing.

I know dozens of female fishers, and I couldn't be happier about what's happening.

Hurry up! Get going! I have four granddaughters that need proper role models.

The Whistle Fish

"Five more minutes," said the old man. "Let's give it five more minutes. We're sure to catch a whistle fish."

"What's a whistle fish?" I asked.

"You'll see," said the old man, smiling.

Another fisherman said, "Come on, let's reel them in. We haven't boated a single fish all day. Hell, we haven't had a strike since sunup. That was nine hours ago."

But because the rest of us were younger and wished to respect his years, the old man won out, and we fished on. We would humor him; five minutes by the clock.

Hemingway's *Old Man and the Sea* begins with perhaps the greatest opening line ever written: "He was an old man who fished alone in a skiff in the Gulf Stream and he had gone eighty-four days now without taking a fish."

Eighty-four days without a fish. An old man.

We ask ourselves, what kind of old man is this? What kind of man persists against such terrible defeat? What keeps him going? Of what is he made that he can stay a chosen course when ordinary men would long since have quit the task? What is in his head or heart that fuels this force, this hope, this constant belief in a thing not caught?

To find the answer we must become like the old man in the story,

Santiago. Now we must keep going, keep reading. His nature is like our nature, and by learning about him we may come to know about ourselves. Of all admirable human traits, it is this grit, this resolve, this relentless pursuit of a goal we most revere. Heros are not so much about inherent greatness as they are about showing up, every time, on time, and enduring. Later, looking back, we call it courage. Mandela's prison time. Gandhi's fasts. Christ's tenacity in the face of certain crucifixion.

The people we most respect believe in the same things we do; the difference between us is not that they are brighter or more gifted or better placed in life than we, but that they outlast us. Sometimes by an hour or a day or a week or a month, but more often by a year or a decade or a lifetime. Can any of us truly hope to lead a great cause, or make a memorable contribution, or even catch a great fish if we quit a ten-year job after ten minutes?

"What's a whistle fish?" I called again to the old man from my perch on the flying deck.

"Oh," he replied, "a whistle fish is the fish you catch when the charter captain blows the time-to-quit whistle. When you hear the whistle you're supposed to quit fishing and reel in. Even though no one has had a bite in an hour, as soon as the whistle blows, someone will get a hookup. It happens every time. You'll see."

As agreed in the morning with the guide, we would quit fishing at four in the afternoon, unless the bite was hot, in which case we would keep fishing until everyone agreed we'd had enough. It was now three minutes to four and we hadn't had a touch since sunup. Only the old man fished on.

In the morning, hopes had been high. The day before, two in our party had fished the same water, the same holes, with the same lures, and done very well on large lake trout and Kamloops rainbows, taking fish all day in a steady bite. But today, under identical skies, and for reasons only the fishing gods can explain, the lake had become a freshwater version of Santiago's sea.

The seconds ticked away.

Those of us who had quit fishing sat on cushioned seats high on the flying deck and enjoyed the North Idaho scenery, while the old man, keeping the angler's vigil, paced slowly back and forth before the trolling rods: two flat-liners, two arched over on downriggers, and a fifth rod, the guide's rod, rigged with leaded line and pulling a silver and black minnow plug. I looked at my watch. Now it was four o'clock sharp, time to put a wrap on it. "Four o'clock!" someone shouted. "Reel them in!"

Instantly, the guide shouted, "Fish on!" and rushed from the cabin below us to help the old man.

But the old fisherman didn't need any help. He'd already grabbed the jumping downrigger rod, and set the hook to put in the insurance. Then he began to fight the fish.

"Well I'll be . . ." someone murmured. Another shook his head in disbelief.

"I told you," said the old man, grinning up to us as he leaned into the rod. "I told you there would be a whistle fish."

This whistle fish turned out to be a bull trout, only a couple of pounds of silvered beauty dappled with God's fingerprints—rare, threatened, and even endangered in some watersheds in the Pacific Northwest. The guide instantly removed the hook with his pliers and released the fish without touching it. The old man beamed.

From somewhere out of a cobalt sky a snow-white cloud drifted between the boat and the sun, shading us for a moment as we rocked on the great blue lake while the guide reeled in the rods and stowed the gear for the run back to port. For a moment there on the fantail, for just a moment, we'd all witnessed fishing's magic show, and proved again the angler's dogged belief in a thing not seen. Some call it faith.

As we headed back across the lake, I made the following note in my journal: "To catch a whistle fish you must never stop believing it exists. Because if you stop believing in it, you will stop fishing, and if you stop fishing, you will never, ever catch a whistle fish."

Question: Is life what happens between the days you spend fishing, or is life the fishing you get on either end of the waiting?

A Small Philosophy Lesson

It's amazing how charming and helpful friends become the instant you announce you're about to embark on an exotic, international fishing trip.

"Need a rod bearer?" they query.

"Someone to carry your camera? Stir your martinis, perhaps?"

"Hey, I know how to unhook fish!"

They are only joking.

But then again, maybe they are not joking.

Is that envy I see in their eyes?

Incredulity?

Fear for my sanity?

Or is it a brief moment of personal reflection? Does the jokester ask, why him and not me?

I don't suppose the answer really matters. But the question I see in their eyes bothers me. Not much, but enough to make me want to tell the following story.

When I was a young soldier stationed in New England and was being reassigned to a post in San Francisco before being shipped overseas, hitchhiking across the United States suddenly seemed like a spectacular idea. Why fly tourist class and miss it all, when you could hitchhike and see it all? When I announced this grand idea to my two best friends, who were being reassigned to the same post, it seemed like a spectacular idea to them, too. With more than two weeks' leave in which to travel, we'd thumb our way across the fruited plain, see what we might see, and take up various and sundry adventures as they presented themselves. We'd be modern-day Huck Finns. We'd do it, by God, we'd do it!

But as the day of departure approached, my friends found a number of pressing responsibilities that needed tending to. They had rounds to make, obligations to fulfill. The list of reasons they could not go was comprehensive, and quite sane.

For my part, I couldn't think of a single good reason *not* to go. So early one fall New England morning near Fitchburg, Massachusetts, I stepped down to the highway that ran by the army post and stuck out my thumb.

By myself.

My first ride was from a woman who took me to some little long-forgotten burg. The next ride took me to the outskirts of Boston. The next on toward New York City. This was in the days before interstates, when hitching rides was easier and maybe safer. I caught rides through Maryland, Virginia, the Carolinas, Georgia, Florida, Alabama before integration, Louisiana, Oklahoma, Texas, and on to Nat King Cole's "Route 66," west through "Amarillo, Gallup, New Mexico . . . Flagstaff, Arizona, don't forget Winona, Kingman, Barstow, San Bernardino." Traveling down one coast, across the South, and up the other coast for two weeks, I landed flat broke but fearless in San Francisco and reported for duty. I saw a lot of country and met a lot of wonderful Americans. Like Lewis and Clark, I kept a journal, but the journal is now lost, and that's okay.

Adventures?

Plenty.

Scares?

A few.

Would I do it again?

Nope.

Would I trade the experience for anything?

Nope.

Would I let one of my children do it?

Not on your life.

What did I learn?

I learned that first you dream, then you do. If you only dream and never do, then your life will pass without much excitement, and certainly without adventure. You may fall into circumstances and have to react to life—and this may be both exciting and adventurous—but it is not the same thing as stepping into an adventure just for the hell of it.

I understand people who would rather dream than do. Doing can be risky, expensive, and even dangerous. Dreaming is secure, cheap, and safe. I don't blame dreamers for only dreaming, but dreaming alone never caught a great fish from a far river.

I have met many people down through the years for whom the dream became more important than the reality. Some of them were psychotherapy patients, some were friends. Safe and sound and warm deep inside their dream, they cannot be pried from it.

A friend of mine who lives in a big city in the East has spent his entire adult life dreaming about the life he would lead if only he lived in Montana or Wyoming or Idaho or next door to me here in rural eastern Washington. He would hunt and fish and hike and camp out and grow a beard. He would be an outdoorsman, even a mountain man. He would be robust and sunburned and wear a red kerchief around his neck. He would don a sweat-stained cowboy hat and learn to swagger when he walked.

But instead he lives in his apartment in the city, stalks the fly shops on his lunch hours, and metes out his days yearning for something he only tasted once and for a short time a long time ago as a young man. And he dreams.

And dreams.

And dreams.

On a visit several years ago he stepped out on my deck and gazed out over the little ponderosa pine forest that covers my acreage. "Oh, I could do this!" he exulted. "Buy a little land, move here. Go fishing and hunting like you do. Oh, yes, I could do this!"

The next day before breakfast—the day I was to take him fishing—he was up early with his nose stuck in a book, an Ivan Doig novel about Montana.

"It's a little windy and cold," I said, "but we'll catch some trout. Let's go."

My friend looked out at the rain lashing the window and the tops of the pine trees pitching in the wind. "Let's wait a bit," he said. "I'm kind of a fair-weather fisherman."

We waited.

We shared a pot of coffee and watched the storm. Then his nose went back into the book about life in Montana.

We didn't go fishing that day. Or the next day when the weather improved. Time ran out. And then he caught a plane home, his fantasy still intact, his dream still undisturbed.

If you want to live life instead of just watch others live it, you can't wait for the weather to clear. You can't wait for a better day, a better time, or a second invitation. The Zulus have a saying: "Because it is always running away from you, you must chase the future if you hope to catch it."

The same is true for living life, for catching fish, for finding out who you are and of what you are made. If you hope to catch an interesting life, you must chase it until your breath comes short from running after it.

Standing on the berm of that highway that fall morning a long time ago with only a rucksack on my back, a few bucks in my jeans, and what many concluded was an ill-considered plan, I stuck out my thumb, smiled at passing strangers, and saw America. However I knew it then, I knew that if I did not want to become a bitter old man filled with regrets I had to stick out my thumb and take my chances.

Snake Oil

Not long ago I was the guest speaker for the Snake River Medical Forum, a group of doctors who get together once a year to see how well they're hitting the old medical ball and socialize a bit. While enjoying free food and wine set up by a pharmaceutical company selling them drugs they'll later prescribe for us, the good doctors also clock a little continuing medical education time while they enjoy themselves. Capitalism rubs up against the Hippocratic oath, and, the way I see it, everybody wins, including you and me.

I work with doctors, lecture to them, respect them, and have one of my own; for the most part I've got no complaints about America's physicians. They're the best in the world. Unfortunately, they have to work in a managed health-care system, a system so screwed up I wonder why we're having a debate about physician assisted suicide when the insurance companies already have a right to kill us. Basically, the insurance companies take the money and the doctors take the heat, which is stressful, and which was one of the reasons I was asked to speak to the Snake River Medical Forum in the first place.

My talk was entitled "Sex, Hope, and the Psychology of Fishing." My purpose was to get the audience to lighten up a bit, pause long enough to reflect on their lives for a moment, and go home with a feel-good feeling. Toward the end of my remarks, I urged what were mostly too-busy physicians to consider that the old American saw "Time is money" might be a mistaken idea and that, from another perspective, just the opposite might be true—that money costs too much time. Given a taste of my snake oil, not everyone left feeling better.

One reason for a negative reaction to my remarks was that I suggested people ought to slow down a bit, enjoy life, and not work so hard. At the end of my career this is easy for me to say. The economic rules that govern most modern general practice medicine are as follows: See nine patients an hour and make a living; see six patients an hour and cut your office staff by half; see four patients an hour and close the doors. No wonder the single most frequent complaint made to the offices of the American Medical Association is "My doctor doesn't listen." What doctor has time? There is only one doctor in America who has time: TV's Marcus Welby, M.D., and that's because he only sees one patient a week.

As my talk wound down and I headed for the closing, I brought up the dirty word: money. I reminded the doctors and their spouses that no amount of money can buy back a missed day of fishing, a day not spent with a son or daughter or grandson or granddaughter, or brother or best friend. I reminded them that fishing is not so much about catching fish, but about being free for a few hours, and spending time with those we love. I challenged them to rethink the old saws that money will buy love, that money will buy happiness, or even that time is money. Hell, money never bought back one second of the time it took to earn it.

I wrapped it up with, "No amount of money can buy back the sunset you missed while you were working. No amount of money can buy back the book you might have read, the love you might have made, the child you might have taken out on the bright waters and helped catch her first fish." A short reading from one of my books on the subject of hope, and I was done.

But not everyone clapped. Some folks resent a psychologist sneaking up on them after dinner and poking around their defenses. Some people don't like being asked to examine the only life they're living. One doctor came up afterward, coffee in hand, and explained in detail why he had to work so hard, why he didn't have any fun, and why he couldn't do anything about it. One apologized for his lifestyle.

I asked myself, "Why is this person, a total stranger, apologizing to me? What did I say that was so upsetting?"

One doc approached me and said, "This has been very helpful. I learned a lot. I'm sure I'll find time to go fishing next year."

It was March.

Whenever I make a speech I make it a point to hang around after my remarks to pick up story material, angling intelligence, and even invitations to go fishing. Not a few folks try to bootleg a therapy consultation, if not for themselves, then for someone else. I'm willing to listen, but not for long. My getaway line is "I don't have the answers, I just ask the questions. We each have to find our own way." Although the last thing I'm looking for is business, once in a while someone will later make a referral or call for a personal consultation.

That evening, when the thank-yous and handshakes and good nights were finished and I was on the road late at night driving up the Lewiston Grade to my home in eastern Washington, I took a minute to size up my own life.

Preachers can slip over into hypocrisy without half trying. Since the line between sound advice and bullshit is a thin one, it's a good idea to look in the mirror from time to time to see if the snake oil you're selling has any redeeming value.

At least for now, for me, it still does.

Because the reason I was driving home late at night instead of staying in a motel was that, early the next morning, I had a date to take two of my granddaughters to Williams Lake for their very first trout-fishing trip. They caught trout, too, and Grandpa hardly helped at all.

In nature, all final solutions are temporary.

Bonefish Felix

I knew him only as Bonefish Felix. He had another name, but in the society of fishing guides and sports you go by the name they give on first meeting, not necessarily the name their parents gave them. It is also understood in this society that, unless something unusual happens, the relationship between the guide and guided will be cordial but restrained. Unless unspoken rules are broken over the time they fish together, neither guide nor guided will come to know much about the other.

"Nice to meet you," he said, extending a hand that offered no return squeeze, no information, no nothing. The handshake seemed to say, "This is as far as things go."

"I'm Paul," I said. "Good to meet you."

"I'm Felix. But they call me Bonefish Felix."

He was a tall, powerful, coal-black Bahamian with gray-tinged hair, whose presence filled the space around him. I joked that he looked as old as me but later learned he had five years on me. I was instantly puzzled by him. What was an older man doing in a young man's job? Was guiding his passion, or did he have to do this work? Was this all he knew? Perhaps he was so uneducated he could do nothing else?

Unless I intentionally set about to find the answers to these questions, my relationship to Bonefish Felix would remain as shallow as the South Andros Island flats we would fish together. Perhaps because a psychologist on vacation must guard against conducting clinical interviews with the help, I put Bonefish Felix down into the "poor, uneducated black man" pigeonhole and let it go.

I'm not sure what is in us humans that causes us to draw hasty negative conclusions about strangers, especially strangers of another race. Perhaps it is because prejudice is cheap and easy and requires no investment of time or personal exploration. Prejudice is a great convenience to the lazy, and even though I try to keep my conclusions about strangers tentative, I have always found that with a reasonably good store of stereotypes at your fingertips, "understanding" humanity is duck soup. I wish I were a better person, but I'm not.

Of course I can't afford this kind of thinking back in the office. A clinical psychologist can't afford to be facile. Rather, your job is to purposely set aside all prejudice, stereotypes, and assumptions, and then to ask probing, personal, information-seeking questions that will lead you to the best possible understanding one human being can have of another. Fail in this task and you fail not only your patient but yourself and your profession.

But with Bonefish Felix how much did I need to know? How much did I want to know? What do you need to know about a fishing guide, besides fish-finding and spotting skills. If I asked a probing question or two, was I willing to respond in kind if Felix asked the same questions of me? The beauty of being a therapist is that you get to ask all the interesting questions but don't have to answer any. But out on the bright waters no such rules are in force. Besides, telling someone you are a psychologist can spoil their whole day.

Still, throughout that whole first day I fished with Felix, unanswered questions about him bothered me. On the water and feeling the strain of the guide-sport relationship relax at the first hookup with a five-pound bone, I complimented Felix and asked, "How long have you been guiding?"

"Twenty-six years. Long time." He laughed as he poled the boat silently over knee-deep water while we searched for the next fish.

I was floored. After a week on the flats I will never confess to being bored, but I'm ready to go home to the Pacific Northwest, see a mountain, feel a chill breeze, and smell pine trees again. I could not imagine doing the same thing in the same place in the same way day in and day out for twenty-six years, even if it was fishing.

Perhaps Felix would feel the same way about my life, but the conclusion I drew about him was that he must require damn little in the way of intellectual stimulation and that, if he had a life of the mind, it must be as barren as the landscape we were fishing. I knew this conclusion might be wrong, and I was momentarily tempted to reach into my tool kit of probing psychological questions to right any misperception. But then I reminded myself that I was on vacation and returned to the important task of focusing on the watery blues, greens, reds, and yellows of dancing light and shadows ahead of me in which the bonefish swims.

Bonefishing is a Zen-like exercise; you must remain utterly silent, looking for nothing so that you can see everything, otherwise you will never spot a fish through the clutter and debris lodged in your mind by a too-civilized life.

"Left! Two o'clock!" said Felix from behind me. "Fifty feet. See them?"

I saw them. Two very big bonefish were moving toward us. I started my cast but mistimed their speed and dropped the fly on top of them. They spooked and streaked away. The biggest fish I'd seen in three days. I think I said "Shit!" or "Goddamn!" or maybe even the f-word.

I can't recall exactly what I blurted out, but I can assure you it was not "Dag nabbit!"

It may be hard to believe, but fishermen occasionally use profanity . . . always justified, of course. Breaking off a big fish, fluffing a cast, snagging yourself with a hook—these are only a few of the triggers that can release what I call pent-up swearage. Pent-up swearage is like a savings account: It contains all the swear words you would normally use at your job back in the city, or in meetings with pinhead county bureaucrats, or with anyone who has it coming, but that you cannot use because of propriety and good manners, or the fear the other guy might pull a gun and shoot you. So you put these oaths into your swearage account, to be drawn upon later when you are on the water chasing fish and something goes wrong, whereupon you are permitted—yes, even encouraged by other fishermen—to, as we psychologists like to put things, "Let her rip!" The therapeutic benefit of shouting great strings of colorful Anglo-Saxon epithets has not been studied much in formal psychological research, but clearly periodic spending down of your swearage account prevents coronary heart disease.

And so it was that, over the week my pals and I fished with Felix and other guides, we spent down our toxic swearage reserves . . . all in the name of an improved final health status, mind you.

At the end of the week my pal Rick and I fished the last day with Felix. We met him at the dock on Little Creek, and while Felix was loading the skiff, I took a spinning rod I carry for barracuda and made a couple of desultory casts into the creek with a chartreuse broken-back minnow plug. As I began to crank in the second cast, a huge barracuda slashed at the plug, hooking himself.

Oddly, Felix motioned for me to hand him the rod. He was the kind of man you don't say no to, so I handed it over and stood back.

People on the way to work—school kids, anglers, and guides—all gathered round to watch the old man battle the big fish. The barracuda ran to the sea, but was cranked back. Then it ran up under the bridge, but again Felix wound him back. Then the brute streaked up the river under a string of moored skiffs in a long, hard run, but Felix fought the beast back to the dock. Just as the fish quit the fight, it rolled to one side and slipped off the hooks. Free again, the 'cuda righted itself and swam slowly to the bottom and out to sea again.

Felix did not swear. He did not erupt in profanity or empty his swearage account. Rather, he mumbled something to himself and handed the rod back to me. "That's fishin'," he said, grinning.

We hunted bonefish late that last day and tipped Felix well for the extra time and effort. He'd worked hard all week. Except for fifteen-minute lunch breaks, he never stopped working. Helpful but never critical, friendly but never officious, Felix was in all the right ways the perfect guide. And I, comfortable with my assumptions, left things between us the way I'd found them.

"Come back some day, Paul?" he asked at day's end.

"Probably," I said, shaking that rough, strong hand that said nothing. "At least you've got a day off tomorrow," I added, knowing he'd not had a day off from guiding for several months.

"Oh, no," he laughed. "Tomorrow's Sunday, and Sundays I work for the Lord."

"Oh?" I said, feeling the ground supporting my prejudice turn suddenly soft.

"You see," he explained, "all the time I'm out there on the flats I'm thinking about Sunday. I'm thinking about my sermon. I'm thinking about scripture and what the people need. I write my sermons in my head, and then write them down at home later. I guess I didn't tell you, I'm the Baptist preacher in this town."

"N-no . . ." I stammered, remembering all the swearage I'd spent down, "you didn't."

"Well," Felix said with a laugh, "you came here to enjoy yourself. Knowing who else I am might have . . . well, you understand, it could have spoiled your fun."

The Gift

When I was a boy my father was hard on me. Not mean, just hard. He didn't like whiners or "gold-brickers." When you worked, you worked hard. When you played, you played hard. If you fell down and scraped your knee, you jumped up and ran off the pain. A hiker and a fisherman, my father marched my brothers and me on long, torturous, high-mountain backpacking trips into the High Sierras of California in search of golden trout. The steeper and more demanding the hike, the better time we were having. Only a lad, I came to believe that unless you had blisters on your feet, aching legs, and altitude sickness, you couldn't be having much fun.

Dad had two formulas to live by: Nothing worthwhile in life comes easy, and pain shouldn't stop you from living. These many years later, I think he was right on both accounts.

Army boot camp made perfect sense to me. After running a mile in full battle gear, a private chugging alongside me groaned, "What are they trying to do, kill us?"

"You mean you're not having fun?" I asked.

The guy shot back, "You need a shrink!"

Dad believed that what doesn't kill you can make you strong, and that it is your attitude toward events that matters, not the event itself. Whatever the task, whatever the job, whatever the goal, whatever the pain or suffering one must endure, attitude is all. Without perspective, the impossible remains impossible, the unacceptable, unacceptable. If you believe something cannot be done, it will never get done because you will never begin; thus do many people bail out of a difficult journey before taking the first step. This holds true for all endeavors, whether they be fishing trips or making money or recovering from life's inevitable injuries.

Years ago I was hired to evaluate a chronic-pain patient who, after losing a couple of fingers in an industrial accident, complained of unbearable phantom pain in the missing fingers. To cope with his pain, he'd become addicted to narcotics. He carried the injured hand in a leather glove filled with Vaseline and kept his whole arm in a sling. Unemployed and with his marriage in trouble, his life had stopped, only to revolve entirely around his wounded hand. His body was injured, but his mind was crippled.

A few weeks after this evaluation I was scheduled to see a woman for another disability evaluation. Her husband accompanied her to my waiting room, and when I met him I noticed his entire left arm was covered with angry red scars and disfigured flesh. Always too blunt when my curiosity has been piqued, I asked him, "Say, what happened to your arm?"

"Caught in a baling machine," the man said with a smile.

"Ouch!" I winced. "That must have hurt."

"Yep," said the man. "Damn near killed me."

"What did you take for the pain?" I asked, thinking of the patient who'd become addicted to narcotics.

"Nothin'," replied the man. "I don't like drugs."

"So what did you do?"

"Shook it."

"Shook what?"

"Shook my arm."

"And that helped the pain go away?"

"Some."

"So how long did you shake it?"

The man turned to his wife. "What was it, honey, 'bout a year?"

These two men differed not so much in the magnitude of their respective injuries, but in their attitudes toward those injuries. I tell this tale to my graduate students in an attempt to teach them what my father taught to me so many years ago: What doesn't kill you can make you strong, and it's your attitude toward events that matters, not the events themselves.

I feel sorry for people who don't fish. They wake up in the morning and know that's as good as they're going to feel all day.

Only Mad Dogs and Fishermen Go Out in the Midday Rain

It has come to my attention that some fishermen do not like to fish in the rain.

Good.

I like to fish in the rain, and sometimes sing in the rain while fishing. If rain keeps some fishermen at home, that is fine with me. Since I am not much of a singer, no audience is a good audience.

Once upon a time I, too, did not like to fish in the rain. If rain was in the forecast, I stayed home. I didn't mind fishing for wet things, but I did not want to be wet while doing it.

Then one day it occurred to me that fishes do not give a damn about rain, except as rain drives food into the water. Rain knocks down insects and washes bugs, worms, caddis larvae, and other such delicacies onto the fish's dining-room table.

The fish's dining-room table is the water in which it lives. Sometimes the dining-room table is full, sometimes it is empty. When it rains, the table begins to fill up. A good, hard rain serves up a banquet, complete with blaring horns to announce the courses.

Only stupid fishermen do not invite themselves to these fish feasts. When the rains fall hard and the fish's cup runneth over, that is the time for the angler to be there serving dishes. When the frenzied fishes are at the table, chins to the linen, jaws agape, chopping, chomping, sucking, and swallowing, that is the time to fool them.

So I fish in the rain, and sometimes sing.

Like Gene Kelly singing and dancing in the rain because he is goofy with love, I sing and fish in the rain because I too am goofy with love—in my case the love of angling and life, whether it be in the sunshine or rainshine.

So the next time you pass a lake or river or stream in the middle of a downpour in the middle of the day, and see some mad fisherman swathed in a sage, waxed-cotton coat and rubber boots above his knees, and if he's wearing a broad-brimmed 4X beaver hat circled with a sheepskin band sporting three classic steelhead flies, do not worry, that madman is me.

Or a madman just like me.

Mad, indeed.

The Dalai Lama on Fishing Guides

The Dalai Lama once described the journey of life as a journey through a great thorny bramble thicket, a journey made safer and more joyous by following someone wise in the ways of the bramble and its twisting, dangerous paths. To guide others through the bramble is to be a priest, a monk, a therapist, a healer, a coach, or anyone who, out of kindness, shows another how to avoid pain and anguish and disappointment.

To become a guide you must first travel the bramble alone, study, learn, and return safely. Only then may you show others the way.

Teachers go to college to earn this right. Priests study their whole lives to merit this honor. Physicians devote themselves to the art of healing to take others through, and fishing guides learn their rivers. Each of us can be a guide to a beginner, a pilgrim, a first-timer.

When you teach others to fish you assume the job of guide, of coach, of mentor. When you show beginners the way through the great bramble patch of fishing, you lead the way by example, keep them on the safe trails, and show them how to avoid the sharp thorns. Most important, you model for them how to keep hope alive.

Your years of fishing translate into study and experience and knowledge. You become expert on the ways of the bramble. You've explored its strange paths and plucked its thorns from your own flesh. Scars teach best. What you know, you either learned the hard way or learned in part from someone older who learned the hard way. The knowledge of fishing is handed down no differently than the knowledge of healing.

Whether it is fishing or life, when you've traversed the bramble and come back again, the Dalai Lama says you are awarded a special pair of leather chaps. The chaps are tanned by the weather of experience. Wearing them over your legs, you can travel the bramble with safety and ease, and almost never be painfully snagged by a thorn.

The chaps are made of practice, learning, and knowledge. You may wear them to protect only yourself, or to protect yourself and others. The choice is yours.

To teach others to fish is to don the leather chaps and show pilgrims the way through the bramble patch. You know it well, they know it not at all. To take them to the other side is a great gift.

If you choose to guide others, put your beginner on the best water, the best riffles, and into the best lies.

Show your traveler exactly where the big fish swims.

Let your apprentice cast first.

Encourage, coach gently, tie the knots, and net the fish, and you, not the novice, will catch the greatest prize of all.

BYOL

If it is only fish you are after on a fishing trip, you must be a beginner. Fishing is only partly about catching fish, and perhaps the smaller part. In truth, fishing is mostly about catching something much more important than anything that swims; fishing is about catching lore.

Although catching a good fish adds to your lore supply, so can getting skunked. Getting zeroed can, all by itself, be a source of considerable lore. Blanked but for breaking off a world-record black bass, for example. Never turning a fish for two days on the Madison River in August for another. Being the only luckless angler in an otherwise highly successful company of fishermen is the stuff of legend, albeit unenviable legend.

Every fishing trip offers the opportunity to snag some lore. It may be a big barrelful of lore, like falling out of the boat or smashing an heirloom fly rod or being driven off the water by a hurricane, or it could be just a little cupful of lore, like, say, hiking through thick timber to a trout stream and having a ruffed grouse go off under your foot like a hand grenade and stop your heart.

Fishing lore isn't like golf or football or tennis lore, or any kind of spectator sport lore. Fishing is a field sport, and fishing lore has to be collected personally. You can't get it listening to an 800 fishing number. You can't ease over to a couple of anglers at your friendly tavern, eavesdrop on their conversation, and pick up any lore that's worth a damn. You can't buy it, steal it, borrow it, or beg it. You have to go get your own.

Fishing lore is lore precisely because it is authentic. The only way to lay hands on the real McCoy is to get out there on the water and wait for it to happen. Sure, you can go looking for fishing lore, but that doesn't mean you'll find any. Lore just happens.

Lore is stepping over a log into what you thought was shallow water only to find yourself chest-deep in a brook trout hole. Lore is accidentally stitching a baseball cap to your skull with a bass fly pushed off course by a sudden gust of wind. Lore is chapped lips, leaky waders, and a twisted ankle.

The finest fishing lore is the kind that almost kills you. Imagine the lore a flats fisherman gathers when he survives a shark attack. Personally, I'd give just about anything for some good shark lore, provided it didn't require suturing. Just avoiding a mauling by an Alaskan brown bear who wants your salmon hole is top-notch lore, and so is being storm-tossed out of your fishing boat, or sinking it.

Top-quality fishing lore lasts a lifetime. If you write it down, we fishing writers know, good lore can last forever—which is why, when we have an eyewitness who may one day actually read our account of some event or other, we scribes are obliged, however painfully constrained, to attempt a description of the actual truth.

Real fishermen can spot phony lore a mile away. It doesn't taste right when you bite into it. When you thump it, it rings hollow. If you drop it, it doesn't bounce the way it should. Bad fishing lore is the work of amateurs. Brown trout that leap like rainbows. Walleyes that leap like brown trout. Sometimes the lore is so phony even nonfishermen can sniff it out. Cheap lore stinks.

If you're a fisherman you have no trouble assaying high-grade lore. Sure, that northern pike may have grown a few inches over the years, but because the angler's finger bear those little white pike-tooth scars that prove the brute bit him where he said it did, you know the guy's lore supply is genuine.

While it's true that a little fishing lore can go a long way with strangers, you need fresh supplies to keep up with your fishing friends and acquaintances—just one more reason why I personally feel compelled to fish as much as I do. There is nothing so pathetic as an angler who has been working so hard he's only gone fishing a couple times in the last year showing up at the annual fishing camp with no more than a thimble full of fresh lore. A couple of quick stories and he's shot his wad. There he sits, staring vacantly into the fire with nothing more to say. Another wasted life. And may God forgive him if he brings up how much money he made last year instead of going fishing, or tries to make up some bogus lore, or, even more deserving of ridicule, falls back on dated material.

If you take good care of it, fishing lore will take good care of you. You never know when you may need a big supply. You could get trapped by a snowstorm in a fishing camp, or get stranded on a desert island with a bunch of anglers, or otherwise be obliged to spend several days, weeks, or months with nothing but lore to fall back on. Running out of food and water and booze may be disastrous, but running out of fishing stories is catastrophic.

Fishing is not so much about catching fish as it is about finding riches you didn't know you were after until you stumbled onto them. At once weightless, ageless, priceless, and as irreplaceable as family photographs, fishing stories are more precious than diamonds. I don't see how anyone can collect too many of them.

One more thing.

If you pass the art of gathering fishing lore down carefully to children and nephews and nieces and the neighborhood kids you take fishing with you, it becomes folk art, oral tradition in its finest form.

Walks home through the woods from the bluegill pond, long rides home from the sea or lake or brook, and especially after-fishing campfires are all lore training schools. Your job as a fisherman is to teach children how to pick up fishing lore for themselves, and how to make it their own and put their signature on it. Your job is to teach them how to care for it, how to keep it dry, how to tell and retell it until it glows with a high luster at life's great yarn-spinning opportunities. As an older fisher your mentoring duties are considerable, and terribly important to the future of fishing. How else will the stories survive?

I have run so many fishing-lore training camps I'm thinking of opening up the Angler's Story Telling and Lore Academy. An informal operation, it will meet every other Tuesday at my place. Free seating around the campfire. No dues. Dress is casual. And there are only two membership requirements: bring a kid, and BYOL (bring your own lore).

Journal Entry: Tying Flies

I have just finished tying seven trout flies. I started out to tie a dozen, but I never hold myself to production schedules when tying flies, or catching fish with them. Production schedules have no place in fishing.

These were soft-hackle flies. Pink-bodied, brown-bodied, yellow-bodied, olive green–bodied flies—I tie them in all likely and unlikely colors to accommodate the whims of trout.

This is the kind of fly you fish in the surface film, or on a sinking line, or trolled slow and deep behind a rowed boat. They're called wet flies, or emergers, and are supposed to pass for any number of swimming bugs. I don't much give a damn what they are supposed to pass for, so long as the trout fall for them.

And they do.

You tie a soft-hackle fly with a few wraps of thread, a little body material, and a partridge breast feather wrapped once or twice at the collar, then tie it off and cement the head, and you're done.

A watchmaker's fingers you don't need. Patience you don't need. Great skill you don't need. Fly-tying sophistication you don't need. All you need is a little time, a good light to tie by, and a small dab of hope.

I like to tie soft-hackle flies partly because I shoot the Hungarian partridge from which the hackles come. I use a classic over-under Beretta Silver Snipe 12-gauge shotgun I bought over thirty years ago.

I kill two or three birds each fall for feathers and meat. I cook the birds slowly in a good white wine and serve them with wild rice and fresh asparagus if I can find it. The feather pelts are dried and become a supply base for the manufacture of trout flies.

About the Beretta: Still in graduate school with a wife and two children and nothing but a poke full of promise, a wagon load of debt, and an apprentice's salary, I could hardly afford a fine Italian shotgun.

But I'd married a rare and magical woman.

Ann has always believed two things about the people she loves: They should never be denied their heart's desire—no matter the cost or consequence; and for those you love, cheap is expensive. The Beretta was my heart's desire and the last thing from cheap.

At the time I desired the shotgun I was making a little extra money teaching a correspondence course for a university, in abnormal psychology. I sent out the lessons, the students wrote essays and such, and they sent their materials in to be graded. When the course ended and a nice check arrived in the mail, Ann said, "Get the shotgun."

I argued with her, but not very convincingly.

Despite our needing everything from a couch for the living room to a decent TV to new winter coats for the children, she insisted I get the Beretta.

I still have the shotgun, and I still have the wife.

Any woman who loves you enough to make sure you have all the expensive toys you think you need and supports your passion to travel the world in search of the fishes is truly an extraordinary and wonderful human being.

I tell this woman I love her at least twice a day.

In fact, I'm going upstairs to tell her right now.

When I Was Young . . .

When I was young and able and had the back of a coal miner, I used to load a heavy twelve-foot, Columbia fiberglass boat onto a set of high roof racks atop a 1965 Chevy Suburban four-by-four. By myself. I'd grunt and groan, but I was a manly bastard and could do it with no more than a half dozen swear words. One day when I was forty-something, a hinge let go somewhere in my back, and I began to rely on the backs of pals and strangers. Eventually, I bought a cheap boat trailer.

Three decades and many boats later, I still own the old Columbia. Though she's not worth much, I've refused all offers to sell her. Rather, as I meet young fishermen without the means to buy boats of their own—and if I like them and believe them to be true fishermen—I just lend them the old Columbia for a year or two, until they can afford their own fishing boat.

An act of enlightened self-interest: By creating this small climate of obligation, I ensure that the fishing invitations never stop. Perhaps when I am too fossilized to go fishing anymore, these youngsters will at least stop by to brag. And wouldn't that be lovely?

A Letter to a Fishing Pal

Dr. Norman Braverman, now a research psychologist at the National Institutes of Health, is an old, old fishing pal. He's also the same "Norm" who appears in several famous cartoons by Gary Larson. In one Larson cartoon a man is headed upstream with a boatload of fish. The caption reads, "Norm's Spawning Service." Many years after the cartoon and its creator became famous, Norm remembered a kid named Gary Larson in one of his psychology classes at Washington State University, where we both attended graduate school. Norm and I taught the same bunch of undergraduates, so Larson may have been in one of my classes too. Because Norm had talked about our steelhead fishing trips with his students, he wondered whether he and "Norm" were one and the same, and wrote Gary Larson a letter asking him this. He received the following reply:

Dear Norm:

Yes.

Gary Larson.

Recently I wrote Norm myself.

Dear Norm,

I tried to go fishing tonight, but failed. I'd hoped for a walleye trip, but when a pal failed to show for our date, I canceled too. You, a gonzo angler, would not have failed me in these circumstances.

I drove out to a couple of local lakes to watch the trout, but seeing no rises or surface disturbances I decided that rather than fish the sinking line one more time this summer, I'd come home and drop you this line.

Regarding that smart-as-a-whip, going-to–medical school, fishing son of yours, I've enclosed an article from *Science News Digest* on the latest developments in medical neuromuscular research, his intended field, as I recall from your last letter. Please carefully memorize the content and thrust of the article, form an intelligent question, and pop him one the next time you take him to lunch. An informed and unexpected question from an unlikely corner is like a good uppercut: You can sometimes get an eight count without half trying.

I make this recommendation on the belief that humility is essential to character development in young people; it helps nourish a spirit of generosity toward others and respect for elders. Elders need respect, and our youth need to respect someone. We elders need to earn it, but they need to pay it. It's a good trade. So create one of those growth opportunities for your son before it's too late.

Just between you and me, I've always found it important to intimidate one's children from time to time, especially after they start growing hair on their privates. As a parent you can do this on the trout stream, around the campfire, or over coffee. Or, you can leave it up to an army drill instructor, provided your kid goes into the military. However the rite and work of passage and acceptance gets done—it must get done—otherwise our children never quite grow up.

If necessary, fake your credentials. There is nothing wrong with the bluff, the tease, or the bloodless challenge to a young whippersnapper. Drill instructors specialize in this, and God bless them for their skill. Alpha males have employed these tools in the raising of youngsters for several million years, and we should not quit now. The world needs tough people, male and female. The worst thing we can do for our children is to go soft on them, bait their hooks, and worry too much about their damned feelings. Feelings are important, but they don't count in the tight spots.

Speaking of feelings, my father died four years ago today, which is another reason I wanted to catch a walleye tonight and decided to write you instead of going trout fishing. Walleyes were Father's favorite fish, to catch, to keep, and to eat. The walleye pike was the dream fish of Dad's Midwest boyhood. I'm glad I was able to help him catch the biggest one of his life in the year before he got sick. He caught it on a Rebel crawdad plug cast tight to a rocky point on Sprague Lake. The pike went about six pounds, with no rounding up.

Norm, my father was a true alpha male: tough on the outside, tender on the inside. Fiercely protective of his family, the poor, and the weak, he would knock a man down for acting badly toward those who could not defend themselves. Despite our educational differences, Dad always knew how to ask me the hard questions. I miss him like the dickens.

See you in August for cutthroat on the dry fly.

Paul

Fly-fishing Beyond the Grave

Unless you've been shopping for caskets lately, it may come as something of a surprise to you that fly-fishing has now invaded the funeral business.

I know it surprised me.

It also relieved me; at least someone is thinking about the needs of anglers finally forced to quit the stream but who want desperately to get in that one last cast—if casting is even possible from the prone position.

These were some of the morbid but humor-tinged thoughts that comforted me as I helped family members shop for caskets recently; not once, but three times in the past year alone. Now chasing sixty, I find that lots of people I've known for years and years are dying right and left, and without so much as a "Mother may I?" As a result, I'm spending a lot of time standing around in funeral homes and listening to eulogies in churches.

In the course of these travels, I've met several funeral directors. I'm told funeral directors have a great sense of humor, although they hide it well. Since they apparently whistle while they do the really grisly work, I'm told the only thing that saddens a funeral director is when the family skips the solid mahogany job at ten grand and cheaps out on the plain steel box at $2,295. Despite their stern faces and hushed public voices, I imagine the really hard work of funeral directors is keeping a straight face while, say, showing caskets for dead fly-fishers.

"Oh yes," the funeral director says, as the family fingers the wood inlay of a fine box, "we understand the special needs of fly-fishermen. Notice the silk embroidered trout, and the still lake, the fine . . . etc."

That the funeral industry anticipated the recent boom in fly-fishing is at once disturbing and comforting; disturbing insofar as nothing is sacred when it comes to grabbing market share, and comforting in that at least the grief-stricken now have the opportunity to connect the joys of fly-fishing with the unpleasantness of croaking.

As a result of my most recent shopping trip for a casket—and as an inveterate fly-fisher increasingly conscious of the time—I'm sorry to report that the needs of dead anglers have not been perfectly met. For example, the fly-fishing scene sewn into the casket linings I studied is at eye level for the deceased. This is a terrible error. Unless they fit you with special reading glasses for very close viewing before they drop the lid, you could end up spending eternity with a headache.

Another thing. Whoever designs the jumping fish to be embroidered on casket linings doesn't know beans about trout. Fish biologists, take a close look: This is not a true rainbow trout, or any other known trout true or false. It is cheap merchandising art and hardly worth a look by the living, let alone the dead.

As the family moved on to study other models, I leaned over the cherry-wood box and gave the fish embroidered in the silk a second study. It was trout-shaped and fishy-looking, but from the coloration I couldn't even tell what kind of trout the manufacturer *thought* it was. Looking up, I trolled for and caught the director's eye.

"For a trout fishermen, eh?" I whispered in Canadian to the man in the somber suit as he swooped in to cashier my interest. A middle-aged gent with a limp as pronounced as Marty Feldman's in *Young Frankenstein*, our director was a study in feigned concern. He wore a hairpiece that fit so badly, I wondered whether it hadn't been lifted off a customer.

"We try to anticipate every need," he assured me with a smile that smelled like old roses.

"I'm no expert," I offered, "but what kind of fish is that?"

The director leaned over the casket and studied the thread work. "I believe it is a trout, sir," he said, apparently satisfied with his piscatorial diagnosis.

"I know it's supposed to be a trout," I said, "but what *kind* of trout?"

A look of puzzlement flashed across the man's face, quickly covered by a wrinkled brow and a voice tuned to perfect concern. "Are you a son?" he queried.

"Son-in-law," I said. "Those people over there are the ones making the decision."

"I see." He smiled, turning his body ever so slightly. "I see. If you'll excuse me, I'll be attending to their needs now."

Apparently a nonfisherman, and in spite of Marty Feldman's limp, our director swiveled his way across the thick carpet as if his hips were made by Mercedes.

Studying the embroidered trout one last time, I called Ann over to the casket and said, "Hon, when I die, don't fall for this fake trout crap. Either bury me like an Egyptian, with all my best rods, reels, a pair of boots that don't leak, and some fine artwork I can enjoy forever, or have me cremated."

Ann smiled weakly; after all, it was her mother's casket we were shopping for. "The kids have already drawn straws for your fishing gear," she said, "so I guess you know what that means."

Before she returned to her siblings I counseled, "Just make sure I'm good and cold before they flick the Bic."

This sad day's work was not for nothing. A casket for my much-loved mother-in-law was picked out and paid for. A fishing person herself, she would have approved skipping the bad art.

Personally, I made an important decision.

When services are held for me, I'm making sure there are lots and lots of fishing snapshots all over the place. Especially around the open bar. I'm rewriting my last will and testament to ensure the following relics are in attendance at my funeral: a pair of old waders, dozens of salmon, trout, and bonefish flies; a favorite rod or two, and lots of photos of true trouts and other game fish. I want the mourners to be able to handle these dear-to-me items of a life well lived. Below the display they'll be able to read—I trust through misted eyes—the following note: "Don't feel sad for me. Hell, I fished hard!"

If You Meet the Buddha on the Road, Take Him Fishing

While waiting for a flight to the Bahamas for a bit of bonefishing on Andros Island, I met a very cordial, articulate, retired English teacher from Malaysia. A native Malaysian, he'd come to America to see his fourth son graduate from the Wharton School of Business. Even though he didn't fish, we fell into easy conversation. Before we parted, I learned why Zen masters never kill themselves.

"I don't fish," he said apologetically. "Never have. My father taught me stamp collecting. I have quite a collection after all these years."

"My father taught me fly-fishing," I said. "After all these years I have quite a collection of flies, but one of us has made the better investment. Tell me about being a philatelist."

Later I broke an old rule and told him that I made my real living as a psychologist, not a fisherman and writer. A sometimes dangerous gambit, this revelation can kill a conversation.

"We don't have many psychologists in Malaysia," my stamp collector responded. "We're too busy building a new country. We need engineers and scientists and businessmen. I don't believe I've ever met a psychologist. What is it that you do?"

I hate this question. No answer seems satisfactory, or even legitimate. Better to be a fisherman and writer than, as one of my non-psychologist friends puts it, "a spook." So I told him I worked with depressed people, and, as a specialty, I tried to keep folks from killing themselves. This last comment seemed to pique his interest.

"Why is it," the gentleman asked, "that so many American millionaires shoot themselves? Are they depressed?"

I began to explain, but wished to hell I'd stuck with fishing. I gave him the rundown on the nature of depression—its most common causes, its signs and symptoms. I even bored him stiff with a lecture on neurotransmitter depletion as a function of acute and chronic stress. Just as his eyes began to glaze over, I paused long enough for him to get in a word.

"Depression is very simple in Malaysia," he said. "In my community we have a Korean Zen priest who gave a speech not long ago about depression. He said, depression is caused by problems. When you have problems, you need to solve them, otherwise you will get depressed. But before you can solve your problems, you must ask yourself two questions."

Eager to learn an Eastern remedy for America's psychiatric common cold, I asked, "What two questions?"

"The first question is, 'Can this problem be solved?' "

I nodded, following along like the student I try to be.

The gentleman smiled. "If the answer to the question is yes, then by all means solve the problem. Because when you've solved the problem, your depression will go away."

That's pretty obvious, I thought to myself, wondering if I'd missed something in this East-West meeting. In America we call it problem-solving therapy and charge plenty for it. "What's the second question?" I asked.

"The second question," said the schoolteacher, "is 'Can this problem be solved?'"

"I thought that was the first question," I said.

"The first question and second question are the same question," said my teacher, smiling. "If the answer to the second question is no, then the problem cannot be solved and you have nothing to worry about. If you can't solve a problem, you don't have a problem."

I waited for my instructor to go on, but he'd stopped talking. I think I was supposed to "get it."

When I did not respond, he continued: "You see, if you can't solve the problem that is causing your depression then it is not a problem, and if your problem is no longer a problem then there is no reason to be depressed."

I must have looked like a slow cow caught in the headlights, because my newfound Malaysian friend offered the following apology: "Zen is very philosophical."

I've studied a little Zen. I read all the hip books on Zen you were obliged to read as a child of the sixties. I know who Alan Watts was. I spent three years in Japan and steeped myself in Buddhist art and culture and Zen archery. For most of those three years my judo instructor was a hundred-pound, eighty-year-old, eighth-degree black-belt gentleman with such perfect balance his spirit ran through his feet and into the earth like the roots of an ancient oak tree. You couldn't budge him and his hundred pounds unless he wanted to be budged. He tossed great big American G.I.s around like rag dolls, never speaking a word of English. As near as I could tell, my sensei was a Jedi knight. Surely I should be able to puzzle out this Zen cure for depression.

"Tell me one more time what the priest said," I asked, making mental notes.

Patiently, my companion explained again why depression is unnecessary.

When my new friend's plane was announced, he bade me good-bye and a pleasant journey. I did the same. Like so many encounters in life, this one would be a one-time thing.

When he was gone I began to think about the last patient I'd seen before going on this fishing trip. A fisherman who hadn't fished in years and the vice president of a bank, my patient was being forced to resign before he would be fired. He had a problem he couldn't solve, was depressed because of it, and was contemplating suicide. He'd promised not to shoot himself before I got back from hooking a few bonefish, and had at least agreed with me that for his particular problem, suicide was too much medicine.

Over a dinner of Japanese noodles, I dictated a short note into my minirecorder, "Zen priest's cure for depression: two questions, same question." I thought about my patient and tried the new formula on for size. If my patient could somehow keep his job, then he would solve his problem and that would cure his depression. But if he was going to be fired and there was nothing he could do about it—the more likely scenario—then he had no "problem." If he had no problem, he was free, and if he was free, then he could do whatever the hell he pleased and should begin to feel better.

Suddenly, I felt that same lightness of being I used to feel as a young judo student when, as an opponent committed to an aggressive move, I would give in to his energy, deflect it ever so gently, and redirect the attack in such a way that my foe landed on his back, not his feet. In judo one does not struggle against what is, but accepts the solution inherent in the problem.

Ten days later I was home again and back in the office. My second appointment was the depressed, suicidal banker. I worked my way around to the problem he could not solve.

"I'm not going down without a fight," he began. "They're not treating me fairly. I won't—"

"Can this problem be solved?" I interrupted.

"What problem?"

"The problem of the president wanting you to resign so he won't have to fire you?"

The man thought a moment. "Probably not. Bill's pretty hardheaded. Once he makes his mind up, there isn't much you can do about it."

"So if the problem can't be solved by you, then do you really have a problem?"

The man stared at me for what seemed a long time. "I have a problem in that I won't have a job. Who's going to hire a fifty-eight-year-old? Resign or be fired, it comes to the same thing. I'll have no job."

"Can you solve the problem of no job?"

"H-m-m," the man puzzled. "I'm too old to start over. But, yes, I guess I could." His eyes lit up. "Oh, I could ask for a big severance package and get out now. They owe me that. Let's see . . . at fifty-nine and a half I could get into my IRAs, that's only eighteen months away. And I've invested well. I have some duplexes and properties. I suppose . . ."

Suddenly, his mood brightened, and before the session was over the depressed banker and I worked out a potential early-retirement plan. He had an old pal in Northern California who wanted him to go into a small business with him. Had no ties to bind him to Washington. I referred him to a lawyer who specialized in golden parachutes, and within a couple of weeks, a deal was struck with his employer and everyone was happy.

I love it when a case works out, especially on the hearsay advice of a Korean Zen priest I'll never meet. The banker and I may have come to the same conclusion, but it's fun to think we couldn't have made it so quickly without a door mysteriously opening in an airport waiting room. And to think my pal has the nerve to suggest what I do is spooky.

I called the banker on routine follow-up a month later. "You were right," he said. "I've never felt better. The heaviness is gone from my chest. It was time to get out and go fishing. Say," he added, "when are you getting out?"

"I haven't found a problem I can't solve yet," I joked back, "but I'm looking for one."

Fishing is a lot like making love—you've never had enough until you've just had some.

Power

When a great fish takes a fly and runs strong and far and jumps to free itself, there is a thing wise anglers do: They bow to the leaping fish.

With the rod extended in supplication, the angler honors the strength of the fish, giving it a length of line and a moment of respite. When the angler bows deeply to a raging fish the fish may not break off and, in time, can be brought to hand on the lightest of tippets.

To master this ritual is to learn not only that fury spends itself quickly, but also the pleasant magic that to acquire great power, one must first yield to it.

The Conversion of Percy Dovewings

The other day I was fly-fishing for bass out of a small boat with my friend Percy Dovewings, when an unfortunate gust of wind sent my popper off its flight plan. When I felt it suddenly stop, I did what any normal fisherman does when he feels his lure acting unusually: I set the hook. As it turned out, this was unnecessary; the hook had penetrated Perc's ear pretty well on the force of my forecast alone.

A gentleman of the first order, Perc took time out from his own casting to show me in which ear I had lodged the fly. "Is the barb in?" he asked.

"No," I said.

"Then would you be so kind as to remove the hook?" he said.

"Certainly," I said.

"Thank you," he said.

That is what I like about Perc: his calm, his cool, his refinement, his sense of humor. That I happen to be the perpetrator of so many minor medical emergencies probably bears some examination, but my misfortunes as a flycaster are not important. Other than suggesting that I invent the Paul Quinnett Casting Helmet, the only remark Perc made was that, after all, "A bass fisherman has to expect these things"—which is, of course, the real yarn here.

If you had known Percy back in his trout purist days, you would have thought him the last man on the planet ever to end up in a bass fishing story. And of course, I'm sure the reader understands that Percy Dovewings is not my friend's real name—his real name is Humphrey Dewcastle—but I promised "Old Hump" I wouldn't use his name in print because, as the reader will soon learn, Old Hump is the sort of guy who is very sensitive about that which is proper and that which ain't.

We're talking full professor of economics. We're talking briar pipe, English sweater, Barbour jacket, Irish wool cap, handmade wading cane, and all the pish-posh airs of the gentleman angler—and this is how he dresses to lecture. You should see him streamside. Percy may be the single exception to the remark that America is the only country that has gone from barbarism to decadence without touching civilization.

I can summarize his preconversion attitudes toward bass and bass fishermen this way: "I had a terrible nightmare," he told me the day after we had argued over the merits of bass fishing. "I woke up in a cold sweat. I looked down and, much to my horror, I found I was wearing one of those 'Kiss My Bass' T-shirts!"

"There's a cure," I said.

"Eh?"

"Go with me sometime. The right bass could change your whole life."

"Bass are a rough fish, like the people who chase them."

On the day of Perc's change of heart, we were lake-fishing for browns and rainbows. While Perc doesn't care much for lake fishing, it was too early in the year for his pilgrimage to Yellowstone and the Golden Triangle. "I guess it would be better than grading papers," he'd said when I invited him along.

Somewhere around eleven o'clock in the morning the mayfly hatch petered out. Spying some likely largemouth cover nearby, I rigged a second rod and pulled my popper box from my vest.

"Good grief," said Perc. "What's that?"

"A bass bug."

"A what bug?"

"Bass bug."

"Uuugh."

Perc made one of those faces budding professors are taught to make when they wish to publicly humiliate an undergraduate who has just made an uninformed observation. (Of Percy's many facial expressions, this is the one I'd most like to see just before his footing gave way and he tumbled headfirst into the Madison River.)

Changing to a bass bug taper, I tied on a 6-pound-test tippet.

"You're quitting the trout?"

"I am," I said.

"Oh," said Perc, his voice trailing off into scorn. "And here I thought you were cut from finer cloth. Why don't you try for carp while you're at it? I've got part of my sandwich left; you could make some doughballs."

Fighting back my fantasy of filling his British fly boxes with nightcrawlers, I tied on one end of those brightly painted balsa-wood bass bugs that look like a Mardi Gras hat and held it under Perc's nose for inspection. Then I tossed it to the edge of a log that protruded into the lake. There followed, on the first twitch, a slurp you could hear at fifty paces.

As bass go here in the Northwest, it was a pretty good fish. The line cut the water this way and that, and on one run the old gal managed to tug the bow of the boat around some fifteen degrees. Twice she broke water. After a while the old hen came up, mouth agape and heavy with roe. I thumbed her up out of the water, removed the hook, and slid her back to the deep.

"Go about two pounds," I said, not too smugly.

"H-m-m," said Perc, lighting his pipe.

Keeping at it, I worked the shoreline, the stickups, the shady spots and dropoffs, taking bass with a minimum of backcasting and almost no smirking. In the meantime, the trout had quit cold. Perc puffed his pipe and watched me in the same way my Brittany spaniels sometimes do—with that kind of cocked head, what-do-you-make-of-that-Charley? gaze.

Now, I'm not the sort of bass fisherman who goes around bragging, but for the next hour or so, everything came together so well that my fishing cap grew uncomfortably tight. Finally, I sat down to "rest my wrist."

After a considerable silence, Perc spoke. "Pretty good fighters. I mean for a nonsalmonid."

"I guess they don't know they're not trout," I said.

"No, I suppose they don't."

I could see that Perc was in trouble: He'd look to the water, then at the open box of bugs, then at the water, then back at the bugs. He was sucking hard on a pipe that had been out for twenty minutes. Finally, he bellowed, "For Pete's sake! Wipe that silly grin off your face!"

"Trust me," I said. "I won't tell anyone."

"I suppose it wouldn't hurt to try just one," he said, picking up his rod and reaching for my popper box. Perc scanned the lake as if he were about to boost a hubcap. "Do you tie these garish things yourself?"

"No," I said. "I buy them."

"How like you," he said. "What do they cost?"

"In the White Elephant sporting goods store, about one dollar. Other places, however, as much as three bucks. Out here on the lake, they run exactly twenty-nine ninety-five."

"Har!" said Perc, fingering the poppers. "What would you suggest?"

"Oh," I said, "bass don't really give a damn. Use that white one there with the rubber legs. And cut your tippet down to at least six-pound-test or borrow one of mine."

"*Rubber* legs? Six-pound-test? My goodness . . ." Perc said, whistling through his nose, "what will you bass people think of next?"

Perc clipped off the mayfly and tied the bug to his leader while I moved the boat into position just off a submerged log. With little fanfare, he then made a short cast to the log.

Then it happened—Percy Dovewings found religion.

The four-pounder that converted Percy came charging through the shallows looking very much like a great white shark headed for the dinner table, wake and all. It took only a split second for the bass to reach Percy's bug, but apparently that was enough time for his entire fly-fishing life to flash suddenly before his eyes . . . or so I gathered when, after the fish made a huge swirl and ripped the popper right off his leader, Percy began to chant "Judas Priest! Judas Priest! Judas Priest!"—which, so far as I can tell, is about as close to swearing as a professor of economics ever gets.

For the longest time, Percy just stood there, his fly rod dangling from his hand. Then his pipe fell from his lips. With glassed-over eyes, he stared at the spot where the bass had disappeared, and his mouth hung open in one of those wide, stupid grins you see on frogs that have just been pithed.

Then, without a word, Percy began to fumble through his fishing vest with both hands—looking, I presumed, for his silver flask.

"You all right, professor? Do you need a drink?"

"No," he mumbled. "A ten-pound tippet! And gimme another one of those things with the rubber legs!"

Improvising

I'd missed my connection. The next bush plane out to the salmon camp wasn't due until the following morning, which left me most of an afternoon and evening in Cordova, Alaska, with nothing to do but make do. So I asked the woman at the airline counter for the name of a reasonable hotel and called a cab.

"Where to?" the cabby asked, setting my luggage in the trunk.

I gave him the name of the hotel and slid into the passenger seat beside him. Most cab drivers are good for a little local color, and some of them can be mined for fishing information.

We traded names and got acquainted. Like most Alaskans, Nino had come from somewhere else and done a bit of everything; commercial fishing, cannery work, coaching kids, even teaching martial arts.

"Ever do any guiding?" I asked.

"Yeah, but not for pay."

"Not for pay is okay," I said. "Anyplace around here you can fish?"

"Sure," said the big Filipino. "Right there." Nino pointed out the window to a river valley cut between great peaks covered by dark-green spruce. "The silvers are running."

"I know," I said. "That's why I'm here. I'm headed out to Camp Kiklukh in the morning."

"Fishing beats watching TV," said Nino. "You know we got too much TV in the world. Too much violence. Too much hatred. Too many bad things and not enough good things. I don't know, man, but it seems to me the world is going to pot."

"Here in Cordova?"

"Well, not so much here. That's one of the reasons I live here. But everywhere else."

We fell into a philosophical discussion of the world's ills, shared a few personal views, and found ourselves simpatico. Approaching town, we crossed a bridge spanning another river, where, as providence would have it, I could see fly-fishermen lashing the water.

"The commercial boys are on strike," said Nino, slowing down. "So those guys are probably doing pretty good. That piece of water they're fishing is for fly-fishermen only. You fly-fish?"

I saw one angler's rod bowed over by a big fish and my blood came up like watching a beautiful woman adjust a stocking high on her thigh when she thinks no one is looking. A plan fell together.

"I'm wondering," I said, "could you drop me at the hotel, let me register and get into my waders, and bring me back here?"

"Sure," said Nino. "I'm off work in a couple of hours. I could come back after dinner with my daughter, say, around sundown. I'll come in my own car, that way I won't have to charge you another fare. Then I could show you a little of Cordova."

I wondered to myself, is this a very good man, or Alaska, or a bit of both?

A half hour later Nino dropped me at the river, flipped a U-turn, and disappeared down the highway leading back to town.

I jointed up my rod and headed down to a big pool below the outlet of a large lake, where several others were casting flies to long dark bullets finning in the green water. After an hour of casting, I hadn't touched a fish.

"Try one of these," said a tall young man, wading over to help and handing me a big purple-and-red marabou fly. He'd landed three nice silvers on the same fly since I'd started fishing. "They like this pretty well," he said with a smile. "Let me know if you lose this one." We talked for a few minutes, and then he moved off to fish below me.

Fly-fishermen must sometimes rely on the kindness of strangers, and this kid from the Midwest fit the old American mold for kindness, offering to help a fellow angler down on his luck. His name was Jake and he'd grown up fly-fishing with his father, as Hemingway might have written, "Up in Michigan." He was happy to be fishing Alaska, pleased that I'd accepted his hand-tied pattern, and proud to be serving his country as a member of the U.S. Coast Guard.

Nino came for me at sundown, just as promised. I'd hooked and lost one good fish and told him about being saved by the young man from Michigan. After I slipped out of my waders and broke down my rod, Nino drove me around town and told me a bit about his life, his children, and his love for Alaska. We shared our concerns about the alarming loss of civility and generosity in the world today. We agreed there was no hiding from the bad news and that, on average, there is too much violence, too much hatred, too much racism, and way too little love, kindness, and understanding in the world.

Back at my hotel we shook hands, smiled warmly, and said goodbye, as if everything we'd just agreed was wrong with the world could be made right again by two strangers like us, and a kid from Michigan.

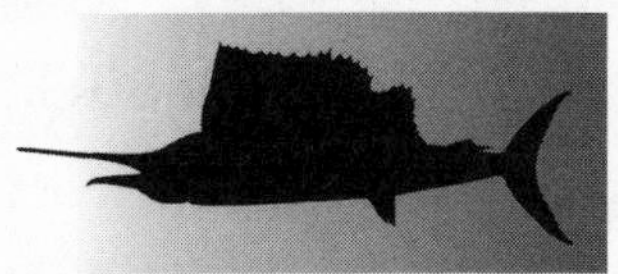

Journal Entry: A Death in the Afternoon

You don't get many of them in life, so you'd better treasure those that come your way. I'm talking here of perfect, warm, blue-sky, windless fishing days when fortune and fish run together, and you are blessed to bear witness. On such days it is good to be thankful, to be respectful, to be spiritual.

Today was one of those days. Here on the Gulf Coast between Cordova and Yakutat, Alaska, the so-called Lost Coast, and thanks to a crackerjack bush pilot, I was not lost today, but was perfectly placed at the mouth of a small salmon river where it enters the Pacific Ocean. I was to be on the river one day, and to live that day, rod in hand, full out from dawn till dark in pursuit of silver salmon.

And it was a perfect day: bright sun, no rain, no wind, the air filled with promise, and with the distant howl of a wolf on the wings of a light breeze. It was a perfect day, perhaps, except for a death in the afternoon.

The salmon that died on this perfect afternoon was a silver salmon, a big buck—a coho, by his Indian name. He came in on a crashing wave at exactly twelve o'clock on an August day in the year of our Lord nineteen hundred and ninety-six. In his swift dash toward natal waters, he missed the river of his birth and stranded himself high on a sandy beach.

A hundred feet away scores of his brothers and sisters and cousins and fry mates rode the same breakers toward the same shallow estuary where, finding just enough water to tail-power themselves toward the freshet, they squirted and spurted themselves over the sand through the receding waves, making safe harbor in the deep throat of the stream that snaked down from the green hills to the blue sea.

But not our buck salmon.

Like the rest, he had aimed for a cold stream and a spawning affair through which he might re-create his heart, his bright silver sides, his dark eyes. He had one chance to make it, and he missed.

Now he lay flopping on his side. Quite helpless. A fish, as they say, out of water.

I stopped casting to watch and wonder whether a great wave might come ashore and rescue him, sweep him back to deep water, give him respite and another chance at immortality.

I waited. The salmon struggled. Waves came, but none so great as to lift him from his dilemma.

Sitting in the sand to rest my casting arm, I studied the buck's predicament. Here was a salmon for the taking. I could walk over, rap him on the head with a priest made of a length of driftwood, and release him quickly from his misfortune, ending his suffering in the bargain.

Or I could provide a more benevolent, divine intervention and help him back to the sea. On a second attempt at his river of no return, he might find his way. He might even give me a shot at him. Would he, I wondered, understand my charity and take the fly I offered him in gratitude? Would he give me an especially good fight?

Looking about as the fish lay still, its gill plates pumping and reaching for oxygen-charged liquid, I could see plainly that every creature in Alaska fishes salmon. Well beyond the breakers I could see a sea lion bobbing in the far waves. Closer in, a pair of seals patrolled the estuary. Brown-bear tracks broader than your hand lined the stream and beach beneath my feet, and wolf tracks trailed away in every direction. For the Alaskan Stranded Salmon Special, there is no "Family hold back," only "First come, first serve."

Soon a squad of seagulls moved in, landing near the fish to gather in the gift. Of all the fishers present and accounted for on that perfect afternoon, only one was torn between the urge to rescue and respect for nature's ways, only one could contemplate this curious crisis.

To act, or not to act?

To aid nature, or not aid nature?

That is the question.

For the last few days I'd been reading *River Out of Eden* by Richard Dawkins, the famous Darwinian biologist. The river of which he writes is the great digital gene pool of life, and of which all living things are made, including you and me and the piece of driftwood my right hand can turn into a priest of death. The unique genetic code that constructed our marvelous buck salmon dying on the beach will not, without my immediate assistance, have any chance to replicate itself. Without help, this salmon will die before mating, and his genes will pass out of that river out of Eden.

Forever.

Unless I put down my rod right now and rescue him, flip him back into the water.

Unless I play God.

I love this perfect day, I love this buck salmon, and I love life with all its wondrous mysteries.

And yet, as I watch the salmon flop again and then lie still, I am immobilized. On what high moral ground do I stand to rescue this fish?

If I save this fish, do I not tug at the threads that stitch the universe together?

Soon to be a scavenger's meal, surely the buck salmon doesn't know all this.

But I do, and the knowing is a burden. Not a heavy burden, but it is of sufficient poundage to keep me sitting on the beach with tension in my chest and confusion in my head.

While saving this salmon's life could not possibly matter in the great scheme of life on this little planet, and saving this one fish could not possibly matter to the thousands of salmon who will die this day, or the millions who will die this season, this year, or this decade, it does matter to one salmon: the salmon dying in front of me.

Should I or shouldn't I?

For what purpose?

To what end?

I came to this river today to catch and then release any fish I hooked. I did not come to kill. To kill this fish is not in today's plan, although our buck would be very good, grilled over open alder-wood coals and lathered with fresh butter and lemon juice.

My mind whirs.

The salmon is dying.

The gulls crowd closer.

I have had no hand in this death. For once, I am innocent. My presence did not affect the buck's fortunes. He missed the river's mouth on his own account. If a crooked chromosome or a bent gene in his guidance system led to his personal disaster, maybe that is how the Big Plan works. Maybe this salmon is supposed to die on this beach, take his bad genes with him, and in the sacrifice save his species from future fatal navigational errors. After all, it wouldn't do for silver salmon to go around beaching themselves, would it?

Time is running out.

To witness the third and final act, I move to higher ground up the beach. It is not higher moral ground, but the view is better.

The flopping stops.

The gulls rush in, cawing and raising a ruckus. There are six of them. They peck and pull, turning on each other with flashing beaks as they fight over the best cuts. They break the thick skin with their hooking bills and rend the flesh. They ignore the few weak flops of the buck, eating him as he dies. Digging in, red beaks dripping, they make a party of it, wings flapping high in noisy celebration.

To witness a death in the afternoon wakes up in me the mild terror that perhaps the universe in which we live and love and spend our lives is indeed without clever design, without purpose or compassion, except as we humans imagine it. What we don't know about how the universe works we invent, attribute meaning to, and call spiritual. Because, perhaps, the alternative is wholly unpleasant. The other option may be as unhappy as A. E. Housman's lines, "For Nature, heartless, witless Nature, / Will neither know nor care."

With me there to keep the bears and wolves at bay, the gulls dine high and handsome. Soon the fresh dead meat is gone, the buck's bony carcass lies drying on the beach. The show is over. I stand, study a pool in which a dozen good fish are holding, and make ready to cast my bright salmon fly.

The buck is gone, and all his futures with him, gone forever out of this river out of Eden. Who swims there still?

Here, and for this one perfect afternoon, six seagulls and I.

A Stone in the River

A long time ago I became friends with another fisherman. We fished together many times and came to enjoy each other's company. New to my area, he always offered to drive, use his boat, and buy lunch. He told me that once he learned about fishing spots I had yet to discover, he would take me to them. In the meantime, I would guide him to all my secret spots, spots that had taken me years to find. Only after I had done so did he betray me—but the betrayal was as much my fault as his, for I had allowed it to happen.

By the second year of our relationship, and for reasons I could not name, I began to feel uncomfortable when my friend called to go fishing. Part of me wanted to say I was busy. I found myself calling him less and less often, and he began to call me less and less often. One day, listening to a gut feeling, I picked up the phone.

"Let's go to Coffee Pot Lake Saturday," I opened, "but I insist on driving and buying lunch on the way home."

"No way, buddy! I owe you big! I'm driving, and that's all there is to it."

I caved in.

The uncomfortable feeling in me persisted, although everything else between us seemed fine.

Then one Saturday morning in early spring I decided I needed a solo to clear my head and drove some sixty miles to a remote, seldom-fished trout stream, a stream I had introduced my friend to the previous fall. Access to the stream, surrounded by private ranch land, is limited. There is only one place to park on the only gravel road that passes near the stream.

Tucked in beneath a small stand of aspen near the parking spot was my friend's car. I pulled in behind, uncased my binoculars, and glassed upstream. There, casting flies to the tail of my favorite pool was a stranger, and beyond him, at the head of the pool, was my friend. Neither saw me and I quickly drove away.

The teacher had been betrayed, the guided had become the guide. Furious wouldn't be too strong a word to describe my emotions at that moment of discovery.

No confrontation was necessary. I'd taken the man fishing, not to raise. Whatever there had been between us was over. For good. I know that's harsh, but once a man crosses a certain line with me, he can't come back over it. Not even if he begs. And I'm not even sure where the line is. Until it's crossed, of course. Then I know.

I'm not proud of this character flaw, but I learned long ago never to waste good fishing time with people who wouldn't know a scruple if they tripped over one. Life is just too short.

A couple of years after this incident a New York publisher wrote to ask whether I would write a book for the lay reader on the psychological merits of forgiveness. I gave the project a couple of days' thought, remembered the betrayal of my former friend, checked my emotional temperature (I was still hot as a pistol), and called her. "Can't do it," I said, "but thanks for the offer."

"Why not?" the editor asked. "It could be a great book."

"Sorry," I said, "I haven't gotten forgiveness figured out yet. Maybe when I'm older and wiser." I said thanks again and rang off.

On little things I am quick to forgive. Forgiving my enemies is a snap, because my enemies' motives are as plain to see as their gunbarrels. Forgiving friends, colleagues, and myself is harder. Much harder. Forgiveness without sincerity is arrogance, and there are times when, because of a violation of trust, my anger and resentment are simply too great to soften my heart. I have fired a half dozen therapists over the years, and intentionally ruined more than one career, for exploiting a patient's weaknesses and violating his trust. And I have slept especially well afterward. After testifying in a major lawsuit against a psychiatrist who slept with his patients, a professional pal remarked to me, "You make a wonderful friend, but a terrible enemy." I took it as a compliment.

I trusted my fishing pal until he betrayed me, yet in a way I betrayed myself. Here, I think, is how it happened.

Consider that every offering, every gift, every token, every gratuity, whether in deed or word, tangible or intangible, has value and a price tag. Just because you cannot see the price tag doesn't mean one isn't there. You ignore this price tag at your peril.

I have also become vaguely suspicious of charity, especially my own. When I give something "freely," what do I want? What is it I am really after? Sometimes it is simply to feel good and to know that, after all, I'm a nice guy and enjoy giving more than I get. At other times my charity is more self-serving, even dubious. Unless it is entirely anonymous, charity creates obligations in others, no matter how subtle or remote the expected payback. Mother Teresa will be sainted for her charity, but I expect God owes her plenty.

Paying back money debts is easy. And clean. Give me a banker with a mean interest rate anytime; at least I know the obligation. But moral debts? Moral debts are treacherous.

Moral debts carry no visible price tag, no quoted interest rate, not even fine print about the balloon payment due years from now.

For money debts we have calculators and bank books and payment slips and fair lending laws to keep things straight between us. For moral debts we have only gut feelings, intuition, and an able little bookkeeper in our heads who, quite out of consciousness, keeps track of what we owe to whom and who owes us what.

The little bookkeeper knows the true price of everything. He wears a little green visor, keeps his head down over his pencil, and writes down every single moral debit and credit that accumulates between us and those with whom we associate.

For a happy life, never ignore this little bookkeeper.

When the bookkeeper says it's time to pay back a dinner, or a fishing trip, or a moral or social debt of any kind, pay it quickly. Don't wait; the interest is compounding.

When the bookkeeper in your head says to accept what is owed you, accept it quickly. Don't wait; the interest is compounding.

Keep these books between you and those you care about balanced, and you will have harmony and long relationships; let these books get out of balance and you will have disharmony and conflict. In the beginning our debtors step on our toes; in the end they step on our hearts.

When we can't pay our moral debts, we are left with only three options: Avoid our creditor, devalue the debt and declare it bogus, or malign the motives of the giver. When, by too much charity, we create debts in others they cannot repay, we force them to avoid us, devalue our giving, and malign our motives. None of this is either smart or noble.

When we do not pay our moral debts in a timely fashion, or discourage others from paying theirs to us in a timely fashion, we break the law of human reciprocity. At least as powerful as the law of gravity, to be human is to reciprocate, to share and to share equally. Sharing means not only to give with grace, but to *receive* with grace. I don't know that my pal intended to rip me off, I just know I ignored my growing sense of discomfort too long and did too little to set right again the debts and obligations between us. Had I been more insistent on equity early on, things might have worked out differently.

Some years after I lost my friend at the stream that day because I could never forgive him, I found the lesson I was searching for. It turned up in a line from Shakespeare. The Bard wrote, "Too much charity turns the heart to stone."

Becoming a fisherman is not as simple as the old formula that fishermen are caught by their first fish. In reality, it is a three-step process. First, the fisherman takes a little fish; then a bigger fish takes the little fish; then an even bigger fish takes the fisherman. If the fisherman is lucky, the big fish doesn't spit him out.

Sometimes You Have to Admire the Fishing Gods

I was only lukewarm about giving up a day of Alaskan silver salmon on the fly for a day of bottom fishing for halibut. But I'd heard stories about the huge, tasty fish, and, what the hell, you ought to try everything once. So the gang of three, Mark, Rick, and me, booked a charter out of Yakutat and set sail the next morning.

There were four other guys on the charter, all midwesterners with a few years on us. They were old pals from high school who'd hung together as fishing buddies their whole lives. They seemed tight and comfortable with each other, except for one thin guy who stood off from the rest of them and who wore a pained expression. He leaned heavily on the rail while his bait was down, and looked out to sea with a thousand-yard stare.

I hooked the first halibut, which turned out to be a ninety-eight-pounder. We're not talking smashing strikes, hot runs, or splashy fights with a halibut. Landing one is more like trying to raise a downed Volkswagen with a hand winch, only with more back and less winch.

The guides don't want you to let these big fish break the surface before they've been gaffed for fear of breaking them off. Once on the surface, these huge slabs of pure muscle are basically uncontrollable, even on 50-pound-test line. Any halibut over a hundred pounds is a "shooter," which means the guide head-shoots the fish with a .410 shotgun to calm it down before bringing it aboard. A wild two- or three-hundred-pound halibut who's been saving his fight for the deck of a boat can snap an angler's leg like a matchstick.

Anyway, for most of the day I held the big-fish record and tried to make as much of it as I could by gently ribbing the other guys, even though halibut fishing is pretty much a no-brainer operation.

Then the thin guy with the pained expression hooked a big fish, and with all of us cheering him on he slowly cranked the great brute toward the surface. For a while it was not altogether clear who was going to win the battle, but no one stepped in to help the man, whose arms were shaking violently as the fish finally came into shotgun range.

The guide leaned over the gunwale and blasted the huge fish. When it was tranquilized, gaffed, and boated, we all congratulated the guy and shook his hand. It was a weak handshake. Standing next to the 112-pounder for the photo, the guy with the thousand-yard stare smiled for the first time all day, and I thought I saw a bit of a twinkle in his dark eyes.

"I'm glad Hal got that one," his friend said to me over coffee as we sat in the cabin while the others fished.

I nodded, not feeling at all bad about losing the lead.

"No," said his pal, leaning in and speaking in a serious tone. "I mean I'm *really* glad Hal got that one. We go home tomorrow. Old Hal's got cancer bad. This is his last fishing trip."

Fishing Interruptus at the Chapel Hole

Far, far away on a distant river there is a stretch of fly-fishing–only, catch-and-release water I consider sacred, or sacred enough that I only go there in midweek when I'm sure there will be no crowds, no bothersome interruptions by strangers—when, to be selfish about it, I can have this little piece of water entirely to myself. I call this water the Chapel Hole and usually fish it alone. I've gone there on special occasions: one time on the day I finished a book I was writing, and another time to grieve my father's death.

To fish the Chapel Hole requires a half-mile hike through ancient old-growth cedar. It is a beautiful, shaded, silent walk under a dark-green canopy. Like a light from heaven, the sun breaks out at the end of the walk where the river curves under a layered stone cliff and cuts a narrow chute against the black rock, a chute barely fifteen feet across. The chute slowly opens into a long deep pool, which, toward evening vespers, is filled with rising wild trout.

There are always good cutthroats in the Chapel Hole. Big ones. On a summer afternoon the best offering is a large yellow-bodied grasshopper fly, cast close to the far bank. Big trout seldom splash to feed, so the rise will be no more than a slurping bulge in the water. If you follow your fly, you may see a wide, dark-green, heavily spotted head push up from the deep, open its white-lined jaw, and suck in your fly. This take only has to happen once, and even if you break off the fish, you will come back. Because you catch the fish and obey the official release rules, the fish will always be there waiting for you at the altar.

The beauty of this remote, unspoiled place is not easy to describe, but it is clear to me that there is nothing any human being could possibly add to this little piece of natural water, land, and sky that would be an improvement.

Except, perhaps, one thing.

I could hear their voices for some minutes. Female voices. They were coming toward me from upriver. Laughing and calling back and forth to one another, they were probably tubers. Lots of people float the river in inner tubes and kayaks and canoes and every manner of watercraft throughout the summer. Like me, they hope to escape the heat and squalor of the city. But not on Wednesdays, and not this far upriver. This is fishing water, not tubing water.

As their voices carried through the canyon, I felt my irritation index rise. I had just teased up one of those big green heads from the far bank of the narrow chute with a Joe's Hopper. The next cast would surely bring a strike. I didn't need a bunch of loud, silly people floating through my sanctuary.

Suddenly, rounding the bend, they were upon me; three beautiful blond young women, probably coeds from one of the universities in the city. I stopped casting. They would pass directly in front of me and right over my fish.

"Sorry," said the first, smiling broadly, as she floated by in her inner tube, her back against one side and her legs draped over the other.

"Sorry," said the second, her lovely hands dappling the water.

"Sorry," said the third, as she brought up the rear. "We're working on our tans." She, too, smiled and then waved good-bye.

I smiled and waved, too, sorry to see them go. Each more lovely than the other, they were as three vestal virgins come to sanctify, consecrate, and dedicate the Chapel Hole to a new and higher order of natural beauty.

Sure, they put my trout down for a few minutes, but I didn't mind. After all, the girls had come to church to worship the sun just the way nature intended, buck naked.

For the trout fisherman there is no fishing light like October light.

A Cast of My Own

A boy's father is larger than life. This is as it should be, otherwise the boy will not look to his father to learn what he must learn to become a man. But as the boy grows to manhood and comes into his own, sooner or later his father becomes only a man. I realized this about my own father the day I accepted one important truth about him: He couldn't cast a fly worth a damn.

Like other boys, I bragged about my father. Still do. And for good reason. My father was a man of three dozen talents—strong, honest, spiritual, at once a fighter and a friend, a champion of the weak, a sportsman, trout fisherman, flytier, and rod builder. He taught me many wonderful things. But how to cast a fly was not among them.

Of course I didn't know this for the first forty-five years I fly-fished. As I understood fly-fishing, the cast was a delivery system for the line and the fly sort of followed along. Casting was but a means to an end. There was something about the line matching the rod, and, oh yes, it was a good idea to taper the leaders because these helped turn the fly over, and thin tippets didn't spook fish.

To get the fly to the fish you whipped the rod vigorously back and forth, back and forth, feeding line as you whipped until you had enough line out to reach your target. You also whipped the rod vigorously back and forth to dry out soggy flies. That's it. That's what I knew about fly casting.

All I learned I learned by watching my father. How else would a boy learn to fly-fish in the 1950s? Not from an Orvis video.

An Iowa farm boy who'd moved to California in the 1930s and discovered golden trout, my father was a self-taught flycaster, and not a very good one, as it turned out. I realized this when I grew up and eventually met and fished with people who actually knew how to cast a fly line. Comparing their loops and distance to mine, I saw I was a poor caster. No, let me be candid here; I wasn't just poor, I was wretched.

True, I had figured out how to get pretty good distance, but at the price of a tailing loop and innumerable wind knots, which for the longest time I believed were tied behind my back by mischievous fishing fairies.

I didn't know how to do the snake cast or the reach cast or how to single haul a cast. When I first heard about the double haul I thought it had something to do with taking the trash out twice a day. I couldn't beat the wind even a little, never looked behind me to see what my loops were up to and, as a result, once clipped the tip off an expensive graphite rod with a lead-wrapped nymph on a backcast. Trout by the millions survived my predations simply by keeping a tongue of fast, unwadable water between me and their lie, and passing on bugs that left wakes like motorboats.

Then came the epiphany. Resting beside a Montana trout stream one afternoon, I watched my father cast to a broad, smooth pool filled with rising trout. I had to admit it, my model for excellence in all things couldn't cast. Piled line, short, dumpy deliveries—there was nothing smooth here to admire. And so I accepted my father as just another man and began my short, uneven journey to become a better caster.

I started with books and articles and watching others. I practiced on the stream, on the lake, and once or twice in my backyard. Never accused of being a quick study, I've taken a dozen years just to graduate the freshman class, and that's by my own grading system—a system unencumbered by reliable judges, helpful coaching, or any semblance of objective criteria that might infringe on the fantasy of those tight, lovely loops and silky smooth casts to which I aspire.

Then, only forty-five years too late, I took my first casting lesson. I didn't intend to, but it just worked out that way. Had it not been freely offered, I would never have taken it in the first place, but Michael C. Maloney offered to give me one. Twice. And for nothing. Only a fool refuses a free casting lesson from the person many people believe to be one of the world's great fly-casting coaches.

Casting in front of his home in Camarillo, California, Michael watched me for a time. Finally he said, "Your backcast is to die for. Your forward cast is perfectly rotten." Then he laughed. "Whoever taught you that by speeding up your forward cast you could get more distance?"

Out of respect for my father, by then deceased, I lied, "I did."

It is not so much that Michael taught me to slow my forward line speed to solve the Great Wind Knot Mystery, or how to make a midair mend to cast around "square rocks," but that he showed me a whole new world of possibilities. As the master put it, "Casting is enough. Catching is fun and good, but casting well is enough."

Later, on one of my favorite rivers, I stopped fishing for a while to watch the slick water slide by. Smooth, glassy, the surface was broken only here and there by small trout sipping duns. I said to myself, "To hell with catching fish, let's cast."

For the next hour, I worked on my cast, on what Maloney had

taught me. I learned to follow the loops and enjoy the bright-yellow line settling on dark-green water. The trout that got in the way were but a pleasant nuisance. I worked on relaxing: slowing down my line speed on the outside, and my speed on the inside.

Then something strange happened, something transcendent. I felt myself slip the old granny knot of casting only to catch fish and side-step into something richer, fuller, and equally rewarding. I felt myself step past my father's cast and into a cast of my own.

A fisherman who doesn't own too much tackle probably can't be trusted in other things.

Something There Is That Doesn't Love a Watch

No man in a hurry is quite civilized.—Will Durant

According to the historian Will Durant, I qualify as a questionably civilized person. Ann is quick to agree. "Slow down," she says, watching me pack for a fishing trip. "An hour one way or the other won't make that much difference."

"This is slow," I say, moving at blur speed and trying not to strike solid objects with my body. "Besides, I'll relax when I get there."

"Sure," she sneers, knowing me too well.

Like a lot of stiffs who work as a slave in the city, I rocket along, doing what I do, pacing myself against the passage of time and the competition, as if I were in some great race to somewhere important. Fact is, if we stand back and study them for a moment, most of our races are not worth winning, let alone running. Some days I worry I might just continue to pick up speed until, around five o'clock, I'll just vanish into thin air.

I don't know about other fishermen, but it takes me a couple of days on the river to slow down, get quiet, and fish at a pace that doesn't disturb the dead. It takes a few days to break free of the artificial rhythm of the time beat out in one-second strokes the way they so happily do it for you back in the city.

On the first day of fishing, I find myself checking the time. I check it as I eat breakfast. I check it as I rig my rod. I check it as I fish an early-morning riffle, run, or hole. This checking lasts a day or two, then gradually disappears, like ankle chains on a slave.

By the third day of fishing, a kind of withdrawal from exact time begins. By the fourth day, meticulous timing has oozed into, "I'll be in after dark"; "If I meet up with you for lunch, okay, but don't wait for me." With each passing day, fishermen begin to swing over to rhythms more natural, more like the fishes. The urban metronome is broken.

The only two speeding tickets I've gotten in the last many years were handed to me on my way to fishing. I got one barreling through a small town on the way to a trout lake, and the other I got on my way to bass fishing. I have never been ticketed for speeding on my way home, or for speeding to or from work.

I call this the Great Outdoors Einstein Effect. The Great Outdoors Einstein Effect works like this: the faster you travel through space toward a fishing hole, the more time slows. At the speed of light, time stops. If you can get your fishing rig moving faster than the speed of light, you will arrive at the river earlier than when you left, depending on road conditions.

Unfortunately, my theory of fishing relativity cuts little ice with sheriffs' officers and their calibrated timing devices. "Makes sense," one said, handing me a speeding ticket. "I like to fish too. Here's your summons."

The Future of Fishing

Many years ago I did a book tour for my first psychology-of-fishing book, *Pavlov's Trout*. This was a cheap book tour. No limo. No driver. No fancy hotels. No spreads in the papers. No unlimited expense account. Since my publisher and I were splitting the cost of the tour out of pocket, I ate a lot of cheese and crackers in cheap motel rooms and tried to convince myself I was a serious literary person working his way up.

I flew tourist class to Minneapolis, rented a cheap sedan, and drove around the upper Midwest for two weeks where, our research told us, 26 percent of all U.S. fishermen live. The deal I had with the publisher, Chris Bessler, was to split all costs fifty-fifty: plane fare, car rental, gas, motels, food, whatever. For my end, I was to drive from town to town, city to city, bookstore to bookstore, read to audiences, give stories to reporters, hang around fishing shops, meet folks, and sell books. We'd make ourselves a best-seller (which actually happened in northern Michigan for three weeks), split all profits, and get rich. And, depending on your definition of rich, that's pretty much how it went down.

But money was only part of the reason for making the trip . . . at least for me. The other part was to fish a bit of the heartland. I try to make it a practice not to mix too much work into my fishing, and the book tour made a pretty good cover for a fishing expedition. Besides, I'd already done the book-tour thing back in 1987 with a trade paperback book with a New York publisher on why it's a bad idea to kill yourself. I'd seen seven or eight big cities first class, answered questions from dozens of radio and TV interview hosts who hadn't read my book, and done several national talk shows without benefit of four fingers of Scotch.

Comparatively speaking, I had a much better time on the fishing-book tour. In fact, a very good time. I met wonderful people. I got a read on middle America's anglers. I met a woman on a little lake in a little Michigan town who was teaching her daughter to fish for bluegills—a soda and box of popcorn set a festive tone. In this post-feminist world, I had lunch with a woman who, in another little town, explained that she had just succeeded in working her way into a men's-only fly-fishing club and, despite some resistance from a few of the Cro-Magnon members, was meeting with wonderful success.

Then—I think it was in Lake Woebegone—I pulled into a Main Street burger joint adjacent to a smooth-flowing river you could toss a fly line across. A clear, fishy flowage, the river ran right through the heart of town. A park had been built on the river's edge, and the river itself was bordered by a cement sidewalk. Ordering lunch, I watched a young man casting a spinner down and across a deep pool.

With my burger finished, I walked across the road and sat down on the grass beside him.

"Any luck?" I asked.

"Nope," said the boy. He appeared to be about thirteen.

"What sort of fish do you have here abouts?"

"All kinds," the boy said, smiling. "I'm trying for pike. They run upriver this time of year. If you keep casting, pretty soon you'll hook one. Want to try?"

"Nope," I said. "I'm from out of town and don't have a license. Just passing through. But I'd sure like to see you catch one."

"Just be patient," said the boy. "Patience is everything."

I nodded.

Together, we kept silent and fished; the boy casting and reeling, I watching. After a while I walked back to my car and retrieved a copy of *Pavlov's Trout*.

"I'd like to give you a book," I said. "What's your name?"

"Jason."

I signed the book "To Jason" and passed it to him.

"Thanks," he said, surprised. He looked the book over, admired the trout on the cover, then quickly put it down so he could get back to the business of catching fish.

"Sure you don't want to sneak in a cast?" he asked again.

"Nope," I said, "but I appreciate the thought."

"There's nothin' like fishing," said Jason. "Nothin' like it in the world."

"Don't I know it," I said.

I lay back on the green grass and let the warm sun beat down on my face. I listened to Jason casting, his bail clicking over and the soft *thrum-thrum-thrum* of his reeling. It was a good sound, soothing and relaxing. I pulled my cap down over my eyes.

After a while, I woke up.

"Any luck?" I asked again.

"Nope. But it's still early," said Jason. "Sure you don't want to try a few casts?"

I said no thanks again, and explained that I had to get on down the road. The future of fishing, I thought, is in good hands.

As I pulled out onto Main Street, Jason stopped casting, turned, smiled, and waved from his wheelchair.

Compared to football, fishing helps build character; when you lose to the fishes, you can't blame it on the officiating.

The Run to Cliff Lake

Cliff Lake was too far to drive to after work. Never having been there, I wasn't sure how far it was. I wasn't even sure I could find it. All I knew was you kept driving straight after you passed the Larder Ranch and didn't turn when the county road turned. According to my informant, "You should see a yellow gate, and something like a dirt road." The lake was supposed to be full of big cutthroat trout.

"Lahontans. They'll hit anything as long as it's green, but don't spread it around; it isn't much of a lake."

I didn't ask anyone to go with me. Too chancy. Too sudden a decision, anyway. I'd left work early to beat the rush-hour traffic, downed a sandwich, tossed my two workhorse fly rods in the back of the truck, and started south.

With a dry spring behind us, the gravel roads billowed high with dust as I pushed the pickup to double nickels between the greening wheatfields. I drove too fast. But then, I always drive too fast going out. Long, deserted dirt roads pull me into a strange place. A race with life? A race against time? A race against death? Fishing may not be worth dying for . . . but minor injuries? You bet.

I mashed the accelerator down. To enjoy the speed I shut the radio off and rolled down the windows. Wind whipped through the cab. I could see dust boiling up behind me into a crystal-blue sky. The tip of a fly rod ticked steadily against a window. I felt as if I were thirty-five again, and getting younger.

I was flying now, even through space and time.

I don't know how fast I got going on the run to Cliff Lake, but I was going too fast to look down at the speedometer. For a time it seemed I wasn't moving past everything, but that I had stopped and everything was moving past me. With the wind howling through the windows, it was as if I were traveling faster than time.

Suddenly it grew quiet in the cab. I was out there in space, suspended, drifting, thinking. Thoughts and memories and scenes from the past flooded over me until it seemed that life did not go forward, but in circles.

Then I saw the yellow gate. I opened it, drove through, and closed it.

Cliff Lake is off the fishing maps. No resort, no reports. Except for word of mouth, you would never know it existed. Midweek, with any luck, I would have the lake to myself.

The road was unmarked and rough as a cob. Lava rock protruded up through dust-filled potholes like dragons' teeth. I risked cutting a tire, but by now I was twenty-five, maybe younger, and I didn't care.

I found the lake under a long, curved lava cliff, hence the name. I quickly got into my hip boots, tied a green marabou leech on a heavy tippet, and began to work what little water was accessible from the small beach. As I began to cast, I noticed a man in a boat fighting a strong fish.

Where had he come from? How had I missed seeing his truck?

The man in the boat and I fished for a time without looking at each other, or so it seemed. But then he would catch another fish and I would find myself watching him, wanting to ask him what he was using. But I didn't. He rowed slowly on the small lake, trolling back and forth at the far end, just out of the range where you can make out a man's features. For the next hour or so, we kept that comfortable distance that sportsmen caught in such circumstances afford each other. Not knowing who he was, I at least liked that much about him.

An occasional fish rose, but I was having no luck with the leech. I switched to a floating line and tried an emerger in the surface film. This produced a seven-inch cutthroat. From time to time, I could see the man in the boat stand to fight yet another heavy fish. He did it quietly and without fanfare, but the noise of the trout's struggle on the surface echoed from the walls of lava surrounding the lake as if some great man-fish battle was being waged. I felt no envy, but took an odd, vicarious pleasure in his success.

So that I could see all of the lake, I hiked to the highest cliff, and when the fisherman in the boat came out of the shadows for a moment and the light struck the aluminum bow just so, I got a better look at his face. He was younger than I had first thought. Whoever he was, he reminded me of someone I had known a long time ago, but whose name escaped me. With sunlight slanting into and mellowing the blue lake to a light green, I took a photograph, framing the young man in the lower left-hand corner. Ann complains I take too many scenery-only shots, but this one would prove I could frame a fisherman in his element and tell a story.

"Hello," I called. "Doing any good?" The young man in the boat didn't answer, but he did wave. Maybe he was one of those fishermen who abhor any noise, who try to keep the rest of us shut up by a quiet example. I don't know; he was too far away for me to read his expression. But then, in one pass, he rowed near enough for me to see that he was not so much a young man as a boy.

Was he a high school kid from one of the local farms? Or a student from the university some eighty miles to the east? Maybe he was a teenager from the city who had come out to this remote little lake for the same reasons I had. Interesting. A boy. All alone. Like me.

We fished for a time, and I saw him land and release another couple of trout. As he made a pass near my end of the lake, a huge cutthroat rose just behind his boat. Turning to face me, he held up his hands and spread them wide to create a slot into which the big fish might fit, but he was still too far away for me to see if he was smiling. I guessed he was.

I shook my head, smiled, waved, and started another cast. The boy rowed by, in and out of my consciousness, like a character in a Fellini movie. When he hooked a fish, I could see that he didn't horse his fish and handled a net well. Still a boy, he knew what he was doing, and I wished that he would pull into the bay I was working and talk to me. But he rowed by and away and, finally, around the corner of the lake until he disappeared into the far cove, giving me one last thumbs-up, as if to say, "Good luck. I hope you catch a big one."

It was getting late, getting to be time to go. Part of me wanted to wait until the boy rowed back out of the cove so that I could strike up a conversation and find out why he was fishing in an out-of-the-way pothole in an out-of-the-way state on a Wednesday evening all by himself.

But I didn't.

A little breeze came up with the last of the evening light. The trout stopped rising. It was quiet now. Except for a lone white gull perched on a black lava bluff against the darkening sky, I was entirely alone. A little tired and feeling all of my years again, I laid the rod down and sat for a long time and listened into the stillness. It was then I realized that when I got home and had the film developed it would, once again, be just another photograph of an empty lake.

About the Author

A man with two careers, Paul Quinnett is both a freelance writer and a clinical psychologist. An award-winning journalist with over 500 stories, essays, and columns published in America's premier outdoor magazines, he has also written four books in psychology for the lay and professional reader. An expert on drug abuse, depression, and suicide, his best-selling *Suicide: The Forever Decision* has also been published in French, German, and Chinese.

His magazine writing credits include *Audubon*, *American Forests*, *Field & Stream*, *Sports Afield*, *Outdoor Life*, *Gray's Sporting Journal*, *the Flyfisher*, *Fly Rod & Reel*, and many others. Several of his stories have been anthologized. Currently fishing columnist for *Sporting Classics Magazine*, he's also published essays in such wide-ranging publications as *Newsweek*, the *New York Times*, and *Psychology Today*. His mentor and best-selling humorist, Patrick F. McManus, in a serious moment, once wrote "Paul Quinnett is one of the finest essayists writing today."

Pavlov's Trout: The Incompleat Psychology of Everyday Fishing was his first attempt to bring the two great loves of his life together. With essays on topics from the phenomenon of why fishermen lie to ethics to the neuropsychology of fly selection, the book has been predicted to become a fishing classic. The sequel, *Darwin's Bass*, is a further exploration of the psychology of fishing man. In his latest book, *Fishing Lessons*, he tackles the philosophy of fishing—a philosophy of enjoying life.

Heavily involved in training younger clinicians, he also serves as Clinical Assistant Professor in the Department of Psychiatry and Behavioral Science at the University of Washington School of Medicine. His specialities include couples counseling, stress management, and consultation to law enforcement agencies in the inland Northwest. He consults on fly-fishing for free.